Return of the Son of Trevor Lynch's White Nationalist Guide to the Movies

by

Trevor Lynch

Edited by Greg Johnson

Counter-Currents Publishing Ltd.
San Francisco
2019

Copyright © 2019 by Greg Johnson
All rights reserved

Cover image:
Caspar David Friedrich, *Moonrise over the Sea*, 1822,
Alte Nationalgalerie, Berlin

Cover design by
Kevin I. Slaughter

Published in the United States by
COUNTER-CURRENTS PUBLISHING LTD.
P.O. Box 22638
San Francisco, CA 94122
USA
http://www.counter-currents.com/

Hardcover ISBN: 978-1-64264-129-5
CENSORED Hardcover ISBN: 978-1-64264-131-8
Paperback ISBN: 978-1-64264-130-1
CENSORED Paperback ISBN: 978-1-64264-133-2
E-book ISBN: 978-1-64264-132-5

Contents

Preface ❖ iii

1. *Alien: Covenant* ❖ 1
2. *Barton Fink* ❖ 4
3. *Batman: The Dark Knight Returns* ❖ 9
4. *Batman v Superman: Dawn of Justice* ❖ 13
5. *Black Panther* ❖ 17
6. *Blade Runner 2049* ❖ 22
7. *Children of Men* ❖ 25
8. Cronenberg's *Crash* ❖ 28
9. *Denial* ❖ 34
10. David Lynch's *Dune* ❖ 39
11. The Sci-Fi Channel's *Dune & Children of Dune* ❖ 54
12. *Dunkirk* ❖ 59
13. *Eraserhead* ❖ 61
14. *The Expanse* ❖ 71
15. *Glass* ❖ 75
16. *Good Kill* ❖ 78
17. *Hidden Figures* ❖ 81
18. *Jodorowsky's Dune* ❖ 85
19. *Jurassic World* ❖ 88
20. *Jurassic World: Fallen Kingdom* ❖ 92
21. *Justice League* ❖ 95
22. *The Loved One* ❖ 98
23. *Mad Max: Fury Road* ❖ 103
24. *The Martian* ❖ 107

25. Miller's Crossing ❖ 110

26. Passengers ❖ 115

27. Princess Mononoke ❖ 117

28. The Promise ❖ 120

29. Rashomon & Realism ❖ 123

30. Rogue One: A Star Wars Story ❖ 133

31. Silence ❖ 138

32. Solo: A Star Wars Story ❖ 141

33. Spectre ❖ 145

34. Star Trek: Beyond ❖ 147

35. Star Wars: The Force Awakens ❖ 151

36. Star Wars: The Last Jedi ❖ 156

37. Three Identical Strangers ❖ 162

38. To Live & Die in L.A. ❖ 168

39. Unbreakable ❖ 172

40. Valerian & the City of a Thousand Planets ❖ 178

41. Watchmen ❖ 180

42. Wild at Heart ❖ 194

43. Zootopia ❖ 206

Index ❖ 213

About the Author ❖ 226

Preface

I usually agonize over books, constantly tinkering with the basic concept, title, and table of contents. Not so with this book. After finalizing the contents for the second Trevor Lynch anthology—*Son of Trevor Lynch's White Nationalist Guide to the Movies* (Counter-Currents, 2015)—I simply opened a file and started pasting in new film reviews in alphabetical order until I got to about 200 pages. Then I fired up the Counter-Currents machine to deliver it to the world. Even the title was a no-brainer, as every Zappa fan understands. The result is the book before you. Since I write film reviews for fun, it seems suitable that everything about this book was free of the pains of labor. I hope that most of you will find it reads the same way.

As you have no doubt noticed, the cover does not follow the formula of the first two Trevor Lynch books, namely their affectionate parody of the *Mystery Science Theater 3000* silhouettes. The copyright holders for MST3K threatened to sue us, and where's the fun in that? So we changed the covers of the first two Lynch books, and I came up with a slightly new concept for this one.

I wish to thank Kevin Slaughter for his work on the cover; James O'Meara and Alex Graham for help with the index; Ron Unz, who first published my reviews of *Three Identical Strangers*, David Lynch's *Wild at Heart* and *Dune*, and *Glass*; and the many writers, donors, and commenters at *Counter-Currents* who made it all possible.

This book is dedicated to a flawless arbiter of taste, my friend and fellow cinephile Petronius.

Budapest
May 5, 2019

ALIEN: COVENANT

I saw *Alien: Covenant* on the big screen in June of 2018 in Budapest. I didn't write a review then, because another reviewer had it covered.[1] But having seen it for a second time, now on Blu-ray, I feel moved to comment.

Covenant is an excellent film, indeed the best in the series since Scott started it with his path-breaking *Alien* (1979) — although James Cameron's *Aliens* is excellent and iconic in its own right.

This is especially surprising and welcome, given that *Covenant* is the sequel to *Prometheus* (2012), Scott's retina-scorching attempt to launch a prequel series. *Prometheus* was not just awful for its portentous, arbitrary, incoherent, and sometimes downright stupid script by Damon Lindelof (*Lost*), but for its vulgar promise to "explain" the xenomorphs rather than just allow them to be menacing mysteries.[2]

Covenant is set 10 years after *Prometheus*. Perhaps because Scott came to realize that *Prometheus* is God-awful, he basically abandoned as much of the detritus as he could, including Lindelof. The only characters who remain from *Prometheus* are Guy Pearce's Peter Weyland (who appears only in the prologue) and Michael Fassbender as the android David. Scott couldn't really abandon the conceit of explaining the xenomorphs, but the end of *Covenant* does not set up the beginning of *Alien*. (The ship that crashes in *Covenant* cannot be the ship that is found in *Alien*.) So we are all left wondering. It is as if, after the debacle of *Prometheus*, Scott decided to simply make the best possible movie, "franchise" continuity be damned. I'm not complaining one bit.

Covenant is not really about the xenomorphs. Unlike *Alien*, it is not a haunted-house movie in space. Nor is it an action mov-

---

[1] Buttercup Dew, "*Alien: Covenant*: An Anti-Semitic Allegory," *Counter-Currents*, June 13, 2017.

[2] See my review in *Son of Trevor Lynch's White Nationalist Guide to the Movies* (San Francisco: Counter-Currents, 2015).

ie like *Aliens*. Instead, *Covenant* is a mad scientist movie. The android David is our modern Prometheus/Dr. Frankenstein/Lucifer figure (originally the movie was titled *Alien: Paradise Lost*), and Fassbender plays him as a cross between HAL-9000 and Hannibal Lecter, right down to his musical taste and exquisite drawings. (Scott, of course, directed 2001's *Hannibal*.)

The script of *Covenant* is intelligent and highly literary, weaving in Wagner, Milton, and Shelley. The music by Australian rock musician Jed Kurzel is effective, utilizing Jerry Goldsmith's haunting, Debussy-like main theme from the original *Alien*. The visual style and effects are simply dazzling, with spectacular location shots, superb sets, models, and paintings, and a minimum of digital trickery. The detail and feeling of realism on the large screen were stunning. I especially appreciated the recreation of Böcklin's *The Isle of the Dead*. Simply as a feast for the eyes, *Covenant* offers scene after scene that will fill you with wonder and delight, as well as sheer visceral terror.

I enjoyed the pacing of *Covenant*. The opening is slow and deliberate, with a good deal of time spent developing characters, although I never really liked or cared about any of them. (It is almost as if Scott wants us to sympathize with David's genocidal misanthropy.)

When we finally set down on a hostile planet, we are nearly an hour into the film. Then things get pretty frenzied, and, aside from a couple of calm interludes, the suspense and action never let up until the end. The aliens are genuinely terrifying: both the classic xenomorphs and the so-called "neomorphs," which are new to us but "paleomorphs" evolutionarily speaking. And although much here pays homage to elements of *Alien* and *Aliens*, where it counts, *Covenant* is a genuinely imaginative and original film.

Scott is a highly PC director. Remember, this is the guy who brought us *Thelma and Louise* and *G.I. Jane*. But there are some subversive elements to *Covenant*. First, the 14-member crew of the *Covenant* consists of 5 women and 9 men. There are at least five married couples, including a black man with a white wife and a couple of macho homosexuals.

This is a plot in which bad decisions lead to disaster. Predictably, when one spouse is in danger, the other becomes emotional and makes bad decisions, and it only gets worse as spouses start dying horribly. The biggest catastrophe, though, happens because two women who are left in charge go completely to pieces in a crisis. Some have pointed out that the race-mixers get their comeuppance, but so does practically everyone else, so there is no moral there.

The final scene of *Covenant* is magnificent and far more terrifying than the giant bugs. Having placed the two surviving crew members into stasis, David, who earlier complained that his experiments lacked only one thing — human test subjects — enters the compartment where two thousand colonists and more than a thousand human embryos are stored in stasis, accompanied by Wagner's magnificent "Entry of the Gods into Valhalla." Then he vomits up two xenomorph embryos and places them among the human ones, like a cuckoo laying its eggs in an unwitting host's nest.

Buttercup Dew is right to see *Covenant* as an unconscious anti-Semitic allegory, and the final scene encapsulates the full horror we all feel at the spectacle of our sleeping race being turned into experimental playthings then corpses by beings that look huwyte on the outside but operate on a misanthropic, genocidal code on the inside.

Frankly, I hope the *Alien* franchise ends here, on the highest note since it began 38 years ago. At the age of 79, Ridley Scott has made more bad movies than good ones. But when he's good — *Alien, Blade Runner, Blackhawk Down, Kingdom of Heaven, The Martian* — hoo-boy. With *Covenant*, Scott can retire with us all wanting more.

Counter-Currents, February 2, 2019

BARTON FINK

There is little satisfying critical literature on the Coen brothers' 1991 film *Barton Fink*. Most viewers are inclined to think that this is because the film is a pretentious, meaningless piece of crap. And *Barton Fink* is surely the most widely detested film by the Coens. The fact that it swept the 1991 Cannes Film Festival, winning the Palme d'Or, Best Director, and Best Actor (John Turturro) can simply be chalked up to French perversity and anti-Americanism. Remember: these people think Jerry Lewis is a genius.

I don't wish to discount the meaningless crap theory, but I think there is more to it. Another reason for the dearth of good commentary on *Barton Fink* is that the conclusions one reaches upon careful viewing are literally unspeakable in polite company, for *Barton Fink* is a profoundly anti-Semitic film.

The Coens wrote the script of *Barton Fink*—in which writer's block is a prominent theme—while experiencing writer's block on *Miller's Crossing*, in which John Turturro plays the most loathsome Jewish villain since Shylock. *Barton Fink* was filmed immediately after the completion of *Miller's Crossing* with Turturro in the title role as another Jewish villain.

And make no mistake, the character of Barton Fink really is a fink. He is not just a nebbish and a victim, he is primarily a villain, whose victimhood is both the just desserts for his villainy and perhaps a barrier to future crimes. Fink's crime is hard to see, though, because he lives primarily in his head. He lives "the life of the mind." Thus he commits a crime of the mind.

The pretentious and meaningless aspects of *Barton Fink* basically arise from the fact that the Coens are making an ersatz David Lynch film, which blends the folksy with the grotesque and supernatural. But it doesn't work, because they are unwilling to make the necessary metaphysical commitments.

As Flannery O'Connor argues in her essay "Some Aspects of the Grotesque in Southern Fiction,"[1] the portrayal of the gro-

---

[1] In Flannery O'Connor, *Mystery and Manners: Occasional Prose*

tesque has metaphysical assumptions. The Enlightenment envisions a world in which evil and abnormality are progressively eliminated. But the artistic portrayal of the grotesque is equivalent to the assertion that evil and abnormality are metaphysical, that they are aspects of reality that can never be eliminated. Thus, as Thomas Mann says, the grotesque is "anti-bourgeois" — anti-progressive, anti-liberal, anti-enlightenment, and also anti-Marxist.

The Coens use the grotesque as a refutation of Fink's Marxist progressivism. But it rings false, because one senses that they are unwilling to affirm the more traditional metaphysical alternative that the grotesque presupposes.

Barton Fink is set in 1941. We begin in New York, backstage in a Broadway theater, in the final moments of *Bare Ruined Choirs*, the new play by the up-and-coming Jewish-Marxist playwright Barton Fink. Fink's character is loosely modeled on Clifford Odets, but the bits of dialogue are a hilarious send-up of Steinbeck. The play is a smash, hailed as a "triumph of the common man." At the celebration, however, Fink is ungracious, boorish, and self-absorbed, reeling off Marxist Popular Front clichés about "real success" being the creation of a "new living theater of and about and for the common man."

Fink's reviews attract the attention of Capitol Pictures, who offer him $1,000 per week to write for the movies. Fink's agent urges him to cash in on his good press, assuring him that the common man will still be waiting for him, and adding prophetically that he might even find one or two of them in Hollywood.

Fink arrives in Hollywood and checks into a dilapidated Art Deco pile the Hotel Earle. With its putrescent palette of greens, mauves, and magentas, its endless empty corridors, its peeling wallpaper, and its grotesque staff, it is pure Lynch. Then Fink meets his new employer, Jack Lipnick (Michael Lerner hilariously playing Louis B. Mayer and stealing every scene).

Lipnik seems to know nothing of Fink, but he is convinced that the "Barton Fink feeling" will be a hot commodity and assigns him to write a wrestling movie starring Wallace Beery. It

---

(New York: Farrar, Straus & Giroux, 1969).

seems a natural fit, given Fink's pronouncements about "the common man." But Barton Fink is a Jewish Marxist from New York. For him, the common man is just an abstraction. Naturally, he gets writer's block.

As he frets in front of his typewriter, he hears laughter from next door. He calls the front desk to complain. The bellman relays the complaint, and the neighbor knocks on the door. Enter Charlie Meadows, traveling insurance salesman, an affable cornfed Midwestern *goy* played by Midwestern *goy* John Goodman.

Their conversation is hilarious. Fink is totally self-absorbed and patronizing, explaining that he writes about "people like you—the average working stiff, the common man." He mentions that people in New York (fellow Jewish Communists no doubt) are creating a new theater "based on the common man," but adding that it must not "mean much to you." Three times Charlie interjects that he could tell Barton some stories, and three times Barton ignores him, ranting on about "empty formalism" and denouncing WASPs and the British class system. Apparently "the life of the mind" precludes empathy for others, or even listening to what they have to say.

The next day, Fink seeks guidance from his director Ben Geisler (Tony Shaloub playing Irving Thalberg) and fellow writer W. P. Mayhew (John Mahoney hilariously playing William Faulkner and stealing every scene). Mayhew is a great Southern novelist who has become a raging alcoholic during his sojourn in the land of the Philistines. When Fink prattles on about writing coming from pain and the desire to help his fellow man, Mayhew replies that he just enjoys making things up.

Fink develops an attraction to Mayhew's secretary and girlfriend Audrey, who offers to help him get over his writer's block. When Audrey reveals that she has actually been ghostwriting Mayhew's recent work, Fink is maniacal in celebrating the unmasking of another WASP hero as a fraud. Audrey chides him for lacking empathy and understanding, but Fink has no idea what she is talking about. Audrey then seduces Fink, and the sounds of their coupling travel the pipes to Charlie's room.

Fink awakens in the morning to find that Audrey has been murdered in bed while he slept. He goes to Charlie who convinces him that he should not go to the police and offers to dispose of the body. Charlie then leaves town, after giving Barton a package for safekeeping. A few days later, two police detectives, Mastrinotti and Deutsch, come to question Fink. Audrey's body has turned up without a head, and their suspect is Charlie Meadows, who is apparently Karl "Madman" Mundt, a serial killer. After the police leave, Fink's writer's block breaks and he completes the script.

Fink then celebrates the completion of the script at a USO dance. When a square-jawed blonde sailor tries to cut in, Fink begins to rant, "I'm a writer celebrating, you monsters [*goyim*]! I am a creator! This is where I serve the common man [pointing to his head]!" Jewish metaphysics makes a distinction between the uncreated creator (God), the created creator (man = the Jews), and uncreative creation, which presumably includes the *goy* monsters. Someone takes a swing at Fink, who falls to the floor and slithers away while the *goyim* fight among themselves.

When Fink returns to his hotel, the detectives are waiting for him. Mayhew has turned up dead and decapitated; they now know that Audrey was Fink's friend; and then there is the huge bloodstain on Fink's mattress. Fink is arrested as Mundt's accomplice and cuffed to his bed frame.

The hotel becomes as hot as a sauna. Fink announces that Charlie has returned. The hallway is filled with flames. Charlie appears, screaming "I'll show you the life of the mind!" and kills the detectives with shotgun blasts, saying "Heil Hitler" before dispatching Detective Deutsch.

Charlie then screams at a terrified Barton that "You don't listen!" and that he is just "a tourist with a typewriter" barging into his world and telling him how to live. Fink naturally thinks the end is at hand and blubbers out an apology. His fury spent, Charlie frees Barton from the handcuffs and goes into his room nonchalantly, as if the building were not on fire.

Are the flames hellfire? Is it all a dream? Is it *symbolism*? I think it is just a meaningless Jewish jerk job.

Fink gathers up his script and flees the building.

A few days pass. Lipnick has read the script. Fink is summoned into his office, where he finds Lipnick dressed in the uniform of an army colonel. The commission is honorary, he mentions, arranged by Henry Morgenthau. The uniform had been run up by the costume department.

Lipnick hates the script. Fink was assigned to do a wrestling movie, and instead delivered "a fruity movie about suffering" — about a man wrestling with himself. Lipnick has fired Geisler, and he informs Fink that he will remain in Hollywood, writing scripts, but none of his scripts will be produced until he "grows up" and realizes the error of thinking that "the whole world revolves around whatever rattles inside that little kike head of yours." Devastated, Fink then goes to the beach, where we are treated to some more pretentious *symbolism*. Then the movie ends.

Barton Fink portrays Jews in an entirely negative light. Fink is a self-absorbed, patronizing, hate-filled, Marxist elitist who talks *about* the common man, and talks *at* the common man, but never *listens* to him. Lipnick is a mercurial, megalomaniacal buffoon. (My friend Petronius suggested he may be a portrayal of Yahweh himself.) The rest of us are just extras in their neurotic psychodramas. And the terrifying thing is that they have the power to make their dreams real. We are ruled by psychotics.

With the character of the Heil Hitlering Madman Mundt, are the Coens suggesting that anti-Semitism is a *predictable reaction* to Jewish behavior? Is National Socialism the comeuppance of Judeo-Bolshevism? Are the flames the "gas ovens" of Auschwitz?

The fact that Mundt is ultimately a big sentimental *schmuck* whose fury can be deflected simply with a tearful apology — sincere or not, we cannot know — takes on new meaning when viewed in light of the tears shed by Turturro's Jewish villain in *Miller's Crossing*, which is a movie about how Jews have hacked the Aryan mind — and how we can erect a firewall.

Why the lack of good commentary on *Barton Fink*? Because one of the unspoken rules of today's society is that if you can't say anything nice about the Jews, you can't say anything at all. Perhaps, one day, it will be the law.

Counter-Currents, May 21, 2015

BATMAN:
THE DARK KNIGHT RETURNS

Batman: The Dark Knight Returns is an animated movie adaptation of Frank Miller's graphic novel *The Dark Knight Returns*. Released in two 76-minute parts in 2012 and 2013, then combined into a 148-minute DVD and Blu-ray edition, this is lame, sclerotic, constipated, Z-grade animation drawn out to paralyzing lengths, completely lacking the visual style and dynamism of the original graphic novel, which is more animated on the printed page than in this adaptation.

Why review it, then? The original graphic novel seems quite paradoxical. The characters of Batman and Commissioner Gordon are highly Right-wing, truly off-the-charts on the F-scale. But this is counter-balanced by a number of features that can only be described as politically correct: anti-racist, anti-sexist, and anti-homophobic. What ties these two dimensions together is Miller's Right-wing individualism. His Rightist values are universal principles that can be followed by anyone, regardless of race, sex, etc., and it is only permissible to go outside the law in service of these values. The film, although it mostly detracts from the graphic novel, also adds a few touches that heighten its Right-wing dimensions.

After the death of Jason Todd (the second Robin), Bruce Wayne retired from the role of Batman at the age of 45. Ten years later, Gotham is at the mercy of the Mutant gang (which is, ludicrously, all-white and practically all-blond, as are practically all the other criminals in Gotham). Commissioner Gordon is 70 and on the brink of retirement. The Joker is catatonic in Arkham Asylum. Harvey Dent/Two-Face receives reconstructive surgery courtesy of Bruce Wayne. Dent is declared sane, released from Arkham, and promptly drops out of sight and returns to crime.

Bored with retirement and appalled by the crime wave, the 55-year-old Bruce Wayne dons cape and cowl and returns to fighting crime. On one of his patrols, Batman rescues teenage girl Carrie Kelley from the Mutants. Kelley then buys a Robin costume and goes into crime fighting, eventually winning the trust of Batman. Kelley's character is an obvious concession to feminism, and with her short hair and tomboyish demeanor, to lesbianism as well.

Batman eventually defeats Two-Face and the leader of the Mutants. Some former Mutant gang members rename themselves the Sons of Batman and become vigilantes. This disturbs President Ronald Reagan—portrayed as a sinister, greenish Frankenstein monster—who asks Superman to step in and stop Batman. Superman threatens Bruce Wayne, telling him to go back into retirement, then zooms off to Corto Maltese to fight the Soviets. Commissioner Gordon retires, and his replacement Ellen Yindel (feminist, lesbian, and very probably Jewish) issues a warrant for Batman's arrest.

Meanwhile, Batman's return has awakened the Joker from his catatonic state. Psychiatrist Bartholomew Wolper, who previously certified Harvey Dent sane and has publicly argued that Batman is actually guiltier than the criminals he fights, now champions the Joker, declaring that he had been cured and should be reintegrated into society. Wolper reintroduces the Joker to the world on a late-night talk show, but it does not go as planned. The Joker slashes Wolper's throat on live TV, then gasses the entire audience to death and escapes.

Batman tracks the Joker to an amusement park and beats him within an inch of his life. Batman knows that he could have prevented every murder committed by the Joker since his release if he only had the strength to kill him years before. But even now, Batman cannot bring himself to simply execute the Joker. Instead, he plans to turn him over to the system that had just let him out to kill again. But the Joker does the right thing for the wrong reason. Out of sheer spite, he snaps his own neck, knowing that Batman will be accused of his murder. Batman, however, makes a narrow escape.

The Corto Maltese war escalates into a Soviet nuclear strike. Superman deflects a nuclear missile to a deserted place, but the detonation causes an electro-magnetic pulse that shuts down all electronic equipment, plunging America into chaos. Batman rallies the Sons of Batman to restore order to Gotham, making it the safest place in the nation. Reagan is embarrassed by this and orders Superman to stop Batman.

Batman and Superman then square off. Batman is strengthened by a mechanical exo-suit, and Superman is weakened by the nuclear blast and a kryptonite-tipped arrow, leading to Batman's victory. (All this is reworked in Zack Snyder's *Batman v Superman*.) Batman then dies of a heart attack, Alfred Pennyworth dies of a stroke, Wayne Manor is destroyed, and Batman is revealed to be Bruce Wayne. In the epilogue, however, we discover that Batman/Wayne faked his death and plans to carry on his crusade against crime in secret.

The portrayals of Wolper and the Joker are the most politically incorrect aspects of the movie, pushing it almost into Alt-Right territory. Wolper is a Jewish name, and he is drawn with a big nose and a black Jew-fro. In the movie, this impression is driven home by voicing him as a smarmy, liberal New York Jew. As for the Joker, he is voiced as a snarky, sibilant, effeminate homosexual.

The most substantive Right-wing elements in the film were already present in the graphic novel, of course, but seeing them on the screen had much more impact.

First, when Jason Todd's death is mentioned, the expectation is that Batman/Bruce Wayne will affirm the bourgeois assumption that nothing is worse than the violent death of a young man. But Wayne rejects this assumption at root, saying that Jason was "a soldier." Wayne's unspoken assumption is that it is appropriate for soldiers to give their lives for a cause, because there are some values higher than the preservation of individual life.

Second, when the retired Commissioner Gordon meets with his successor Ellen Yindel, he makes an extraordinary case for going outside the law for reasons of state, to pursue a higher good. He recounts how the Japanese attack on Pearl Harbor shocked Americans into entering World War II and recounts how it was later revealed that Roosevelt knew the attack was coming and did nothing to stop it, precisely to get the United States into the war. Many innocent men died, but Gordon clearly believes that Roosevelt did the right thing, even though he is not willing to come out and say it. Instead, he says that he could not judge it, because "It was too big. He was too big." Yindel only sees the relevance to Batman later, when she gives up her pursuit of him because "He's too big."

Of course, Roosevelt's ploy to get the United States to bleed for Jewry in another World War became the template for the conspiracy to get the United States to go to war with Israel's enemies in the Middle East. This, coupled with Miller's politically correct views of race and sex, gives *The Dark Knight Returns* a distinctly neoconservative ideological flavor: a marriage of liberal-democratic and globalist values with Schmittian political realism. But this is consistent with the larger superhero genre, in which Nietzschean Supermen, or just plain Supermen, always work to promote egalitarian humanism.[1]

It's time for Batman to shrug.

Counter-Currents, May 5, 2018

---

[1] See Greg Johnson, "Schmitt, Superheroes, & the Deep State," in Greg Johnson, *Toward a New Nationalism* (San Francisco: Counter-Currents, 2019).

BATMAN V SUPERMAN:
DAWN OF JUSTICE

In any matchup between Batman and Superman, I side with Batman. I've never liked the character of Superman, because he is not a man at all. He's basically a god. He's not a human being who has raised himself to the pinnacles of human excellence. He's an alien who is simply endowed with superior abilities. There is nothing heroic about Superman, because he is almost invulnerable. He faces no risks. There's nothing he must struggle to overcome.

Batman, however, is a true Nietzschean superman, a man who has made himself more than a man. He's a man who faces injury, death, and imprisonment night after night in order to fight evil. I don't want to live in a godless universe, but frankly I would prefer that we make ourselves into gods rather than find them readymade.

I didn't like Zack Synder's first Superman movie, *Man of Steel*, so I had very low expectations for *Batman v Superman: Dawn of Justice*. That said, for the first 80% of *Batman v Superman*, I found myself thinking this is a pretty good movie. Zack Snyder would be a great silent movie director, and the opening credit sequence (based on Frank Miller's *The Dark Knight Returns* graphic novel) is pure poetry. The first appearance of the Batman is genuinely terrifying. There is a great nightmare sequence in which Batman fights against Superman's henchmen who are dressed as Nazi soldiers while giant cockroach-Valkyries whisk the fallen to some sort of hellish Valhalla. The directing, editing, and special effects throughout are superb. Hans Zimmer's score, moreover, is one of his better efforts. But for all that, at about the 2-hour mark, the movie became ludicrous, unintelligible, and uninvolving.

The movie is set about two years after *Man of Steel*. The public is souring on Superman. Sure, he saved the earth from the Kryptonians, but a lot was destroyed in the process. And maybe the Kryptonians came here because of him. And he is one of them too. How can we trust him? How do we know he will always be benevolently disposed to us? Is Superman outside the law? Shouldn't he have to follow the same laws as the rest of us? Superman may look human, but he is not. Shouldn't we fear a god who has no real attachment humanity?

Three of Superman's critics are Senator June Finch (Holly Hunter), billionaire Lex Luthor (Jesse Eisenberg, whose characterization is a cross between Zorg from *The Fifth Element* and the Joker from *The Dark Knight*), and billionaire Bruce Wayne (Ben Affleck), who moonlights as Batman. For his part, Superman's alter-ego, Clark Kent, sees Batman as a dangerous vigilante. There are also conflicts between Luthor and Senator Finch, who refuses to allow him to import kryptonite, and between Luthor and Batman, who steals the kryptonite after it is smuggled in.

Conflict, of course, is the stuff of good plots. But characterization is essential too. Unfortunately, Luthor's motives are the murkiest, which is unfortunate, because he drives the entire plot. Luthor gets Lois Lane taken hostage by African revolutionaries, knowing Superman will come to her rescue. Then he has mercenaries massacre the guerrillas, and Superman is blamed. Luthor tries to acquire kryptonite to use against Superman, but it is blocked by Finch then stolen by Batman. Luthor bombs a Senate hearing at which Superman is testifying. Superman, of course, survives but is humiliated and disappears for a while.

When Superman returns, Luthor gets Batman and Superman to fight one another. Batman, however, is prepared for the fight with new armor and kryptonite weapons, which significantly weaken Superman. However, when Batman is poised to kill Superman with a kryptonite spear, he pauses at the last minute when Superman says "Martha," his mother's name—which, coincidentally, is the name of Bruce Wayne's mother as well. Then Lois Lane arrives to explain that Superman has been blackmailed into fighting Batman by Luthor, who has kidnapped Martha Kent. Then the two superheroes unite to fight Luthor and rescue Martha.

Now, this sort of peripety is the stuff of classic drama and grand opera and Bollywood. Yes, it is ludicrous when stated baldly, but it doesn't have to seem that way. It could have been handled well. It almost works as it is. But it also marks the point when the movie stopped working.

After Superman and Batman team up to fight Luthor, he unleashes his final assault. Using technology from a crashed Kryptonian vessel, Luthor has created a monster (basically an electrified version of Peter Jackson's cave trolls) that is capable of destroying Superman.

Batman and Superman are then joined in their epic battle by Wonder Woman, played by Israeli actress Gal Gadot. Although I admit that my reaction is not entirely rational, given the amount of disbelief I had already suspended, I found the addition of another superhero intensely annoying. I had the same reaction to *Twilight*. I was fine with the vampires but thought the whole thing was ruined by adding werewolves.

Superman realizes that the troll, like him, is vulnerable only to kryptonite, so he uses Batman's kryptonite spear to kill it. Unfortunately, using the spear also weakens Superman, whom the beast kills in its death throes.

To my great surprise, when Batman began to deploy his kryptonite weapons against Superman, weakening him to the point that he could have been killed, I found myself *liking* Superman more. It makes sense, though, because to be vulnerable is to be human. But to fight on in spite of vulnerability is true heroism. Before this, Superman may have been super, but he was no hero, because he was invulnerable. Invulnerable men, however, do not face risks, require virtues, or make sacrifices. And when at the movie's climax Superman *risks death* and then *actually dies* to save us, it had a real emotional punch. And when all the whooshing and zapping dies down and the movie shifts into *dénouement* mode, it somewhat recovers.

Lex Luthor is imprisoned (and when his head is shaved looks like a rat), Superman is memorialized, Clark Kent is buried back in Kansas, and Batman joins Wonder Woman to search for other "metahumans" like herself, since after Superman's death the earth is vulnerable to other threats that lie beyond. I smell franchise.

But it appears that they will have some help after all, for in the last shot of the film, a few particles of earth thrown on the lid of Clark Kent's coffin begin to levitate. Yes, that's right, Superman did not just die to save mankind, he will rise from the dead to continue the fight. This confirms Gregory Hood's reading of *Man of Steel* as offering Superman as an Aryan warrior Christ.

Superman's experience of vulnerability to kryptonite was, in effect, his incarnation — his descent from being an immortal god to being a mortal man — in order that he could die for our salvation. And his impending resurrection is a return to divine status, although this time he will also have a connection to humanity, because he lived and died as one of us, which makes him far less threatening.

Zack Snyder is an extraordinarily talented director. *Watchmen* remains the greatest superhero movie ever made. But it had an excellent script, a script that even improved upon the original graphic novel. The best director in the world can't overcome a bad script though, and Snyder's recent works, from *Sucker Punch* to the Superman movies, suffer from bad scripts.

In terms of performances, Jesse Eisenberg's Luthor was more a collection of quirks than a character. Henry Cavill and Ben Affleck look better than they act. Gal Gadot's Wonder Woman isn't even good-looking.

The Christian allegory in Snyder's Superman films is an interesting dimension. *Batman v Superman* is relatively free of political correctness. But it is also free of the philosophical depth and Rightist political themes of Nolan's Dark Knight Trilogy. Although the portrayal of Luthor as a shrimpy, neurotic, fast-talking Jewboy who manipulates two hulking white superheroes into trying to kill each other does have an archetypal quality that gives one pause.

After a strong opening week, *Batman v Superman* sank like kryptonite. Let's hope it is the end of the franchise and Zack Snyder finds a better outlet for his considerable talent. He's actually talking about remaking *The Fountainhead*, for instance. (Snyder and Christopher Nolan would be among my top picks for a proper *Atlas Shrugged* adaptation as well.) Until then, he remains on artistic probation.

Counter-Currents, May 25, 2016

BLACK PANTHER

I saw *Black Panther* with a friend in Seattle last week. Judging from the reverent silence in the theater—broken only occasionally by our laughter at unintentional bits of humor—it was an all-white audience. The serious tone of *Black Panther* is a departure from recent Marvel movies, which constantly undercut heroism with ironic humor. But *Black Panther* is a movie about numinous, magical Negroes, and some things are sacred. God is not mocked. (Unless he is Thor.)

Given the massive media hype and grotesque, fawning patronage of white liberals, I was prepared to hate *Black Panther*. But it really isn't a terrible movie, although I would not see it again.

The premise of *Black Panther* is ludicrous, but no sillier than most superhero movies. The superhero known as Black Panther is the hereditary monarch of a remote African kingdom called Wakanda. Wakanda, like Ethiopia, Lesotho, and Swaziland, was not colonized by whites. Wakanda also possesses a unique natural resource, a magical metal of extraterrestrial origin called "vibranium." (One has to ask: when Stan Lee and Jack Kirby created the Black Panther character in 1966, was "vibrant" already a euphemism for non-white?) Because of their isolation and vibranium, Wakanda developed the most advanced technology on the planet. To protect themselves from white colonizers, the Wakandans used this technology to hide their futuristic capital city—complete with flying cars—behind some sort of ray shield, like an African Galt's Gulch.

Black Panther is a deeply feminist film, even though feminism is as common in the real Africa as flying cars. Sometimes the costumes and set design look like they could have come from the pen of A. Wyatt Mann, especially the guy with the green zoot suit and matching lip plate. There is a hilarious scene in which some Wakandans shut up a white man by oogaing. (I pray that this catches on.) When a Wakandan flying car shows up in Oakland, the local urban youths immediately start talking about stripping it and selling the parts. Naturally, the white liberals around me were terrified to laugh at any of this.

But at a certain point, I simply decided to view *Black Panther* as a science fiction movie set a long time ago, in a galaxy far, far away, and this suspension of disbelief allowed me to relax and enjoy the spectacle.

The plot of *Black Panther* deals with the rise of a new king/Black Panther, T'Challa (played by Chadwick Boseman), who faces two challenges to Wakandan isolationism.

The first challenge is the liberal welfare statism of T'Challa's ex-girlfriend Nakia (Lupita Nyong'o), a spy who roves around Africa doing good deeds for impoverished and oppressed Africans. She thinks that Wakanda needs to become a humanitarian superpower like Sweden, sending foreign aid and taking in refugees. (Let's call this option "Dem Programs," for short.)

The second challenge is represented by T'Challa's American-raised cousin N'Jadaka/"Killmonger" (Michael B. Jordan), who wishes to spark a global black revolution by exporting Wakandan weapons and technology to black revolutionaries and gangsters around the globe. (We'll call this option "Kill Whitey," for short.)

There has been a lot of debate about the politics of *Black Panther*, most of it wrong-headed.

Wakanda is a black, isolationist ethnostate which cultivates a fierce patriotism. When T'Challa shares Nakia's suggestion to open Wakanda to refugees with W'Kabi, a tribal leader played by Daniel Kaluuya, the response is simple: Refugees would inevitably bring their problems to Wakanda and destroy their way of life. I was shocked that such sentiments made it to the screen, but the reason soon became clear: W'Kabi is a villain, and *Black Panther* only voices such Trumpian sentiments to dismiss them.

To repeat: *Black Panther* is not an ethnonationalist, isolationist movie. To be sure, it shows how such policies created a great society. But the message is that it is selfish for Wakanda to keep its treasures to itself. It must share them with the world, even at the risk of losing its identity and independence.

Furthermore, although Killmonger is an eloquent advocate

for the global extermination of white people, *Black Panther* is not Walt Disney's *Kill Whitey*. (There's a good meme in there, through.) Indeed, Killmonger is the main villain of the movie, and he is defeated and killed by T'Challa, who does not take his cousin's ideas the least bit seriously. Instead, he regards them as merely a symptom of the malaise of black people under colonial oppression. He even blames his cousin's downfall on his father's decision to abandon him in America rather than raise him in Wakanda. This mistake, of course, was rooted in Wakandan isolationism.

Black Panther isn't even anti-white *per se*. Yes, the only colonial oppressors mentioned are whites. Nary a word is spoken about the vast Arab slave trade. Yes, one of the principal villains is a white South African with the subtle name Klaue ("claw") played by Andy Serkis. But one of the heroes of the movie is a white man, Everett K. Ross (Martin Freeman), who is an agent of the CIA no less. Yes, the good white guy works for the American deep state. Let that message to black America sink in for a minute.

So what is the political message of *Black Panther*, once both isolationist ethnonationalism and global white genocide are rejected? Dem Programs, of course. T'Challa comes to think that Wakanda has been wrong to selfishly guard its independence and hoard its wealth. Thus, at the end of the movie, T'Challa and his sister go to Oakland, California, one of America's vibrant murder capitals, to outline his plans to uplift blacks around the world with Dem Programs. No doubt with the aid of their good friend in the CIA and other liberal white (((or whitish))) allies. Roll credits.

Black Panther is an entertaining spectacle, but in political terms it is a sinister fraud. It draws its energy by exciting black audiences with two Black Nationalist visions that, like it or not, resonate deeply with them: the advanced, isolationist, nationalist African Shangri-La of Wakanda and Killmonger's project of global white genocide. But in the end, *Black Panther* rejects both forms of Black Nationalism and channels these energies into support for the present system of racial integration and liberal-managerial welfare statism under the tutelage of the Democratic Party and the globalist deep state.

Colonialism runs deeper than you think.

But this should come as no surprise, given that the creators of the original *Black Panther* comic are Jews. Writer Stan Lee was born Stanley Lieber, and artist Jack Kirby was born Jacob Kurtzberg. Moreover, both Marvel Studios and Walt Disney are completely loyal to Lee and Kirby's Jewish vision of black-white race relations. As Kevin MacDonald outlines in his classic essay "Jews, Blacks, and Race," Jewish organizations and individuals took a leading role in promoting black civil rights in America:

> Jews have played a prominent role in organizing blacks beginning with the founding of the National Association for the Advancement of Colored People (NAACP) in 1909 and, despite increasing black anti-Semitism, continuing into the present. The NAACP was founded by wealthy German Jews, non-Jewish whites, and blacks led by W. E. B. DuBois. The Jewish role was predominant.
>
> But Jews have promoted a very specific vision of black uplift, namely racial "integration" under the tutelage of the Democratic Party and the managerial state, which are dominated by a white and Jewish elite. Thus Jews have consistently opposed all forms of black separatism and isolationism, from Marcus Garvey in the first decades of the 20th century to Malcolm X in the 1960s to Louis Farrakhan today.[1]

Wakanda is basically a black Switzerland: an neutral, isolationist society protected by high mountains that has grown wealthy and advanced by minding its own business. From the liberal-democratic-globalist point of view, Wakanda has no more right to exist that way than Switzerland does. Thus the fruits of its isolation must be shared. Its borders and bank accounts must be opened to the needy of the world. But there are just too many of these people. Thus global altruism can only

---

[1] Kevin MacDonald, "Jews, Blacks, & Race," *Counter-Currents*, February 15, 2012.

tear down the advanced nations, not raise up the backward masses.

Only ethnonationalists oppose this globalist agenda. When White Nationalists come to power in the United States, we will create a black homeland on this continent, and we will call it Wakanda. Forget liberalism, the Democratic Party, and the managerial-welfare state. Only White Nationalism will make Wakanda real.

Counter-Currents, February 24, 2018

BLADE RUNNER 2049

It is dangerous work, making a sequel to a classic like *Blade Runner*, Ridley Scott's 1982 *magnum opus*. French Canadian director Denis Villeneuve's *Blade Runner 2049* is a very good film, but it inevitably falls short of the original.

I first discovered Villeneuve's work with his 2016 science fiction film *Arrival*.[1] *Arrival* impressed me as a highly imaginative science fiction film with an original visual style, told with an appealingly deliberate art-film pacing, with a stunning plot twist and a powerful emotional payoff. Villeneuve's 2015 film *Sicario* is an excellent thriller/crime drama.

Blade Runner 2049 is more like *Arrival* than *Sicario*, and that is something of a problem. At 2 hours, 43 minutes, *Blade Runner 2049* takes art-house pacing and style to Tarkovskyesque lengths. It is a real artistic gamble, and not an entirely successful one. I think this would have been a much more effective film—and yet also more commercial—if directed more like *Sicario*, i.e., edited down/sped up to 2 hours.

It would have been more like the original *Blade Runner* as well. I suspect, however, that Villeneuve may have rejected such a course because he felt intimidated by the prospect of doing a sequel that would invite too many comparisons with the original, so he struck out in a direction that would be more likely to please middlebrow critics and the sort of people who enjoy sitting through *Solaris*, *Stalker*, or *2001: A Space Odyssey*. I generally like such movies, but I felt that *Blade Runner 2049* runs out of steam near the end and fails to deliver the powerful emotional punch toward which it was building.

But this problem may have been inevitable, for there was probably no way of doing this movie without including Harrison Ford, and frankly, I wish they had done it without him, or pared his role down to a brief Yoda-like encounter in the second act, where he imparts some useful information to the questing

---

[1] See my podcast discussion with John Morgan, "A Sci-Fi Trifecta: *Arrival, Passengers, & Rogue One*," *Counter-Currents*, January 27, 2017.

knight and then is left behind.

I also wish they had replaced Ford with Ryan Gosling's character for the third act, which would have eliminated all the gimpy appeals to nostalgia. I think a much more emotionally powerful conclusion could have been crafted with Gosling alone, for he undergoes the same transformation from egocentrism toward disinterestedness and detachment that Roy Batty does in the original. (I won't explain this point, because it would entail spoilers, but watch the movie, and you will see what I mean.)

Gosling, frankly, is ten times the actor that Ford is. Gosling's performance as K, a replicant and a Blade Runner, is stunningly subtle and sensitive, whereas Ford is capable of nothing but being a two-fisted, hard-drinking, crotchety old scene-chewer. Frankly, after he was on screen for 3 minutes, I wanted to run him through with a light saber. (Science fiction will not be safe until the entire casts of the original *Star Wars* and *Star Trek* are dead.)

I liked most of the other performances in *Blade Runner 2049*, particularly Ana de Armas as Joi, Sylvia Hoeks as Luv, and Carla Juri as Ana Stelline.

Jared Leto's performance as the Mephistophelean businessman Niander Wallace doesn't really compare to the original's Eldon Tyrell, and frankly I don't understand his behavior in the first act, when he casually kills a new replicant while monologuing. Nor does his behavior seem rational in the third act. If Rachel gave birth to a child, and Wallace can create a whole new Rachel, and he has Deckard, then he has both parents. So why does he need the child? Can't he discover the secret of replication reproduction with the parents alone? And if the child really is a "miracle"—an event that we can't replicate with natural causes—then even if he had her, there's nothing he could do.

In short, the basic problem with this move is the script. Which is a pretty big problem.

The script also lacks the poetry and mythic dimension of the original, which is not just a sci-fi dystopia but an allegory about Satan's rebellion against God—see my essay on *Blade Runner* in *Son of Trevor Lynch's White Nationalist Guide to the Movies*—

whereas here we just catch glimpses of a Marxist revolt of the masses, which is a myth as well, in the superficial sense of the word.

The film touches on the same issues of personal identity as the original, but does not add any depth to them.

Blade Runner 2049 extrapolates from the dystopia of the original, incorporating ecological elements from Philip K. Dick's novel *Do Androids Dream of Electric Sheep?*.[2] But other updates make no sense, such as the vast orphanage where predominantly white children dig through garbage. Isn't this replicant work? And where are all these white orphans coming from? It doesn't make sense that there are lots of surplus white children on an ecologically devastated planet.

The visual style of *Blade Runner 2049* is stunning. Of course it is based on the original, but it develops it in interesting and original ways. It is truly the most successful element of the film. Like Terrence Malick, Villeneuve underscores the fact that cinema is inescapably a visual medium. Unfortunately, also like Malick, he also underscores the fact that a good movie needs to be *more* than just a series of striking images.

The music by Hans Zimmer and Benjamin Wallfisch effectively incorporates Vangelis' original themes, but what is new is not memorable.

What this all seems to add up to is: *Blade Runner 2049* is a superficial movie, but it is still successful as such. It held my attention for 2 hours and 43 minutes, but it lacked a powerful emotional payoff. It is good, but it could have been so much better. Still, it is definitely a movie that I will watch again, in the hope of glimpsing something deeper. I recommend it to fans of *Blade Runner* and science fiction aficionados in general. Take in a matinee with friends, then go out to dinner. I guarantee you will discuss nothing else.

Counter-Currents, February 2, 2019

---

[2] Greg Johnson, "Philip K. Dick's *Do Androids Dream of Electric Sheep?* as Anti-Semitic/Christian-Gnostic Allegory," *Counter-Currents*, February 15, 2012.

CHILDREN OF MEN

Mexican director Alfonso Cuarón's *Children of Men* (2006) is loosely based on P. D. James' 1992 novel of the same name. Cuarón is solidly Leftist, but *Children of Men* seems more and more like a Right-wing vision of dystopia with each passing year. (Cuarón's 2001 film *Y Tu Mamá También*, is basically Marxist propaganda and soft-core porn, but his 2013 hit *Gravity* could be seen as an argument against putting women in the military or space, although I don't think this was the director's intention.)

Children of Men is set in 2027. For unknown reasons (surely none of them related to feminism), the human race has become infertile. The youngest humans on the planet are 18 years old.

In the Introduction to *The White Nationalist Manifesto*, I have a thought experiment about what would happen if a particular people, or the whole human race, were to discover that they have no genetic future, i.e., that they are going extinct. (I had not seen the movie at the time I wrote it, but I remember reading about James' novel in 1992, and the premise stuck with me.)

James and I both speculated that impending human extinction would lead to rises in anti-social, short-term, self-destructive behaviors and well as intense religiosity. James also predicts the rise of Left-wing terrorist violence, which makes sense, since Leftism is a form of religion for unbelievers.

In James' scenario, the nihilism and fanaticism unleashed by impending extinction have left the planet devastated by wars, insurrections, plagues, and migrations. But sea-girt Britain has managed to maintain order with an authoritarian government. Because Britain is relatively stable, however, it is a target for massive waves of illegal immigrants and refugees from the rest of the world.

In Cuarón's film, entire cities have been walled off as refugee camps ruled by violent gangs. The Fishes are a Left-wing pro-refugee terrorist sect, who, in the name of love and kindness, want to unleash the refugee tide so it can drown Britain like the rest of Europe.

I am not sure if 2006 audiences and critics saw Cuarón's dystopian vision of Britian's future as outlandish and unlikely. But today his depictions of ruined English cities swarming with non-whites, parades of Muslims chanting "Allahu Akbar" and firing guns in the air, and brutal urban firefights between terrorist gangsters and the British army seem more like current events than prophecy—especially after the migrant crisis began in 2014, applauded by Europe's elites as a humanitarian duty but also urged as an economic necessity—because of low European fertility. After all, Mammon is our god, and if Europeans fail to keep the economy afloat, they must be replaced by non-Europeans. The economic system is absolute. The people are fungible.

The story that James and Cuarón set in this world is, frankly, less interesting than the world itself. I won't spoil the plot except to say that it centers around the first glimmer of hope for humanity in 18 years, namely a woman has become pregnant. But she is a refugee, and unfortunately, her life and that of her child are imperiled because they have become pawns of the Fishes terrorist gang, who want to use them as symbols to spark an uprising. The hero, Theo Farin (*Sin City*'s Clive Owen), another pawn drawn in by the Fishes, tries to spirit the pregnant woman away to safety.

Cuarón portrays British police and soldiers as Nazi-like sadists and martinets who seem to delight in senseless acts of violence. But the Fishes are also portrayed as a pack of treacherous, hysterical, homicidal freaks and degenerates.

From a White Nationalist point of view, the most repugnant aspect of the film is that the pregnant woman is a very black African. This is Cuarón's invention, not James'. Thus we are treated to the spectacle of a white hero risking life and limb to save a black woman and her child who are the hope of the human race. At the end of the film, we are left wondering: Does this child perhaps mean that the curse of infertility can be lifted for the entire human race? Or will Africans alone inherit the planet? Frankly, the latter is hardly a happy ending, and the whole film would end up being just a disgusting exercise in glorifying white racial altruism. Normies are supposed to feel hope at the end, but racially-conscious whites will still feel despair.

Nevertheless, happy ending or not, *Children of Men* is still worth seeing. It is an intense and gripping action film set in an increasingly realistic dystopian future. It is brilliantly directed with an excellent script, striking images, solid performances (including Michael Caine as a lovable old stoner), and some well-chosen music. Its images of a race facing long-term extinction and fighting off non-white hordes are especially relevant to whites today, thus *Children of Men* might be a useful teaching tool to get white "normies" to start talking about the most pressing issues of our time. After all, 2027 is right around the corner.

Counter-Currents, December 10, 2018

CRONENBERG'S *CRASH*

I remember the moment in 1996 when I first heard about David Cronenberg's *Crash* on National Public Radio. I exploded in outrage. I thought the story of a group of people who made a sexual fetish of car crashes had to be the stupidest movie concept of all time. Not decadent or perverted, mind you—although it was obviously *trying really hard* in that respect—but just stupid. I had the sense that Western decadence, like a 16,000-page burlesque by the Marquis de Sade, was finally running out of perversions, and Cronenberg was desperately trying to come up with a novel tab and slot combo, perhaps by employing some sort of random content generator, like picking words from a book at random. "Sex and . . . car crashes. Yeah, that's the ticket."

Of course, I was wrong about all that. Culturally, things have gotten so much worse since 1996, that a film about attractive white people who get off on car crashes seems almost wholesome in retrospect. As for where the story came from: *Crash* was based on a novel by J. G. Ballard, which explains the try-hard geekiness of the concept. But maybe Ballard was the one using the random perversion generator. I have not read the novel, and I don't know how faithful the film adaptation is, but I am commenting here on the movie alone.

Of course, the connection between sex and car crashes is not random and accidental. Both are objects of voyeurs, which is what *Crash* makes us, the audience. But most viewers rebelled, and *Crash* was a huge commercial and critical flop. Virtually everyone, audiences and critics alike, found *Crash* unintelligible, unsexy, repellent, and sometimes downright ludicrous.

Thus it was some years before I actually saw *Crash*, and to my surprise, it is truly an excellent movie. I would rank it as Cronenberg's best, alongside *A History of Violence*.[1] The story of

---

[1] See my review in *Trevor Lynch's White Nationalist Guide to the Movies*, ed. Greg Johnson, Foreword by Kevin MacDonald (San Francisco: Counter-Currents, 2012).

Crash is much less satisfying, but I give it extra points for *avant-garde* audacity and sheer visual style.

Crash had me from the opening credits, which loom up like signs along a nighttime highway, accompanied by Howard Shore's spiky, metallic, percussive theme scored for an ensemble of electric guitars.

Then we are inside an airplane hangar. The camera languidly stalks and caresses the bulging, sleek, riveted surfaces of small planes. Then we see Catherine Ballard (Deborah Kara Unger), a beautiful but cold and ferret-faced blonde, expose one of her breasts and press it against the surface of the plane as a lover takes her from behind.

Then we are inside a television studio. People are looking for Catherine's husband, director James Ballard (James Spader at the peak of his attractiveness and charisma), who is in the camera room having a quickie with a crewmember, which is interrupted.

Next we are on the balcony of the Ballard's posh modern apartment in a high-rise overlooking a busy expressway near the Toronto airport. Catherine is looking out over the expressway. The couple tell each other of the day's sexual adventures, as a prelude to their own love-making. As James takes her from behind, Catherine commiserates with her husband about his interrupted tryst. "Maybe the next one," she repeats consolingly.

Maybe the next one will work out, for there will always be a "next one." James and Catherine are clearly compulsive serial sexual adventurers. Both of them are highly attractive, affluent young professionals in a large city. Birth control and abortion have separated sex from procreation. Sexual liberation has unchained hedonism from morality. At thirtysomething, they have already racked up hundreds, if not thousands, of partners and are beginning to get a little jaded. As long as they avoid venereal diseases, though, they can keep rutting until they look like Keith Richards.

Many critics have remarked on how unsexy, unarousing, and unpornographic *Crash* is, citing it as evidence that Cronenberg is an inept director. But they have missed the point. *Crash* is not a "sex positive" film. It is an anti-sex film. It is a film about addiction and degradation. Expecting *Crash* to make sex addiction sexy is like expecting *Requiem for a Dream* to make drug addiction alluring.

In the next scene, an indeterminate time has passed. James is driving home from work on a rainy night. Idiotically, he is trying to read through papers as he navigates the freeway. Suddenly, he loses control of his car, heads down an embankment, and ends up in oncoming traffic. He collides head on, and the man in the front passenger seat of the other car shoots like a projectile through both windshields and into the passenger seat of James' car, dead. Seriously injured himself, James sits stunned as the female driver of the other car claws away her seat belt and exposes her breast.

Next we see James in the hospital, black sutures spiking up from deep, blue-black bruises, a shattered leg being held together by a hideous metal contraption with spikes buried in his flesh. Catherine tells him that the driver of the other car, Dr. Helen Remington (Holly Hunter), is also in the same hospital. Sometime later, James is up and walking and encounters Dr. Remington in the hallway, walking with a cane, her body horribly twisted. He speaks to her, and she grips her cane in rage, as if she wants to thrash him with it, then totters on, silent.

With her is Vaughn (Elias Koteas, who looks like Chris Meloni's homely brother), a tall, lurching figure in doctor's whites with horrible scars on his face. He carries a file filled with photos of lacerated and sutured accident victims. Vaughn remains behind to inspect James' leg brace and examine his other injuries, deeply invading James' personal space, smirking and leering at his injuries, and ending with an inappropriately long gaze directly into James' eyes. One is left feeling this is not so much a medical examination as a pick-up.

It becomes clear that James has been changed by his brush with death. While in the hospital, he rebuffs Catherine's sexual advances. While convalescing at home, he says to Catherine, "Is the traffic heavier now? There seem to be three times as many cars as there were before the accident." Helen Remington later reports the same experience to James: "[The traffic is] much worse now. You noticed that, did you? The day I left the hospital

I had the extraordinary feeling that all these cars were gathering for some special reason I didn't understand. There seemed to be ten times as much traffic."

Crash is masterful at communicating the sense that through their trauma, James and Helen have, in effect, entered a new world. Of course they are still on planet earth. They have entered a new world in the Heideggerian sense of world: a new context of intelligibility. The same things surround them, but their *meaning* has changed completely. The crash is what Heidegger calls an *Ereignis*, an event that transforms the meaning of everything.

When James and Helen meet the second time, they are at the police lot where their wrecked cars are impounded. James has revisited the accident not only by seeking out his wrecked car, but also by buying a new car of the exact same make and model. Because of his crash, James cannot relate sexually with Catherine, but he can with Helen, because they have shared the same experience. They end up having sex in James' car in an airport garage. Then, when James returns home, he has sex with Catherine in the same seated position.

Then the movie gets really weird. Vaughan reappears as the impresario of a reenactment of James Dean's fatal car accident. After the crash, the police appear, the spectators scatter, and Helen and James escape with Vaughan and the driver of the Dean car, Seagrave (Peter MacNeil), who is seriously injured. When we arrive at Vaughan's lair, we meet Gabrielle (Patricia Arquette), another crash victim who wears hideous braces that look like bondage gear over black lace lingerie. All of these crash victims live in the same altered world of meaning, in which they reenact their traumas—and historic versions of their traumas, like the deaths of James Dean and Jane Mansfield—until first Seagrave then Vaughan are killed.

Catherine, who is the only member of the cast who has not been in an accident, wants to join the rest of them, and they want to bring her in as well. Catherine is run off the road by Vaughan, but she is not injured. Then, after Vaughan is killed, James fixes up the car that Vaughan died in and uses it to run Catherine off the road again.

All these crashes are interspersed with increasingly kinky sexual encounters: James fucks Helen (again). Vaughan feels up Helen in his car while James watches. Vaughan fucks a prostitute in his car while James watches. (Creepily, Vaughan flexes one of the prostitute's legs, clearly taking pleasure in it simply as a hinged object, like a pocket knife.) Vaughan fucks Catherine in a car while going through a car-wash while James watches. (With his greenish corpse-like complexion and scars, Vaughan looks like Frankenstein's monster deflowering his bride among the instruments of Dr. Frankenstein's laboratory.) Then James fucks Vaughan in Vaughan's car. (Followed by Vaughan ramming his car into James.') James also has sex with Gabrielle in a car, skipping her vagina and inserting his penis into a deep scar on Gabrielle's leg. Then Helen and Gabrielle have a bit of lesbian action in the back seat of the wrecked car in which Vaughan died. And despite the physical hotness of the various actors (under all the scar tissue and prosthetics), none of it is remotely arousing, and a lot of it is downright distasteful—which, I maintain, is Cronenberg's brilliantly realized intention.

If *Crash* is just a movie about sex and car crashes, it rapidly becomes tedious, then ludicrous, then just meaningless, then people stream toward the exits. For *Crash* to hang together and be meaningful, there has to be a deeper connection between sex and car crashes than just the word "and."

And no, the fact that both are subjects of voyeurism is not enough. People move quite comfortably from sexual voyeurism to sex, but nobody moves from accident voyeurism to accidents.

Also, when people have brushes with death, they often snap out of self-destructive behavior patterns, such as sex addiction. But in *Crash*, brushes with death simply lead to the intensification of addictive behaviors, infusing the accidents themselves with sexual energy so that they too are obsessively repeated until some of the characters are actually killed. And no, I don't think it is enough to simply trot out some Freud talk about neurotics being drawn back to and repeating primal traumas, because that is just a description of what is happening in the film not an explanation of *why* it is happening.

So what is the connection between sex and car crashes? My

answer is simple: In *Crash* the car crashes are not car crashes, they are sex acts too, specifically unsafe sex acts that lead to the transmission of HIV. For me, the meaning all fell into place on the second viewing when James, lying in his hospital bed, says, "After being bombarded endlessly by road-safety propaganda, it's almost a relief to have found myself in an actual accident." James, of course, is a sex addict, and sex addicts are also bombarded endlessly with safe sex propaganda, especially AIDS awareness propaganda. And while road safety propaganda does not make driving less pleasurable, safe sex propaganda does cast rather a pall over things, since condoms reduce pleasure and addicts cannot simply stop having sex. This means that they often feel relieved once they catch HIV, so they can cease worrying about it and really throw themselves into their addiction. Once you crash a car, you don't want to crash a car again. But once you have unsafe sex, you want to have it again, and if you no longer fear HIV, you are free to make a fetish of unsafe sex with HIV positive people. Indeed, even though most of the couples are male-female, I think *Crash* is really about homosexual men, for the simple reason that practically every sex act in the film is from behind.

This interpretation throws a lot of light on the end of the movie. Vaughan has died. James buys the car in which he died and gets it running again. Then he runs Catherine off the road. Her car goes down an embankment and flips. She is thrown out of the car. James rushes to her side and asks if she is hurt. Although dazed and bloody, she says that she is all right. James then slips her panties down and enters her from behind, repeating her consoling words from earlier in the film, "Maybe the next one, darling, maybe the next one." None of this makes any sense psychologically if car crashes are just car crashes, but it makes perfect sense if Catherine is "bug-chasing," because there will be a next one, and a next one, and eventually she too will crash through the disease barrier and enter the realm where hedonism, shorn of its last inhibition, is free to become a full-blown death cult, in which its devotees grind themselves into oblivion.

Counter-Currents, September 12, 2017

DENIAL

Denial is a very boring and deceptive movie about a legal case, *David Irving v Penguin Books and Deborah Lipstadt*, in which British World War II historian David Irving sued American Jewish historian Deborah Lipstadt and her British publisher for libel over allegations made in her 1993 book *Denying the Holocaust*, in which she accused Irving of being a "Holocaust denier" and a bad historian who distorted history to conform with his ideological agenda, namely the vindication of Adolf Hitler.

Of course, this being a movie, distorting history to forward a Left-liberal agenda is apparently fair game. For example, since people associate beauty with goodness and ugliness with evil, the frumpy, mannish, 50-something Deborah Lipstadt is played by the beautiful 40-something fashion-model/actress Rachel Weisz. (I seriously doubt that Deborah Lipstadt could jog, even to escape the SS, and she surely would not look as good as Rachel Weisz in tights.)

The evil Nazis and Holocaust deniers, by contrast, are uglied up by the casting department. David Irving, who was quite the ladies' man, is played by a short, chinless, jowly, bug-eyed, thoroughly repulsive actor. The same is done to lawyer Martin O'Toole, who has a bit part (but not to lawyer Sam Dickson, whose name appears as Dixon in the credits).

In 1996, Irving filed his libel suit in Britain, where the burden of proof falls on the defendant. Thus Penguin and Lipstadt were forced to defend the truth of Lipstadt's claims about Irving being a "denier." And, to gild the lily, they argued that Irving was a racist and anti-Semite to boot.

Irving ended up representing himself in court. Little wonder that he couldn't find an attorney. It was quite possibly the dumbest libel suit since Oscar Wilde sued the Marquess of Queensbury for calling him a sodomite in 1895. It was, of course, child's play to prove that Wilde was a sodomite, just as it was child's play to argue that Irving, by any reasonable definition of the terms, was a racist, an anti-Semite, and a Holocaust denier.

The real issue, of course, is whether being a racist, an anti-Semite, or a Holocaust denier are necessarily bad things. Irving, like Wilde, apparently wanted the court to rule that he was really not a bad person. But law courts are not the place to seek moral vindication. That is something that outsiders—whether homosexuals or Holocaust deniers—must have the courage to give themselves.

The one thing that *Irving v Lipstadt* did not establish is that Irving is a bad historian, which is probably why the defense focused on racism and anti-Semitism. I followed the trial closely as it unfolded and carefully read historian Richard Evans' report on Irving's scholarship. The long list of "errors" adduced by Evans consisted mostly of differences of interpretation rather than matters of fact. Evans and two research assistants went over more than 20 of Irving's books with a magnifying glass and found only two or three actual errors of fact. One wonders if any other historian could acquit himself as well before such minute scrutiny. Even an amateur like me can find that many mistakes on a random page of William L. Shirer's *The Rise and Fall of the Third Reich*.

Unfortunately, Irving's politically incorrect convictions, combined with Evans' handwaving and quibbling, were enough to convict him in the eyes of the judge who decided the case. It is utterly galling that virtually every account of the trial claims that Irving was "discredited" rather than vindicated as a historian.

It is even more galling when one compares Irving's work to the plodding, unimaginative, clichéd, and conventional writing of his accuser, Deborah Lipstadt. David Irving educated himself, authored more than 20 books, and made a modest fortune by dint of sheer talent and hard work. Lipstadt, by contrast, would never have been a professor or an author based on her modest talents alone. She was raised up and propped up by feminism, political correctness, and Jewish ethnic networking.

Moreover, Lipstadt's *Denying the Holocaust* really is a work of defamation. It is every bit as tendentious as she accuses Irving of being. And Lipstadt was just one player in an organized Jewish campaign to destroy Irving's reputation as an author because he lent that reputation to the cause of Holocaust revisionism.

Ironically enough, Irving was never a blanket Holocaust denier, and the Holocaust was never a focus of his work. But Irving's historical spadework did raise questions and problems for the mainstream Holocaust narrative. These problems were no threat to honest scholars, but for Jews, the Holocaust is not a matter for scholarship but the object of a religious cult, and, as is typical with offshoots of Mosaic religion, dissenters are not to be tolerated or debated but to be defamed and destroyed, often with the most self-righteous, hysterical, and swinish verbal—and sometimes real—thuggery.

In one scene, Lipstadt and Robert Jan Van Pelt decry the desecration of the purported gas chambers at Auschwitz by Fred Leuchter, which rather begs the question, since Leuchter's whole point was to determine if something sacralizing had occurred there at all. Later they pray over the ruins.

It is not hard to see why Irving wanted to squash Lipstadt—and the system that created her—like an insect. But it is hard to fathom the naïveté of thinking that he could get justice in a law court. And even if he had won, Lipstadt was just one head of the hydra, whose control over the mass media and academia would have been unshaken. His reputation as an author would not have been restored. Mainstream publishers would not have come courting.

Granted, Irving had used lawsuits before with good effect to harass his enemies. But when Penguin refused to knuckle under or settle, he should have dropped the suit before it went to trial. Really, Irving should simply have accepted his downfall, counted his blessings, and continued to write books for the ages, knowing that history would judge him in a better light and that would be the best revenge. But that course proved psychologically impossible.

It is odd that not even Rachel Weisz and a sympathetic director and script can make Deborah Lipstadt seem like a likable character. At every step of the way, she kvetches and complains as people do her huge favors. (She must be hell on waiters.) Absurdly, she complains that Holocaust survivors are not being allowed to tell their tales at the trial. In one scene, yet another Jew who was not exterminated by the Nazis portentously rolls up her sleeve to reveal her camp tattoo and asks Lipstadt to promise that her voice will be heard.

When I lived in Atlanta, I always fantasized about going to one of Lipstadt's occasional public lectures and asking her, "Professor Lipstadt, don't you think it is time for Jews to stop being silent about the Holocaust?" You know very well that she would not say, "Actually, I think we're doing an adequate job of talking about it." Really, does a moment go by when somewhere on the planet, some Jew is not remaining silent about the Holocaust?

Lipstadt is probably still kvetching today about being misunderstood and unappreciated, having dined out for two decades on her trial, with a book deal, this movie, well-paid speaking engagements, and various awards for her "courage." It really took a lot of courage to go up against the lonely and reviled David Irving with a six-million-dollar war chest, the mass media, and the full weight of the most privileged and powerful tribe on the planet behind her.

Irving has not fared so well. Like Wilde, he was ruined by his folly. Wilde was imprisoned, which broke his health. He died at the age of 46, not long after his release. The world will never read the books that he could have written if he had made a wiser choice and lived a long and productive life. Irving's case ran from September of 1996 to April of 2000, when the judge ruled for the defendant. Irving was held liable for Penguin's trial costs (£2 million, about $3.2 million) and eventually forced into bankruptcy, losing his home and access to many of his research materials.

Moreover, since his defeat, Irving did not accept his fate, buckle down, and focus on completing his life's work before death or senility still his pen forever. Instead, he has thrown himself into ever more frantic and sordid attempts to relive his glory years when he was a millionaire author living and traveling in luxury.

Irving recorded it all in his online diaries: renting and being evicted from homes he could not afford; increasingly grueling and seedy tours of the United States in rented vans, speaking in restaurants and hotels; rows with waitresses, journalists, protestors, and movement people; creepy stalking behavior directed at young female ex-assistants; his repulsive attempt to shake down a German movie studio for "plagiarism" for using his research on Rommel (you can't copyright historical truth); being thrown out of restaurants, hotels, and countries, etc.

More than 20 years have now passed since Irving filed his fateful suit, but for an author, the true measure of that time is all the books he has failed to write. Irving is almost 80 now. He's basically wasted the last quarter of his life. He has betrayed his talent, his calling, his readers, and the cause of historical truth. This is a tragedy in the true sense, the story of a man with genuinely great talents undone by a terrible character flaw, in this case overweening vanity now curdled into bitterness. And, sadly, it's too late to turn things around.

But *Denial* is not a tragic drama, a movie that evokes fear and pity for David Irving. Tragedy is an Aryan form of literature, after all. Instead, *Denial* attempts to be an extended exercise in typically Semitic wound-licking, ritualistic denunciation, and gloating over the suffering of tribal enemies. But it fails even in that ugly ambition. In truth, *Denial* is just portentous, boring, and sometimes unintentionally funny. Skip it, stay home, and read *Hitler's War* instead.

Counter-Currents, January 16, 2015

DAVID LYNCH'S *DUNE*

David Lynch's third feature film is his 1984 adaptation of Frank Herbert's science fiction classic *Dune*. Herbert's *Dune* is widely hailed as a masterpiece, while Lynch's *Dune* has a much more mixed reputation, tending toward the negative. When I first saw Lynch's *Dune*, I was deeply disappointed. Herbert's novel had left a powerful and vivid impression on me, and Lynch's vision was not my vision. It took a good ten years for Herbert's novel to relinquish its grip on my imagination, allowing me to appreciate Lynch's *Dune*, which I now regard as a worthy adaptation of the novel and a truly great but not unflawed film.

Lynch's *Dune* was a critical and commercial flop. Lynch's lack of creative control over the project left a deep bitterness, which is why there will probably never be a director's cut, even though Universal has offered Lynch the opportunity. But *Dune* was still very good for Lynch's career. It was his first big-budget film, and his director's fee allowed him to hire his own staff which played an important role in supporting all of his subsequent creative efforts. Moreover, Lynch's deal with Dino De Laurentiis was to do two movies: *Dune*, under De Laurentiis' control, and a second one, under Lynch's creative control, which became *Blue Velvet*, the quintessential David Lynch film. Even the failure of *Dune* was probably good for Lynch in the end, for had it become a big-budget sci-fi blockbuster, Lynch might have been sucked into creating more conventional Hollywood fare at the expense of his own unique vision. Indeed, before the failure of *Dune*, Lynch was scheduled to direct two sequels, *Dune Messiah* and *Children of Dune*.

As a rule, science fiction is progressivist whereas fantasy literature is reactionary. Frank Herbert's *Dune* saga—which eventually sprawled into six volumes—is the notable exception to this rule, for *Dune* is one of the most reactionary works of the human imagination. Herbert believed that feudalism, not liberal democracy, was the social system best adapted to mankind's ascent to the stars. Feudalism was a decentralized system adapted to a society in which population centers were widely separated and in which transportation was costly and slow. Such conditions no longer exist on earth, but they certainly would pertain between inhabited planets scattered throughout the galaxy. The exploration and settling of the universe is a project requiring immensely long time horizons, which are characteristic of medieval institutions—dynasties, holy orders, guilds—but absent in liberal democracies, in which few people plan past the next election cycle.

Herbert also imagined other ways in which advanced technology would lead to the recurrence of archaic values and ways of life. For instance, in the distant back story of *Dune*, mankind had been enslaved by its own creations, artificial intelligence and robots. But the machines were overthrown in a massive religiously-inspired revolt known as the Butlerian Jihad, which created a syncretic religion combining elements of Christianity and Islam, as well as Hinduism, Buddhism, and Taoism.

Artificial intelligence was banned, forcing mankind to develop its own mental and spiritual powers. For example, "mentats" used highly developed mnemonic and calculative techniques to become "human computers." Genetic engineering was also banned, forcing mankind to adopt selective breeding projects— spanning millennia—to improve the human race.

Herbert mentions three hierarchical, initiatic orders: the Bene Gesserit sisterhood, which practiced eugenics; the Spacing Guild, which developed prescient navigators for space travel; and the Bene Tleilax, which trained mentats, created clones, and developed the arts of mimicry to unimaginable heights or depths. ("Bene Gesserit" is a Latin motto that can be interpreted as "well born"—i.e., "eugenic." It might also be meant to bring the Jesuit order to mind.)

In addition to psychic powers, mnemonic tricks, and eugenics, the Bene Gesserit and Bene Tleilax also used the techniques of "prana-bindu yoga" to develop superpowers or *siddhis*. For instance, in *Dune*, the Bene Gesserit practiced the "weirding way" of battle, a form of martial arts. They perfected "the voice," the power to make their commands irresistible. They also developed minute conscious control of the body's involuntary and voluntary muscle systems alike. They even had the power to reflectively analyze and control the body's chemical processes. To normal people, of course, it all seemed like magic, hence the Bene Gesserit were widely disdained as "witches."

Not only did Herbert envision technology—and its rejection—bringing back sorcery, he imagined how it might bring back swordplay as well. Atomic weapons had been banned, with planetary destruction as the penalty for breaking the pact. Laser-like weapons had been neutralized by the invention of shields. When lasers contacted shields, the result was an immense explosion that would kill both parties. Shields also neutralized projectile weapons like guns. But a slow blade can penetrate a personal shield. Thus high technology has returned us to a world of hand-to-hand combat with swords and daggers.

Herbert's *Dune* universe is thus an example of what French New Right thinker Guillaume Faye called "archeofuturism": a combination of futuristic technology and archaic values, social forms, and practices. One could say the same about *Star Wars*, of course, but George Lucas was simply riffing—or ripping—off Herbert, from the galactic empire to initiatic knightly orders, down to desert planets and even spice mining, although without Herbert's deep thinking about how such things could all hang together.

Now this is just the merest sketch of the world that Herbert conjures up in *Dune*, and it is an enormous challenge to recreate this world—and a story within it that sprawls over more than 400 densely printed pages—into a movie of manageable length. But Lynch does a superb job.

A beginning, we are told in the opening narration, is a delicate time. The novel begins with an old witch, the Reverend Mother Gaius Helen Mohiam of the Bene Gesserit, arriving at castle Caladan to test 15-year-old Paul Atreides, the son of the reigning duke Leto Atreides. Stripped of any mention of space travel, of course, this could be a scene from a fantasy novel. It would be an interesting cinematic bait and switch to see just how deep one could go into the story before revealing that it is science fiction set in the distant future.

Lynch's dramatization of this scene is one of the best sequences of the film, but it is not how he begins. First, there is a narration by the princess Irulan, whose words actually begin the book, for the chapters usually begin with epigraphs drawn from her own books on the story Herbert is telling. Irulan establishes straightaway that this is a science fiction movie. The time is the distant future, where the known universe is ruled by the Emperor Shaddam IV, her father. In this time—Irulan almost says "in this period"—the most precious substance in the universe is the spice mélange, which extends life, expands consciousness, and is vital to the Spacing Guild which knits the empire together. The sole source of the spice is the planet Arrakis, also known as Dune, which is the home of the Fremen, an oppressed and marginalized desert-dwelling people who believe in the prophecy of a messiah or mahdi who will lead them to freedom.

The setting of *Dune* of course brings to mind the deserts of the Middle East. The Fremen are Arabs. The spice is oil. Arrakis sounds like Arabia + Iraq. Shaddam even sounds like Saddam Hussein, who wasn't a force when the book was written. The distant and corrupt empire could be Byzantium at the time of the rise of Islam or the Ottoman empire at the beginning of the 20th century. Moreover, the story of Paul Atreides stirring up a Fremen revolt against the Imperium has parallels that are worth a closer look to the story of T. E. Lawrence, better known as Lawrence of Arabia.

The Fremen have many Arabic loan-words and Islam-derived beliefs. They practice circumcision. But, rather disturbingly, Herbert envisions these as part of the general fabric of the galactic empire and its syncretic religion. Indeed, in the final two novels, *Heretics of Dune* and *Chapterhouse Dune*, Herbert reveals that the Bene Tleilax practice an esoteric form of Islam, taking Muslim misogyny to truly monstrous extremes. But the Bene Gesserit are well-versed in Islamic lore too, although they merely regard it as a topic of study and a tool of statecraft.

After Irulan's narration and the opening credits, another narrator summarizes "A Secret Report within the Guild," concerning a plot that might jeopardize spice production, which establishes that Arrakis is the source of the spice, Caladan is the home of the Atreides, Giedi Prime is the home of the Harkonnen, and Kaitain is the capital of the known universe. Frankly, this narration strikes me as clumsy. Can you name another science fiction movie that utilizes it? The names of planets can simply be introduced in passing, as part of the dialogue, or overlaid on the screen (as Lynch later does anyway with Caladan and Giedi Prime). Both narrations are undramatic ways to establish in advance information that Herbert himself introduced quite successfully in the story itself, and Lynch should have just been confident enough of Herbert's skill and his own to do the same.

The first actual scene of the movie is one of the most iconic: the audience of Shaddam IV with a third stage Guild navigator. This scene is entirely Lynch's invention, although it was inspired by a very different audience with a Guild navigator in Herbert's sequel, *Dune Messiah*. Visually, the scene is both sumptuous and surreal, although the Guild navigator seems rather fake and mechanical.

My favorite touch is the departure of the Guild navigator's locomotive-like tank, which, like a great metallic slug, leaves behind a trail of orange spice slime, some of which is perfunctorily hoovered up by his retainers, who shuffle along dressed in shapeless black boiler suits hiding who knows what mutations. Before they depart, the retainers look back at the Emperor from the doorway, the lintel of which bears the words "Law is the Ultimate Science," then we hear what sounds like an electronic raspberry before they turn and follow the tank.

In terms of the plot, the audience scene gives the Emperor the opportunity to explain *his* plot, which is also a good part of the film's plot. The Emperor feels threatened by the popularity and growing military power of the Atreides of Caladan. To destroy them, the Emperor has ordered them to take control of Arrakis, a prize rich enough to lure them off the security of their home world and onto alien soil, where they will be vulnerable to an attack from their hereditary enemies, the Harkonnens, the former rulers of Arrakis, who will enjoy the secret aid of the emperor's elite Sardaukar troops.

Ironically, the Emperor is sending the Atreides into the one place in the universe where the harsh environmental conditions have created a fighting force capable of defeating the Sardaukar—namely the Fremen, who, unknown to the Imperium, exist in vast numbers and have effective control of Arrakis and with it the spice, the most precious commodity in the universe.

The Fremen have been quiet under Harkonnen rule, stealthily pursuing a project of terraforming Arrakis into a more livable world. The Harkonnens are basically merchant princes. They measure power in terms of wealth and treat Arrakis simply as a colony to be exploited. They regard soldiers simply as mercenary muscle, Pinkertons to keep the workers in line. Thus they have overlooked the Fremen and have no idea of their numbers and military potential.

One of the themes of the novel, which did not make it into the final cut of the film, is that the leader of the Harkonnens, Baron Vladimir, for all of his Byzantine plotting, is really rather thick, because he is blind to the whole realm of warrior virtue and how it is cultivated. He is entirely a creature of his appetites, which are monstrous. He has grown so fat that he has to be buoyed by suspensors to move around. He is the embodiment of the bourgeois ethos of hedonism and preferring dishonor to death. Lynch's characterization intensifies these traits almost to the point of parody. Lynch's Baron—played by Kenneth MacMillan with unfortunate traces of a New York accent—is not only fat, but also covered with hideous suppurating sores. His doctor is always near, to keep his carcass alive for further pleasures.

The Emperor and his close confidant Count Fenring suspect that the Baron wishes to use Arrakis to create fighting men, because that is what they would do. The Emperor simply refuses to believe that the Baron has overlooked the superb fighting skills of the Fremen. But such matters simply did not occur to him.

The Atreides, however, are very different. They are a martial elite, tracing their descent from the ancient house of Atreus. They measure power in terms of the size, the power, and especially the loyalty of the military forces they command. The Atreides are renowned for their ability to inspire loyalty from their men by *giving* it to their men. They are masters at the delicate art of creating camaraderie and brotherhood within a hierarchical, military order. The Harkonnen's soldiers will kill for money. The Atreides and the Fremen and the Sardaukar will die for honor. All the Fremen need for them to rise up against the Imperium are a catalyst and a leader—both of which are provided by the Emperor's plot.

Another important element established in the audience scene is that in the *Dune* cosmos, the leading institutions of society—the ruling houses, the Bene Gesserit, and the Spacing Guild—have worked together for a very long time while keeping immense secrets of great importance from one another. Only the Emperor is allowed to see the Guild navigator. The ruling houses, moreover, are kept in the dark about the ultimate aims of the Bene Gesserit, even though they accept their sisters as wives, concubines, and mothers of their heirs. Indeed, in all six *Dune* books, Herbert never really tells us what the Bene Gesserit's goal is, beyond serving humanity. To maintain such levels of secrecy in vast organizations carrying out plans that span thousands of years presupposes remarkable levels of both idealism and discipline.

The Guild navigator tells the Emperor that they want young Paul Atreides, the ducal heir, killed. This too is not in the book, but it gives a motive for Reverend Mother Mohiam's visit, which begins the book. It is an unnecessary move. Herbert's beginning was fine as it is. But Lynch wished to present the Guild as the ultimate wire-pullers, whereas for Herbert they are just one player.

But there are three more scenes before we actually get to the test. The first is cleverly compounded out of three separate scenes in the novel. It introduces Paul as well as three Atreides retainers: the mentat Thufir Hawat (Freddie Jones), Doctor Wellington Yueh (Dean Stockwell), and sword master Gurney Halleck (Patrick Stewart). All three characters are wonderfully realized. Paul is played by Kyle MacLaughlin, one of Lynch's favorite actors (*Blue Velvet, Twin Peaks*), who in truth is a bit old to depict the fifteen-year-old of the novel. But Herbert had a disturbing pattern of creating sexually precocious teens and even preteens, which simply cannot be portrayed on screen, necessitating casting older actors.

Paul is introduced studying what today look like large, clunky computer tablets. This sequence is perhaps the clumsiest in the film. As Paul reviews the relative positions of Caladan, Giedi Prime, and Arrakis (all unnecessary given the Secret Report), little voices insert bits of background information. For instance, we are told that Bene Tleilax is where mentats come from, that they are human computers, and one can know them by their red-stained lips. We are also told that Baron Harkonnen has vowed to destroy House Atreides and steal the ducal signet ring for himself.

Was Lynch unable to work this information into the script in a more natural way? And why include the detail about the signet ring at all? This is not *Lord of the Rings*. There is no magic in Leto's signet. If we really needed to know about mentats, why not include the scene where it is revealed that Jessica and Thufir have been training Paul to be a mentat, without him even knowing it? This bit of information is actually quite relevant to the development of Paul's character as the story unfolds.

Another oddity in this sequence is the introduction of the "weirding modules," which is also a Lynch invention. In the novel, the weirding way of battle is a Bene Gesserit martial art. It is a yogic superpower. In Lynch's hands, it becomes a weird looking hand-held device that turns sound into a killing force. It seems likely that Lynch introduced this concept simply to pander to sci-fi fans who expect laser guns, which Herbert took pains to replace with swords and daggers. (Moreover, the Sardaukar use lasers in the final battle scene anyway.)

It would have been far more faithful to Herbert to depict the weirding way in the manner of Chinese *wuxia* movies like *Hero* and *Crouching Tiger, Hidden Dragon*, which have just as much audience appeal as laser battles anyway. This is essentially how it was treated in the Sci-Fi network productions of *Dune* and *Children of Dune*. Frankly, such an approach would have made Lynch's climactic battle scene far more interesting. Let's hope Denis Villeneuve is taking notes.

Then, after two brief scenes, the first introducing Duncan Idaho (Richard Jordan), the second introducing Paul's father, Duke Leto (Jürgen Prochnow), we finally get to the test. Lynch's handling of this scene is truly virtuosic. His script masterfully distills everything essential from Herbert's text, and the settings, casting, and performances are all first rate.

Welsh actress Sian Phillips (Livia in *I, Claudius*) is a superb Reverend Mother, capturing every facet of Herbert's character: her steely ruthlessness and fanaticism in the pursuit of her ideals as well as her very personal attachments, disappointments, and hopes — and even such bizarre and disconcerting details as her metal teeth.

Francesca Annis plays Paul's mother Jessica, a Bene Gesserit sister who broke her vow to the order to bear only daughters to the Atreides, bearing Paul instead. Annis looks exactly like Herbert's description of Jessica: tall, willowy, beautiful, with reddish brown hair and an aristocratic bearing that makes everyone think she is high born, when in fact she was the illegitimate child of a Bene Gesserit of unknown rank, and her father's identity was kept secret from her. (Which is just as well, because he turned out to be Vladimir Harkonnen.) A sign of the great care that went into casting is that Kyle McLaughlin actually looks like he could be the son of Francesca Annis and Jürgen Prochnow.

So why are the Guild and the Bene Gesserit interested in young Paul Atreides? For 90 generations, the Bene Gesserit have been running a selective breeding program, blending the best bloodlines of the empire, both aristocratic and common (introduced through Bene Gesserit wives and concubines), to produce a superman, whom they call the Kwisatz Haderach, the "shortening of the way," the one who can be many places at once.

The Bene Gesserit have perfected a way of tapping into and passing on the memories of their maternal ancestors and fellow sisters. This presupposes that memory is somehow stored in a realm outside the individual mind that can be tapped into by different minds — akin to the Theosophical idea of the "akashic records" encoded in the ethereal realm. This is also the presupposition of the idea introduced in *Dune Messiah* that a clone (or "ghola") can recover the memories of the past physical incarnations of its genotype.

But the Bene Gesserit cannot access male ancestral memories. The Kwisatz Haderach, however, will be able to do so, in addition to female memories.

The Bene Gesserit, however, are not interested simply in mastering the past. They also wish to see into the future. Like the Guild's navigators, they gain prescience by consuming the spice. The Bene Gesserit clearly expect the Kwisatz Haderach to share in this power as well, since the Reverend Mother asks Paul quite pointedly if he has prescient dreams.

Thus the Kwisatz Haderach will be a Janus figure, both surveying the collective memory of mankind and peering into the future. Such knowledge would bring enormous power, to the Kwisatz Haderach himself, and to the sisterhood that controlled him.

After the test scene Lynch takes us to the Harkonnen planet Giedi Prime. Lynch's depiction of Giedi Prime is his own invention. It is a hideous industrial hellscape, built over bubbling black filth that is a nod to the "matmos" of another sci-fi flop, *Barbarella*, also produced by De Laurentiis. Black smoke belches from the mouth of a huge, fat face, perhaps a nod to H. R. Giger's design for the Harkonnen keep for Alejandro Jodorowski's abortive *Dune* adaptation. Unlike the novel, Lynch's Baron does not live in sybaritic splendor. His palace looks like a factory or a slaughterhouse, a maze of roofless green-tiled rooms lost inside a vast industrial box. (Herbert actually incorporates Lynch's depiction of Giedi Prime into *Heretics of Dune*.)

When we enter the baron's presence, we first hear a humming, then the bubbling of the matmos, then a sickening slurping sound. The baron's grossly fat body lolls on a chair while is doctor sucks gunk out of the sores on his face, aided by retainers whose ears have been sewn shut and whose vision is restricted by hideous goggles. The Harkonnens stamp their tyranny into the very flesh of their servants. Indeed, every Harkonnen subject has a "heart plug" installed that allow him to be murdered with no more effort than flipping a switch.

The scene also introduces the twisted mentat Piter De Vries, played by Brad "Wormtongue" Dourif, as well as the Baron's nephews Feyd (Sting) and Rabban (Paul Smith). Jack Nance plays the Baron's henchman Nefud. After Piter pedantically explains the plan to destroy the Atreides to Feyd and Rabban, the

Baron—half devil, half child—exultantly activates his suspensors, shooting into the air like a whirring blimp while laughing manically. Then he descends, painted toenails delicately *en pointe*, pausing a moment to bathe in the matmos drizzling down from the glowglobes in his audience chamber, then pounces on a terrified twink, pulling his heart plug and bathing in his blood. It is a bit much for most people. But one has to give Lynch credit. I can't think of a grosser and more loathsome villain in all of cinema.

The Atreides departure for Arrakis is a highly imaginative sequence. The costumes and accoutrements of the Atreides bring to mind the British Empire in the early 20th century, right down to their pug. (When Gurney Halleck charges into battle against the Harkonnens, he carries the pug with him. In the final scene of the movie, the little dog reappears, having somehow survived the Harkonnen attack and subsequent years of guerilla warfare in the desert.)

The Guild spaceship, with its ornate entrance and mysterious, Gigeresque innards, is intriguing. Lynch's machine and ship designs in *Dune* do not look like extrapolations on present day technology. They are not sleek and "space age," but weirdly clumsy and clunky, covered with tubes, pipes, wheels, and spikes that look archaic, not futuristic. (Some of them are apparently dwarf-powered.) It is frankly impossible to envision how they might work, which adds to their uncanniness.

A historian of design needs to explore the question of whether we are witnessing the birth of the Steampunk aesthetic in Lynch's *Dune*. It makes sense, because immediately before *Dune*, Lynch directed *The Elephant Man*, which is set in Victorian London. There are even some design continuities between *The Elephant Man* and *Dune*, for instance the gas wall sconces in *The Elephant Man* have equivalents in the Emperor's throne room. The worst aspect of Lynch's design is dressing the Sardaukar troops in shapeless hazmat suits.

Many people complain about the spaceship effects in *Dune*, and on DVD and Blu-ray, they do look bad. But I have seen *Dune* in the theater, and they look just fine on the big screen. George Lucas, of course, could have done better, but that's the only thing he could have improved.

The sequence in which the Guild navigator "folds space" is bizarre, but how would you depict it? First, it should be noted the "folding space" is another Lynch invention. Herbert only ascribes the power of prescience to the Guild navigators. Second, Lynch's depictions of the navigation sequence and Paul's visions are based on Herbert's descriptions. In the novel, after Paul takes the water of life and is finally transformed into the Kwisatz Haderach, Jessica leads Paul into the place where Reverend Mothers—women—are terrified to go, "a region where a wind blew and sparks glared, where rings of light expanded and contracted, where rows of tumescent white shapes flowed over and under and around the lights, driven by darkness and a wind out of nowhere."

Once the Atreides are on Arrakis, two scenes stand out for their faithful and inspired adaptation of the novel: the spice harvesting sequence and the attempt to assassinate Paul with a hunter-seeker. The spice harvesting sequence introduces the imperial planetologist, Dr. Liet Kynes, a natural aristocrat and the true leader of the Fremen (superbly realized Max von Sydow). It also gives us our first glimpse of the sandworms of Arrakis, Lynch's trifold design for which follows Herbert's description of the sandworm mouth as opening like the petals of a flower. Finally, it establishes an important aspect of the character of Duke Leto: he values loyalty more than money, and the loyalty goes both ways, to his men and from them. In the interests of economy, Lady Fenring's conservatory, a long dinner party, various short military conferences, and a subplot about Hawat's suspicions of Jessica are omitted, as are the Giedi Prime subplots from later in the book. A conversation between Jessica and the Shadout Mapes (Linda Hunt) was filmed but cut.

Dr. Yueh's betrayal, the Harkonnen attack, the death of Leto, and Paul and Jessica's escape are all quite faithful to the book and realized in a compelling and often quirky manner. (I especially enjoyed Piter's strange hand gestures in his conversation with Nefud.) But in the interest of time, Lynch abridges Paul and Jessica's flight. The capture of Hawat and the deaths of Duncan Idaho and Dr. Kynes are also abridged, to no great loss.

Lynch's treatment of the second part of *Dune*, Paul and Jessica's adventures with the Fremen, however, is highly abridged. It turns out that Lynch actually filmed a number of scenes that were later cut. First, there is Paul's duel to the death with the Fremen Jamis, which leads to the scene where he is given the name Usul and chooses the name Paul Muad'dib. Then there is the deathstill scene, removing the water from Jamis' body, which leads to the scene where Paul and Jessica are shown a vast Fremen water cache. There are also scenes where Chani learns of the death of her father, Dr. Kynes, and the Fremen drown a tiny sandworm to produce the water of life. These scenes really should be restored in a director's cut. They would allow the Fremen world to breathe a bit and disclose some of its wonders. Theater running times are no longer an issue, and every fan of the novel and Lynch film would rejoice.

Everett McGill, who also appeared in *Twin Peaks* and *The Straight Story*, plays Stilgar, the Fremen leader. Oddly, McGill manages to make his voice sound like a dubbed Italian film from the 1960s. Sean Young plays Chani.

Aesthetically, the second half of *Dune* is the least satisfying. Lynch's depiction of the deserts and mountains of Arrakis, as well as the underground lairs of the Fremen, are frankly ugly and often unpleasantly dark and murky, often verging on the unintelligible. They fail miserably at capturing the sublime splendor of the desert in Herbert's descriptions. One wishes that Lynch had watched *Lawrence of Arabia* before shooting *Dune*, or simply visited the high deserts of Arizona, Utah, and New Mexico for some inspiration. Let's hope that Denis Villeneuve does not neglect the opportunity to include some dazzling nature photography in his forthcoming adaptation. It is a cheap and easy way to enchant moviegoers.

The third and final part of *Dune* depicts Paul and the Fremen's defeat of Shaddam and the Harkonnens and Paul's installation as the new Emperor. Generally, Lynch's adaptation is quite faithful. There are some engagingly quirky and bizarre touches, such as the Sardaukar generals, a racially diverse collection of scarecrows and tin woodsmen with metal plates in their heads, or the Emperor's strange rotating control center, where

Shaddam and his generals rain down fire on their attackers as if they are playing a video game. The worst special effects in *Dune* are in the climactic battle, which has dreadful process shots and bizarrely skewed color contrasts.

The final scene, in which Paul defeats Feyd in hand-to-hand combat, is brilliantly done. Sadly, it was heavily cut. The touching death of Thufir Hawat was removed, which rendered somewhat pointless the scene on Giedi Prime where the captive Thufir had a heart-plug installed and is told that a poison has been introduced into his body in order to make him dependent on the Baron for the antidote. The terms that Paul dictates to Shaddam, including marrying his daughter Irulan, are also cut. Finally, Lynch omitted the strange but moving final words of the novel, in which Jessica reassures Chani that they may bear the rank of concubine, but history will remember them as wives.

Instead, Lynch ends with another of his inventions: a miracle. Paul causes rain to fall on Arrakis. Herbert himself chided Lynch on this ending, claiming that Paul was not actually a messiah. He was just pretending to be one. But in fairness to Lynch, *Dune* is the story of a superman who is taken as a messiah. If the messiah could not make rain, perhaps the superman could. Furthermore, both the project that bred Paul and the prophecy he fulfilled were set in motion by the Bene Gesserit. The confluence of these schemes on Arrakis might merely be a freak accident, but readers can also be excused for seeing it as some sort of Providence. Herbert himself makes such a reading possible with his genre-bending fusion of science fiction and fantasy tropes.

Irulan's narration also speaks of how Fremen prophecy predicted Paul Muad'dib's ascension would bring peace and love to the galaxy. This comes off as bitterly ironic to the readers of the novel, because there Paul knows better. His prescient vision shows only civil war and untold suffering as the Fremen spill off-world and subdue the cosmos in a new *jihad*.

There is no reason why Lynch could not keep his ending and restore Herbert's and the other deleted bits of the final scene in a director's cut.

What lessons should Denis Villeneuve learn from the successes and failures of Lynch's *Dune*? First and foremost: if Herbert's novel was good enough to enthrall millions of readers over more than fifty years, a faithful film adaptation will be good enough to produce a classic beloved by millions of viewers. Second, incorporate nature photography for the desert scenes. Nature is more beautiful than anything that can be created with CGI or on soundstages. Third, don't over-explain. Lynch's greatest mistake was not to follow Herbert's example of merely intimating the back stories while unfolding the main story. Of course this technique filled the readers' minds with questions. But that is one of the reasons we just kept reading. There's nothing wrong with mystery, after all.

The main cause of Lynch's tendency to over-explain was lack of faith in the novel and in the audience. It is hard to tell how much of this was Lynch's own mistake and how much was a result of pressure from De Laurentiis. We can infer that the latter played a large role from watching the extended version of *Dune* that De Laurentiis produced for television after the movie's theatrical failure. Lynch insisted that it not bear his name. This production contains a great deal of footage that Lynch cut, as well as even more back narration, using extremely ugly drawings. The clear intention was to make *Dune* intelligible to complete morons, the kind of people who could not see a simple cut between locations and infer that someone had traveled between them.

Viewing this abomination is a painful experience. Many good scenes were dropped and should be restored to a director's cut. But also a great deal of fat was trimmed, particularly in the audience scene, where every single cut removed even *more* over-explaining—adding back in some of the atmosphere of mystery and wonder that made Herbert's *Dune* a classic. If only Lynch had gone further. Lynch's *Dune* is not a classic like the original novel, but it remains superior to the Sci-Fi Channel mini-series, which is far less artful, while remaining much more faithful to the book. If Denis Villeneuve manages to combine artfulness and fidelity, he may well surpass them both.

The Unz Review, April 16, 2019

The Sci-Fi Channel's *Dune* & *Children of Dune*

David Lynch's *Dune* (1984) is a flawed masterpiece. When I first saw it, I was deeply disappointed. Frank Herbert's original novel made a powerful impression on me. I could *see* Herbert's world, and Lynch's vision was not my vision. But when my initial impression faded and I returned to Lynch's film with an open mind, I found it immensely imaginative and compelling. Even the score by Toto managed to grow on me.

Yes, Lynch changed some things about *Dune*, but the changes were for the better. For instance, the audience with the Guild navigator is not in *Dune*, but a similar scene takes place in the sequel *Dune Messiah*. It was too visually interesting a scene for Lynch not to steal, and he used it to advance the plot in crucial ways. *Dune* also combines a cynical materialism with genuinely mystical ideas like prescience. Lynch downplays the materialism and focuses in on the magic.

Dune deals with the explosive results of combining religion and politics. Young Paul Atreides is the product of the Bene Gesserit sisterhood's centuries-old project to breed a superman. When he just happens to fulfill the prophecies of a messiah implanted in a superstitious desert people by the same sisterhood, he uses religion as a tool to raise an army and restore his birthright, but as we learn in the sequel *Dune Messiah*, the holy war takes on a life of its own and scorches the galaxy.

In Lynch's telling, Paul really is a messiah. Oddly though, Lynch goes in the exact opposite direction in his treatment of the "weirding way," turning it from a yogic *siddhi* into a kind of technology.

Lynch did not have control of the final cut of *Dune*, and many scenes were removed. There will never be a director's cut, but some of the missing footage has surfaced in an abomination that appeared on television. In truth, though, nothing essential was lost, and each time I view this film, I marvel anew at how masterfully and concisely Lynch relates the essentials of the story.

Lynch's *Dune* has many critics and skeptics. I quell their qualms in my much longer analysis of Lynch's *Dune* in the previous chapter. In the meantime, if you want to develop a better appreciation of David Lynch's *Dune*, I suggest you try the alternative, the Sci-Fi Channel's 2000 miniseries *Frank Herbert's Dune*, directed by John Harrison. Every Herbert fan will want to see it, but few will enjoy it. In truth, it is pretty bad. Let me count the ways.

First, the special effects are abysmal, far inferior to Lynch's which predate the age of computer animation.

Second, although some of the interior and exterior sets are imaginative, the costumes are mostly bad, especially the silly headgear.

Third, something is wrong with the sound. There are patches of the film where the dialogue is unintelligible, and not just because of the exotic accents of some of the Czech actors. The worst offender, actually, is William Hurt as Duke Leto Atreides, who sounds like he is mumbling through wooden teeth. To make matters worse, the DVD set I have does not have subtitles.

Fourth, the script is wordy, a flaw that stands out in the scenes that have direct equivalents in the Lynch film.

Fifth, the Fremen's various gestures and rituals are muddled and clumsy, lacking in the stark simplicity one would expect of such people.

Sixth, the only decent music sounds like Brian Eno's "Prophecy" theme from the Lynch film.

Seventh, I don't like a lot of the cast. Some of them are ugly and others are terrible actors. Most of the casting and acting is far inferior to the Lynch film, particularly the characters of Duke Leto, Lady Jessica, Reverend Mother Mohiam, Stilgar, Dr. Yueh, Dr. Kynes, Thufir Hawat, Piter de Vries, Mapes, and Chani.

Alec Newman is actually good as Paul Atreides, but there are precious few scenes where he plays off anyone equal to him. I also liked Julie Cox as Princess Irulan, whose role is expanded from narrator to agent. This bit of tampering did not bother me, since it sets the stage for her more prominent role in the subsequent novels, and some of her lines are taken from characters in the original novel. I also liked Ian McNeice as Baron Harkonnen, whose portrayal is faithful to Herbert, whereas Lynch's unforgettable Grand-Guignol Baron owes much to his own sick imagination. P. H. Moriarty's Gurney Halleck is not bad, but he is no improvement on Lynch's Patrick Stewart. The same is true of Giancarlo Giannini's Emperor Shaddam IV and Matt Keeslar's Feyd: not bad, but not better.

After 295 underwhelming minutes of the Sci-Fi *Dune*, I was not exactly eager to pop in the sequel, 2003's *Frank Herbert's Children of Dune*, directed by Greg Yaitanes. In fact, it took me more than a decade to get around to it, a decision that I regret bitterly, because it is an absolutely brilliant series.

The Sci-Fi *Children of Dune* is actually an adaptation of Herbert's two followup novels, *Dune Messiah* and *Children of Dune*. Watching it, I felt completely vindicated in my objections to the original series, because virtually every flaw that had rankled me had been removed: the bad actors, the ugly actors, the muffled sound, the pedestrian music and directing, the terrible special effects, even the silly hats. Both series had the same budgets, but the second one looks infinitely richer. Truly the worst sort of poverty is lack of taste.

The best actors in the first series are back: Alec Newman as Paul, Julie Cox as Irulan, P. H. Moriarty as Gurney Halleck, and Ian McNeice as Baron Harkonnen. Even a couple actresses whom I disliked in the first series — Barbora Kodetová as Chani and Zuzana Geislerová as Reverend Mother Mohiam — were much better under Yaitanes' direction.

Edward Atterton's Duncan Idaho, Steven Berkoff's Stilgar, and Alice Krige's Lady Jessica are all huge improvements over the first cast. (Krige is an astonishingly regal and charismatic woman. You have seen her as the Borg Queen.)

The new characters are exceptionally well-cast and acted: James McAvoy as Leto II, Jessica Brooks as his twin sister Ghanima, and Daniela Amavia as their aunt Alia. All three are exceptionally attractive and charismatic. They are all a bit older than in the books. Alia is about fifteen in *Dune Messiah*, whereas in the series she is an adult. The twins are nine in *Children of Dune*, but in the series, they are seventeen, on the cusp of legal adulthood. Frankly, these were good choices, because in Herbert's novels, all three characters are sexually precocious, which is something that even today's entertainment industry balks at putting on the screen. More mature actors are also more believable.

The big surprise is Susan Sarandon, who camps it up a bit as Princess Wensicia, the scheming younger sister of Princess Irulan. Sarandon, of course, is probably old enough to be Julie Cox's mother. To add unity to the adaptation of the two novels, and probably also to get more out of Sarandon, Wensicia is made one of the conspirators in *Dune Messiah*. She is the only character who gets to wear silly hats.

The theme of *Dune Messiah* is Paul's attempt to free himself from the terrible consequences of his own ambition, which have turned him into the God Emperor of a fanatical religion and ignited a universal conflagration. The theme of *Children of Dune* is freedom. Like a fugue, the two themes run through both books, the theme of freedom emerging at the end of the first; the theme of religion concluding at the end of the second. Thus it is quite natural and satisfying to have the two novels worked into a single 266 minute miniseries.

Paul's power of prescience means that mankind is not free, for free acts cannot be foreseen. But there was something that Paul did not foresee: the fact that his daughter Ghanima had a twin, a brother, Leto. Leto, therefore, was a free being. Leto's goal was to free mankind from the prescience of his father—the prescience he inherited from his father. This freedom was the gift of a particular kind of blood, a particular genetic code. Thus Leto had to oversee a breeding program as long and as ambitious as the Bene Gesserit's, and toward the opposite aim: the creation of a truly free race. This is Leto's "Golden Path."

To fulfill the Golden Path, Leto must become the greatest tyrant the world has ever seen, an immortal God Emperor. To this end, he allows "sand trout"—the precursors of the giant sand worms—to fuse with his skin, turning him eventually into a giant worm-human hybrid who is virtually indestructible, as long as he avoids a bath. It is an astonishingly imaginative and downright weird story arc that finds completion in Herbert's fourth installment, *God Emperor of Dune*, which I hope I will live to see brought to the screen. Yaitanes could certainly do it justice. In truth, I am saddened that the Sci-Fi Channel did not see fit to do it years ago.

Children of Dune is high-concept science fiction, but it is not space-opera. There aren't a lot of laser battles or space-ships whooshing around. It is more like opera-opera: grand conflicts hinging on grand moral and metaphysical themes, enacted in grand settings by grand heroes and villains dressed, of course, in grand costumes.

But none of it rings hollow and melodramatic. Nor is it undercut with irony and camp, except in the case of Sarandon, who sometimes acts like she is too good for the story. (In one scene, she swings her arms like a cloddish farm girl carrying pails of milk. A princess would know better.)

Overall, Yaitanes' direction is characterized by an unapologetic commitment to beauty and emotional warmth and sincerity. There are many genuinely moving scenes, highlighted by the lovely score by Brian Tyler (Enya meets Elgar). No matter how far out Herbert's imagination can swing, it always remains grounded in the constants of the human heart.

If you are just beginning to explore the *Dune* universe, I would recommend that you skip the Sci-Fi *Dune* miniseries entirely. Begin with Lynch's *Dune*, then watch *Children of Dune*, its worthy sequel.

Counter-Currents, October 23, 2018

Dunkirk

Dunkirk is Christopher Nolan's most emotionally powerful movie. It deals with the evacuation of 400,000 British, Canadian, and French troops trapped on the beach at Dunkirk after being defeated by the Germans in the Second World War.

Dunkirk is a strange work, especially for Christopher Nolan, who typically directs long films with complex plots, extensive character development, and lots of dialogue. *Dunkirk*, however, is only 106 minutes long. There is no single storyline. The movie consists almost entirely of action sequences. There is a large cast, but most of the characters have no names. Most of the actors are unknowns. The few big names have small parts. There is no real character development. There is hardly any dialogue.

The story simply begins at Dunkirk. There is almost no context. The Germans are referred to simply as the "enemy." German aircraft are seen during the movie, but German soldiers appear on screen only in the final minutes, and I never saw a swastika. It is mentioned that the enemy tanks stopped, but no reason is given. (The answer is that Hitler was too kind to the British.)

Instead of a single storyline, there are three: soldiers trying again and again to escape from the beach, fighter pilots providing cover for the evacuation, and a private boat joining the rescue flotilla. The storyline of the beach escapees is the most harrowing and depressing. The stories of the pilots and the boat are the most inspiring. The film moves between the three storylines, but in a non-linear fashion, made most clear when daytime and nighttime scenes are intercut.

Dunkirk is masterful at creating suspense. The cutting between the three storylines makes it feel less like a story and more like a musical fugue. The soundtrack by Nolan's frequent collaborator Hans Zimmer is dreary, electronic, and industrial. The music and the sound effects are shockingly loud. Again and again, I found myself wincing and squirming in my seat. This is aviation, industry, war, and speed as music—Italian Futurism on film.

But as the movie reaches its conclusion, all the elements fall into place in a series of emotionally shattering climaxes—when Zimmer's electronic noise melts into Elgar's Nimrod variation, when we see that the single boat we have followed is part of a vast flotilla, when two young evacuees look out a train window and once again see England's green and pleasant land, when the wheels go down on a fighter that has run out of fuel. *Dunkirk* will wring tears from the flintiest hearts. This film is a masterpiece, and Christopher Nolan is one of our greatest living directors.

Naturally, those humorless culture-killing religious fanatics of the diversity cult are complaining that *Dunkirk* is too white and too male, since not only must white men be engineered out of England's future, they must be airbrushed out of her past. But Leftists are right to dislike this film. Unlike virtually every other movie about the Second World War, *Dunkirk* does not serve as propaganda for multiculturalism. It is not a movie about those dirty, Jew-killing Germans, whose deeds—we are constantly told—are somehow the refutation of every nationalistic sentiment, even in the people who fought against them.

Instead, *Dunkirk* is a movie about England. It is a movie about coming home. It is about the patriotism, social solidarity, ingenuity, hard work, and bravery of countless humble white people whose primary mistake was to trust the leaders who delivered them into two World Wars and are now overseeing their replacement with the scum of the Third World. Leftists fear *Dunkirk* because it gives white men a glimpse of a nice white country we could someday restore, and the virtues we must find again if we are to defeat the real enemy this time.

Counter-Currents, July 22, 2017

ERASERHEAD:
A GNOSTIC ANTI-SEX FILM

David Lynch's first movie *Eraserhead* (1977) combines surrealism, low-budget horror, and black comedy. It rapidly became a staple of the midnight movie circuit and provided endless fodder for coffee-house intellectuals and academic film theorists.

Eraserhead is quite simply a gnostic anti-sex film. The film is premised on a gnostic dualism, which holds that the material world—including sex and childbearing—is fundamentally evil, a prison in which the spirit suffers. The solution to suffering is to free ourselves from the trammels of matter, including sexual desire.

Eraserhead was filmed intermittently, on a shoestring budget, over a period of five years (1972–1977). Although the meaning of the film is self-contained, it is illuminated by some details in Lynch's biography.

For instance, beginning in 1973, Lynch began his lifetime engagement with Hinduism and Transcendental Meditation. He has reportedly described *Eraserhead* as his most "spiritual" work.

From 1966 to 1970, while studying at the Pennsylvania Academy of Fine Art in Philadelphia, Lynch lived in a hellish urban environment like the one seen in *Eraserhead*.

In 1968, Lynch's first child, Jennifer, was born while he was still in art school. The pregnancy was unplanned, and Jennifer was born with severely clubbed feet, which required extensive corrective surgeries.

In 1974, Lynch's marriage broke up, due in part to his infidelity.

Eraserhead opens with a planet in space. Then the sideways face of the main character, Henry Spencer (Jack Nance), floats up from the bottom of the screen in front of the planet (which can be seen through him) and drifts out of the frame. A throbbing sound grows louder and louder as we zoom in on the rough surface of the planet. Then we follow a trench until the screen is utterly dark. Next we see a metal-roofed shack on the surface with a huge hole in its roof. We enter the hole. Inside, we see a man with horribly disfigured skin seated in front of levers. In the background is a cracked and broken window.

We then cut to Henry's face. His mouth opens, and what looks like a hypertrophied sperm cell comes out. Then the Man in the Planet pulls a lever, and the sperm whooshes out of the frame. Another lever seems to start a huge machine. The camera moves to a pool of water. Then a third lever sends the sperm splashing into the pool. Then we see bubbles and darkness. After that, we move toward a white circle of light, which seems to be glimpsed through a hole in gauze, fringed with hairs or threads. At which point the prologue ends.

The meaning of the prologue becomes clear when we learn a bit later that Henry has fathered a baby with his estranged girlfriend Mary—or at least a hideously deformed *something* that they *think* is a baby. Henry's head and mouth of course are stand-ins for his penis, from which sperm cells actually emerge. The pool of water into which the sperm falls is Mary's womb. And the movement from darkness to light is the birth of the baby.

The fact that this process is under the control of the so-called Man in the Planet gives it all a sinister cast. Sex and reproduction are material (the planet is a great hunk of matter, pulled into a spherical shape by the force of gravity), mechanical (produced by a huge machine), and directed by the malevolent will of the Man in the Planet, whose deformities emphasize his materiality and who is a kind of Gnostic Demiurge figure, imprisoning the spirit in matter.

After the prologue, we see Henry's face, looking back over his shoulder anxiously, as if he is being stalked. He is dressed in a suit with a pocket protector. His hair is teased up in a huge bouffant. He carries a brown paper bag through an industrial hellhole back to his tiny apartment. Before he enters, a beautiful brunette emerges from the apartment across the hall. The brunette is a temptress figure, who in this scene calls to mind Franz von Stuck's *Sin*. The brunette tells Henry that someone named Mary called to invite him to dinner at her parents' house. After an awkward silence, he thanks the woman and goes inside.

Henry's apartment is a strange place. It is furnished with a table, a record player, a dresser, a tabernacle-like cupboard, a bed, a night stand, and a couple of lamps. What seem to be grass clippings are piled on top of the dresser and on the floor under the radiator. The night stand is decorated with a mound of dirt from which protrudes a denuded branch. A tiny picture of a nuclear mushroom cloud hangs above it. In the top drawer of his dresser, Henry finds a picture of Mary torn in two. Obviously their relationship has been strained.

The next scene, dinner at Mary's house, is the dark comic high point of the film. The scene begins with Mary's worried face peering out of the window of her house, which is set in an industrial hellscape with a front yard filled with dead flowers. Like Henry's apartment, the interior is drab and depressing. There are grass clippings here, too.

Henry's meeting with Mary's parents is filled with excruciatingly awkward silences, during which we hear constant mechanical rumbling and hissing, as well as the loud sucking sounds of a litter of nursing puppies. Both Mary and her mother have spastic episodes. Mary's father Bill has a loud voice, a benumbed arm, and a demented grin frozen on his face. The less said about the chicken, the better.

Then an electrical socket begins sparking, and a lamp glows brightly, then burns out, which in Lynch's cinematic language signifies the presence of the supernatural. The mother then confronts Henry with a very awkward question: "Did you and Mary have sexual intercourse?" The question is followed by some intensely awkward nuzzling from the mother.

The reason she asks is that Mary has had some sort of . . . baby. Mary questions whether it is a baby at all, but the mother insists that it is a baby, a bit premature perhaps, but a baby. She also insists that Henry and Mary get married and raise the child. Henry takes the news by getting a nosebleed. All told, dinner could have gone better.

The next scene takes place a short time later. Henry and Mary are apparently married and living together with the "baby" in Henry's little room. The "baby" is a grotesque creature. It looks more like a fetal puppy than a human being. Basically, it is a hypertrophied sperm cell with eyes and a mouth. Its body is hidden in bandages. Apparently it has no arms or legs. Mary is becoming increasingly frustrated feeding the "baby," which writhes, fusses, and spits out its food.

Henry goes to the lobby to check the mail. He finds a tiny package in his mailbox. Furtively, he ducks out to the street to open it, finding a tiny worm inside. He returns, a hopeful smile forming on his face, and lies down on his bed to soak up this scene of domestic bliss, staring into the hissing radiator. When Henry looks into the radiator, a light shines from inside it and an empty stage appears. Henry is pulled back from his reverie by the baby crying. When Mary asks if there is any mail, Henry lies and says no.

Cut to a dark and stormy night with the baby crying. Henry gets out of bed and places the worm in the tabernacle-like cupboard, which emits a hum that grows louder when Henry opens the doors. Mary lies awake, tense, frustrated, and sleepless, listening to the baby cry. Finally, she loses her cool, leaps out of bed, and screams "Shut up." Then she dresses and declares she is going back to her parents' for a good night's sleep.

Before she departs, Mary kneels at the foot of the bed, peering between the bars of the metal bedframe like a woman in prison, yanking on the bed, causing it to rock and squeak. Is she pantomiming her imprisonment to the baby and the material realm? Is she having another spastic episode? No, she's just trying to dislodge her suitcase from under the bed. After Mary departs we see the temptress coming down the hall looking wet, tired, and sultry.

On his own, Henry wonders if the baby is sick and decides to take its temperature. The temperature is normal, but suddenly the baby is covered with vomit and hives. Its breathing is labored. So Henry rigs up a vaporizer. At one point he glances at the tabernacle, then moves toward the door, perhaps to check to see if any new worms have arrived in the mail, but the baby starts crying whenever he tries to leave.

Cut to Henry in bed, at the beginning of another sleepless night. The radiator hisses. We hear metallic grinding. Two metal panels part, and we see the stage in the radiator, footlights coming on one after another. Then the Woman in the Radiator appears. She is blonde and wears a white dress. Her face is disfigured with huge round cheeks whose wrinkled texture makes them look like a scrotum. She begins dancing to the organ music that Henry played earlier on his phonograph. Her manner is girlish and demure.

Then sperm cells begin to fall onto the stage. The Woman in the Radiator regards them with childish excitement, but when the organ music stops, she gleefully squishes one beneath her shoe. The music resumes, then stops, whereupon another sperm is crushed. The wind then howls, and the Woman retreats back into the shadows.

Is the Woman in the Radiator's girlish and demure behavior just an act put on by a dominatrix who excites fetishists by crushing things underfoot? Perhaps. But if so, this is only a minor element of her role. Instead, I see her as an embodiment of asexuality and innocence, a Vestal Virgin whose purity is guarded by deformity, whose role is to crush and reject the deformed products of Henry's sexuality. If the Man in the Planet represents bondage to matter and sexuality—which is embodied by the hideous and demanding "baby"—the Woman in the Radiator represents freedom from matter and sexuality, as well as the responsibility of parenthood. If the Man in the Planet is the Demiurge, the Woman in the Radiator is Sophia, the divine spiritual/intellectual principle that allows us to be saved from the bondage of the material realm.

Metaphysically, the realm in the radiator is the opposite of the planet in the prologue. The light is the opposite of the darkness of the planet. The stage suggests a realm of imagination, spirit, and freedom, rather than the planet's realm of matter, gravity, and mechanical compulsion. The music in the radiator contrasts sharply with the mechanical rattle and hum of the planet. If the radiator is heaven, the planet is hell. These contrasts point to a neat gnostic dualism of matter and spirit, bondage and freedom.

When the Woman in the Radiator fades into the shadows, we see Henry tossing and turning in his bed. He wakes up to find that Mary is back, locked in a deep slumber, her face glistening with sweat. Her teeth are clicking together. She rubs one eye, making a gross squishing sound. She is hogging the bed, and Henry tries to force her onto the other side. Then, in horror, he reaches down and finds a sperm cell in the bed. He throws it against the wall, causing it to explode. Then he finds another and another and another. At this point, it is clear that the sperm are coming out of Mary, that she is writhing in the pangs of labor. This is how the "baby" was brought into the world. Mary's bed hogging, writhing, sweating, teeth chattering, and eye rubbing—as well as the fact that she is unconscious the whole time—emphasize her corporeality and make it thoroughly revolting.

The sperm cells have been splattered against the wall next to the tabernacle cupboard, whose doors now open to reveal the worm, which springs to life and begins squealing. It retreats into the darkness of the cupboard and then appears to be on the surface of the planet, squealing, writhing, doing somersaults, plunging into one hole and then emerging from another. On its last emergence, its end opens up in a vast, all-devouring maw, not unlike one of the sandworms of Arrakis. Mechanical noises grow louder as we plunge inside and then see Henry—apparently from the point of view of an observer in the planet, perhaps the Man in the Planet himself.

The worm is sensate flesh, deprived of all higher faculties, capable only of cavorting and suffering on the material plane (the planet) where it is imprisoned, without hope of release. But Henry is more than just a worm. He has higher faculties (Sophia) that might just save him. But he's due for another test, which the Man in the Planet has dispatched. Cue a knock on the door.

The temptress across the hall has locked herself out of her apartment. It's late. She wants to spend the night at Henry's. When the baby begins to cry, Henry stifles it, lest the woman be repelled. Then we see Henry and the woman kissing in his bed—not *on* it, literally *in* it. They are sinking into a pool of white liquid in the middle of the bed. She sees the horrifying baby out of the corner of her eye, but continues to kiss and sink. In the end, only her wig is visible, floating on the surface of the white pool. Then we have a shot of white paint separating into two distinct white waves that flee one another. This effect was accomplished by sloshing two waves of white paint together, then reversing the film. The unity between the two has been broken. Coitus interruptus? Then the temptress' face appears, looking into a sharp, narrow beam of light. Then we see the planet, which seems to force her back into darkness. She is, of course, both an instrument of the planet (a temptress) and a victim of it, since she, too, feels desire.

Then the Woman in the Radiator steps forward from the darkness and begins to sing in a lilting, slightly Southern accent:

> In Heaven
> Everything is fine
> In Heaven
> Everything is fine
> In Heaven
> Everything is fine
> You got your good things
> And I've got mine
>
> In Heaven
> Everything is fine
> In Heaven
> Everything is fine
> In Heaven
> Everything is fine
> You got your good thing
> And you've got mine
>
> In Heaven
> Everything is fine

This is a pretty clear statement of the dualism between the material/sexual/hellish realm represented by the planet and the Man within and the spiritual/asexual/heavenly realm represented by the Woman in the Radiator. Henry then steps onto the stage in the radiator, entering the Woman's liminal space between hell and heaven—the realm of suffering and the realm of release. They look into one another's eyes. Smiling, she opens her hands toward him. We heard a loud humming and twice see blinding white light. A glimpse of the stainless void? Then she is gone.

Now we hear the baby crying and, in a flash, see the Man in the Planet. The dead sperm cells blow away. We hear a squeaking sound, and a mound with a dead tree in it is wheeled out onto the stage, an enlarged version of the mound with the dead branch on Henry's dresser. Henry then steps into what appears to be a witness box, grasping the rail and nervously turning the pipe in its housing. Henry is clearly on trial, torn between the Man in the Planet and the Woman in the Radiator. It's enough to blow a guy's head clean off.

So next, Henry's head blows clean off, while his hands continue to grip and turn the railing. The head of the crying baby emerges from Henry's neck. Blood begins to pour from the tree and pool up on the floor where Henry's head has landed. Then his head disappears from the puddle of blood. It falls through the air and lands in an industrial alleyway, where the top of Henry's skull breaks off. An urchin picks up the head and takes it to a pencil factory. A core sample of Henry's brain is used to manufacture erasers. A factory worker sharpens a pencil and tests it by drawing, and then erasing, a line. The eraser bits are then just . . . brushed away. It is a bizarre but brilliant image of rampant dehumanization and materialism. Modern man doesn't just use the whole buffalo. We *are* the buffalo. Today a man, tomorrow dust in the wind. Eraser dust in the wind.

Fortunately, it was just a terrible dream. Henry awakes and finds the temptress gone. He spends the whole day waiting for her to return. He hears a sound, goes to knock on the temptress' door, but there is no answer. The baby seems to be laughing at him. Hours pass. He hears the elevator and opens the door. The temptress is there, entering her apartment with a hideous old trick. She looks at Henry disdainfully, seeing his head replaced with the baby's. Humiliated, Henry shrinks back and closes the door.

Henry feels he has been rejected because of the baby, which fills him with hatred. He goes to the dresser and finds a pair of scissors. He cuts open the baby's bandages and finds nothing but a pile of entrails. The kid has no body. Obviously, this is not a viable organism. And it is utterly repulsive. And it is ruining Henry's life. Henry then resolves to kill it, stabbing its pulsating entrails with the scissors. Fluids squirt and then ooze out, followed by enormous amounts of foam. Henry retreats to the other end of his room. The electricity begins surging. Sparks fly out of the sockets. Something uncanny is about to happen. Then we see the head of the baby grown monstrously large, moving around the room, illuminated in the flickering lights. Then everything goes dark, and we hear a thud. Is it the baby? Is it Henry?

Next we see Henry standing in a cloud of eraser dust. (It is the image on the film poster.) Then we see the planet, which explodes. After that, we see the man in the planet, his face in agony, sparks flying from his machinery, which he can no longer control. Finally, the screen is filled with white light as the Woman in the Radiator embraces Henry. Henry has been liberated from the sufferings of the material realm. The end.

But what kind of liberation did Henry achieve? I would argue that it is not liberation through *spiritual attainment*. Henry has not overcome the desires that cause suffering. He has just killed his baby because it got in the way of satisfying his desire for the temptress across the hall. You can't get much more sordid than that. Thus I believe Henry's liberation was achieved simply by death. Hence the cloud of eraser dust, a symbol of the evanescence and ultimate meaninglessness of human life. Henry tried killing the baby, and the baby ended up killing him.

Life is hell. Death is heaven. But there hardly seems to be any sort of moral order governing this arrangement. Heaven certainly does not seem like an appropriate *reward* for killing one's child. But maybe heaven isn't something *after* death. Maybe it simply *is* death. And death is simple annihilation, not a passage from one realm to another.

It is hard to escape the conclusion that the message of *Eraserhead* is pure nihilism, albeit of a spiritual/mystical variety.

It is, however, doubtful that this is David Lynch's full and final philosophy of life, considering that he ended up fathering four children. When Lynch was in Art School in Philadelphia, his father was so disturbed by some of his artistic experiments that he urged his son not to have children. Just as I'd love to know what Freud's mother thought about the Oedipus complex, I'd love to know what David Lynch's kids think about *Eraserhead*.

Counter-Currents, December 12, 2018

THE EXPANSE

The Expanse is a SyFy network original series that is now nearing the end of its third season. *The Expanse* is the most imaginative and absorbing science fiction series since the reboot of *Battlestar Galactica* (2003–2009).

The Expanse is based on a series of novels by S. A. Corey. I have not read them, so I cannot judge the accuracy of the adaptation, but I am delighted that there are eight, soon to be nine novels, which will provide material for future seasons. SyFy canceled the series after the ongoing third season, but Amazon Video has picked it up. So I hope that we will all be binge-watching *The Expanse* for years to come.

The Expanse is set more than 200 years in the future. Mankind has colonized Mars, the Asteroid Belt, and the moons of Jupiter and Saturn. The Earth is ruled by the United Nations. Former nations are referred to merely as "economic zones." Once gifted with abundance, the Earthlings thought only of present, personal indulgences, not the future of mankind, leaving the world massively overpopulated and polluted. A lot of the population is unemployed and exists on the dole.

Mars, by contrast, has a forbidding environment which has bred a Spartan ethos. The entire planet is dedicated to terraforming Mars to create a livable environment for distant future generations. The Earthlings, of course, regard the Martians as fascistic.

In the Asteroid Belt and beyond are the "Belters," the frontiersmen of the system. They do not, however, resemble American pioneers so much as the proletarian rabble one would find in seaports. Their culture seems like a fusion of Irishmen, Juggalos, and the global South, forever haggling, carousing, toasting, and complaining about injustice in a sing-songy, Irish-Jamaican inflected pidgin English.

Like all cultural products today, the casting of *The Expanse* is maximally politically correct and diverse, with whites, blacks, Asians, Middle Easterners, South Asians, and all manner of mystery meat. There is also maximum cultural eclecticism and confusion. An Iranian actress plays an Indian woman named Crisjen Avasarala. A white man is named Sadavir Errinwright. A Chinaman is named Jules-Pierre Mao. A mulatto bears the name Naomi Nagata. And, most ridiculously, an Iranian actor plays an Arab from Mars who talks like a good old boy from Texas. You get the picture.

The Expanse, like other such science fiction, projects a future that is a bit more diverse and exotic than the present, ignoring the fact that if present trends continue, in 200 years, there will be no diversity. There will just be a despoiled earth swarming with a homogeneous population of brown hominids who are too dumb and violent on average to sustain and advance technological civilization.

Politically correct science fiction defers the ultimate consequences of diversity to a still more distant future because viewers would be revolted by a vision of panmixia. They would not watch shows populated exclusively by people with whom they feel no identification. Beyond that, whites today cannot be taught to miscegenate our race out of existence if we cannot identify with people on the screen doing the same thing 200 years from now.

Thus *The Expanse* features two very white Alpha Males James Holden (played by Steven Strait) and Amos Burton (played by Wes Chatham), both of whom regard the mulatto Naomi Nagata as a sexual prize. Holden, the main hero, actually ends up sleeping with her (of course).

In short, the purpose of politically correct science fiction is not to *portray* the homogeneous dystopia of "diversity," but to *promote* it by treating miscegenation merely as a way of expanding individual sexual options while veiling the ultimate collective consequences from us.

But if you can set aside the odious racial politics of *The Expanse* (which is no worse than anything else on TV) and just focus on the story, the series is highly rewarding.

The plot of the first three novels/seasons deals with mankind's first contact with an intelligent and deadly alien life form, and the almost complete inability of our ruling elites to deal with it in a rational, prudent, and ethical manner. Instead, *The Expanse* offers a portrait of a civilization whose political, economic, and scientific elites are almost entirely sociopathic.

When the alien life form is first encountered by industrialist Jules-Pierre Mao, it is simply a blue goo which is dubbed the "proto-molecule." Mao's first reaction is to weaponize it and sell it to the main rival powers, Earth and Mars. To do that, however, human guinea pigs are required, and to remove any moral qualms about such experiments, a group of scientists voluntarily undergo a procedure that turns them into sociopaths. And once they become sociopaths, well, there's no limit to the scope of their experiments.

The proto-molecule, however, apparently having assimilated a sufficient number of human test subjects, attains a kind of emergent intelligence. It develops a mind and agenda of its own, which sets the system reeling.

Mankind is standing on the brink of the greatest discovery—and the greatest danger—in its history, so naturally the imbeciles who run Earth and Mars go to war. It is all extremely bleak and chilling, but highly imaginative and involving.

Of course there would be no story without some good characters who do their best to save mankind from the proto-molecule and an even more formidable enemy—our own leaders. The good guys are the crew of the spaceship *Rocinante*: James Holden, who is a morally earnest knightly hero; Naomi Nagata (Dominique Tipper), the engineer; Alex Kamal (Cas Anvar), the pilot; and Amos Burton, a mechanic and thug.

Other good characters are UN Deputy Undersecretary Crisjen Avasarala, played by the Persian actress Shohreh Aghdashloo; Avasarala's faithful paladin and spy, Cotyar Ghazi, played by Lebanese actor Nick Tarabay; Martian soldier Roberta Draper, played by a Polynesian actress Frankie Adams; Methodist minister Annushka "Anna" Volovodov, played by Elizabeth Mitchell; and Joe Miller, a detective on Ceres Station in the Belt played by Thomas Jane.

All of them stand out by having a moral center and working to prevent humanity's (self-)destruction.

My favorite characters are Avasarala and Amos. The husky-voiced Avasarala dresses and comports herself like a Bollywood diva. She is a powerful woman who has not masculinized herself in the least. She is shrewd and ruthless, capable of using Machiavellian means to moral ends. She ends up saving the world—and ruling it—and deserves it.

Amos is a thug with a sketchy past from Baltimore, which has not mellowed in 200 years. A lot of viewers probably regard him as a "psycho," and perhaps they are meant to. But Amos clearly has a moral compass. He is capable of loyalty, justice, and righteous anger. What makes him scary to most people is that he is quintessentially Aryan: taciturn, cold, hard, unsentimental, and utterly ruthless in meting out death to evildoers. Played by the hulking, charismatic Wes Chatham, Amos steals every scene he is in.

Like many series, *The Expanse* had a bit of a wobbly start before getting its stride. I confess, for instance, I find the *noir* gumshoe *shtick* of Miller, who is prominent in the first season, to be annoying and often ridiculous. But after the second episode, I found myself binge-watching to the end of season two.

With its complex characters and plots and its gritty, near future setting, *The Expanse* has much of the same appeal as *Firefly*—and given that *Firefly* is one of the best science fiction series ever, that is a strong recommendation indeed.

Counter-Currents, February 2, 2019

GLASS

M. Night Shyamalan's *Glass* is a sequel to two of his films, *Unbreakable* (2000), which is my favorite of his works, and *Split* (2016), which I found to be quite unpleasant, although I must concede that it is brilliantly acted in the lead role(s) by James McEvoy.

Unbreakable is a deeply moving film about how David Dunn (Bruce Willis)—once a brilliant college athlete who has been emasculated by his wife, an overprotective physical therapist—discovers that he is not an ordinary man. David Dunn is actually a superhero, and *Unbreakable* is his origin story.

The famed Shyamalan "twist" is that the film's art-film pacing, frequent low-angle shots, and glossy, sensuous images of the ordinary have lulled us into thinking that *Unbreakable* is set in the world that we all live in, the world where the extraordinary is impossible.

Split is a deeply distasteful film about Kevin Wendell Crumb, a psychopath with 23 or 24 personalities, who kidnaps three teenage girls and eats two of them. *Split* is disturbingly close to being a just a slasher flick, and it was enormously popular with precisely that audience.

I was delighted to learn that David Dunn and his archnemesis Mr. Glass (Samuel L. Jackson) would be returning in *Glass*. I was not thrilled that James McEvoy's Kevin Wendell Crum *et al.* would be back as well.

And that, frankly, is the primary flaw of *Glass*. David Dunn and Mr. Glass should be the central characters. They have spiritual depth, tragic grandeur, and unfinished business. But the movie is hogged by McEvoy's giddy cycling through his various personalities, chewing up the scenery and some of the extras in the process. Seriously, Mr. Glass didn't even utter a word until half way through the movie.

Split partisans will of course disagree. But they probably find the movie unsatisfying as well, with David Dunn and Mr. Glass hogging McEvoy's spotlight from time to time.

The bottom line is this: *Glass* is not a great movie, because the plot tries to synthesize too many elements and fails to do so in a satisfying way. Imagine a movie that tries to be a sequel to *2001* and *A Clockwork Orange* at the same time. Not even Kubrick could have made that work.

But is *Glass* at least good—good enough to see in the theater? Yes, emphatically yes. For in the end, Glass has a very important message. I won't spoil the plot, so I will only mention things that are apparent in the trailer and other advertising.

Mr. Glass, David Dunn, and Kevin Crumb all end up in an institution for the criminally insane. Yes, Dunn has saved countless lives over the years, but he's a criminal, because he took the law into his own hands. The police frown upon that. They'd rather have dead citizens than vigilantes running around.

In the institution, the trio are placed under the care of Dr. Ellie Staple (Sarah Paulson), who specializes in treating patients with delusions of grandeur. Her goal is to talk Mr. Glass out of thinking he's a supervillain, David Dunn out of thinking he's a superhero, and Kevin Crumb out of thinking he's a bit of both, perhaps. She tries to persuade them of mundane, materialistic explanations for what seems to set them apart from the rest of humanity.

But Mr. Glass is a mastermind, and masterminds are always a few steps ahead. And suffice it to say, Dr. Staple does not talk him out of his "delusions."

I am not going to stay any more about the plot. But the takeaway message of Glass seems to be that Dr. Staple's brand of psychological materialism is nothing but an ideology of social control. And just as in *Unbreakable*, Mr. Glass reasons that if there is a person like him in the universe (a supervillain with brittle bones), there is his opposite (an indestructible superhero), if there is a group of people dedicated to attaining superhuman excellences, for good or evil, then must also be a group of people dedicated to crushing superhuman excellence to maintain control of a flat and mediocre world.

Glass is a battle between the Superman and the Last Man, and Shyamalan is clearly a partisan of human excellence against the leveling forces of modern liberal democratic society. That makes

Shyamalan in essence a man of the Right. Thus it should come as no surprise that *Glass* has received overwhelmingly negative reviews in the mainstream media. People on the Dissident Right, however, are better equipped to appreciate it. Thus I give *Glass* a qualified recommendation. *Glass* fails to be a great movie. It is sometimes deeply frustrating and distasteful. But it nevertheless deserves praise for offering a defense of human greatness from modern egalitarian mediocrity. I found the ending genuinely moving. *Glass* is a noble flawed film.

The Unz Review, March 1, 2019

GOOD KILL

Good Kill is an OK movie starring Ethan Hawke and directed by New Zealander Andrew Niccol, who also directed Hawke in *Gattaca*, the dumbest anti-eugenics movie ever made (beautiful but dumb). Hawke plays Major Thomas Egan, an Air Force pilot assigned to pilot drones in the "war on terror." (Can we have the word "terrorism" back now that George W. Bush is no longer around to mangle it?)

Instead of living in a war zone, where his life is constantly at risk, Hawke lives with his hot wife (January Jones, a.k.a., Betty Draper) and two beautiful children in a subdivision in Las Vegas. Instead of taking off and landing on the pitching deck of an aircraft carrier, he commutes to work in a sports car. His office is a trailer on a military base where he is part of a team of five who carry out drone strikes in Afghanistan and Yemen for the Air Force and the CIA.

Apparently these drones fly at 10,000 feet and cannot be seen from the ground by the naked eye. They have cameras with sufficient resolution to allow operators to recognize people on the ground. They carry multiple Hellfire missiles that can obliterate a building, a convoy, or a group of people 8 to 10 seconds after launch.

The movie's recreation of drone warfare may or may not be accurate, but it is certainly dramatic and emotionally compelling. It is terrifying that people on the other side of the planet can stalk you with eyes in the sky and in seconds obliterate you and your family and your neighbors and anyone who might rush to the rescue.

The two most disturbing strikes were under CIA command. In the first, the drone crew blows up someone they are told is an enemy commander along with his house and family. Then, when neighbors rush to the smoldering ruins to render aid, they are blown up with a second missile. (They use the Mafia term, a "double tap.")

In the second strike, a house and family are blown up, but instead of blowing up the rescuers, the drone crew watches as neighbors piece together seven dead bodies, and then, at their funeral the next day, they are blown up again along with their extended family who have come to see them off.

Frankly, I wish Saddam Hussein had such technology in 2001 and used it to pick off the Wurmsers, Feiths, Perles, Krauthammers, and Kristols who brought untold death and misery to Americans and Iraqis alike. But Saddam was clueless about the real enemy and probably would have blown it.

The movie dutifully rehearses the arguments for and against the use of drones. Jack Johns, the Lieutenant Colonel in charge, argues that drones are cheaper in terms of American dollars and lives and more discriminating about targets (and thus less destructive) than conventional warfare.

The token female non-white, Vera Suarez (Zoë Kravitz — who is half Jewish and about half black) offers the standard liberal talking points: the use of drones constitutes "war crimes"; it is indistinguishable from terrorism; it is a recruitment tool for terrorists. This is all true, but it is even more true of conventional warfare.

First of all, we need to separate the case offered for the particular wars we are fighting in the Muslim world from the case for drone technology in general. We don't need to be fighting in Afghanistan and Yemen. We just need to cut our special friend Israel loose. (After sending her 6 million Jewish-American reinforcements.)

But in themselves, drones strike me as a good weapon. The drone crews agonize about collateral damage more than old-fashioned bomber crews, simply because, although they do less damage, they *see* it better. But if they can see it better, they can also avoid it better. No matter how terrible drone strikes are, do they really compare with the indiscriminate terror bombing of Dresden and Hamburg or Hiroshima and Nagasaki? Viewed dispassionately, drones represent moral progress in warfare.

Ethan Hawke's character just doesn't think drones are sporting. He thinks of warfare as a duel, and if the enemy can't kill you back, there is something wrong with it. He wants to risk shedding his blood, and the only Purple Heart he can win in his trailer is for carpal tunnel syndrome. But of course, warfare is not a duel. We do not seek to equalize our risks and weapons, but to gain every possible advantage. But all of that is "cheating" if war is subjected to the rules of dueling.

Hawke's crisis of conscience is supposed to seem honorable and manly, but it strikes me as weak and self-indulgent. Unable to put his family through hell with long absences in war zones, he puts them through hell in other ways: by developing a cartoonishly excessive drinking problem, having spats with the missus, and flirting implausibly with the ugly Zoë Kravitz character. Frankly, the weakest part of the film is Hawke's character, his crackup, and his redemption at the end. And given that he is the central character of the film, I can't really recommend *Good Kill*, despite the fact that it is very well-made. Like *Gattaca*, *Good Kill* is beautiful but dumb—and not nearly as entertaining.

Counter-Currents, May 27, 2015

Hidden Figures

Hidden Figures, a.k.a., *We Wuz Astronautz*, tells the story of three black women who worked at NASA in 1961 struggling for equal rights both as blacks and as women. The movie tells us that it is "based on true events," and the three women—mathematician Katherine Johnson, computer programmer Dorothy Vaughan, and engineer Mary Jackson—actually did exist. But it is not clear if any of the struggles and achievements depicted actually happened, or if they are just-so stories. The moral of the movie, however, is quite clear: three unsung black women played an essential role in the US space program.

Now hold on just a minute. European man's conquest of space is one of our greatest achievements. So of course the Left wants to find or create non-whites who contributed to the process. It is called Afrocentric "cultural appropriation." "Kangz," for short.

Given that intelligence is distributed on bell curves, even though African blacks have an average IQ of 70 and African-American blacks—many of whom have a significant percentage of white ancestry—have an average IQ of 85, there will always be some outliers: extremely intelligent and extremely stupid blacks. And in a society with some extremely intelligent blacks, they can of course be employed in projects like the space program. This was particularly the case in the US during the Cold War, which sought to mobilize all available talent in the race against the Soviets.

But that does not change the fact that the conquest of space was a white achievement. It could have been done without any blacks, and left to their own devices, blacks never created the wheel, much less conquered space.

Of course, the true unsung heroes of the American space program were not African Americans, or Americans at all. They were German Nazi rocket scientists. But in *Hidden Figures*, the only foreign accent belongs to Dr. Zelinsky, who informs us that he is a Polish Jew who survived a Nazi concentration camp. Naturally, he encourages one of the black women, Mary Jackson, to pursue an engineering degree. If you were a "white male," he asks, would you pursue a degree? If she were a "white male," she replies, she'd already have one.

Not only were blacks not essential to the space program, they were actually overwhelmingly hostile to it. No sooner had Americans landed on the moon in 1969, than blacks and their Jewish and liberal allies were calling for an end to the space program and a new focus on minority uplift. Gil Scott-Heron even blamed the rent hike on his rat-infested apartment on "Whitey on the Moon."

Unfortunately, while it is possible for white men to conquer space, it is not possible to make blacks our equals. More than 40 years and trillions of dollars later, rats are still biting black children, but whitey has not been on the moon since 1972.

Hidden Figures basically plays like a made-for-cable-TV movie, for one of those channels that idle housewives and welfare queens watch during the daytime. It is slow-paced, light on science and math, and full of soap-operatic domestic and romantic interludes, montages set to vintage R&B music, and similar filler. The acting throughout is effective but unremarkable.

The message to whites is: black people are just like us, only sassy. Thus doing away with segregation and traditional gender roles will unleash talents and creativity that will lead us to a better society.

But it didn't really work out that way. And actually *Hidden Figures* subtly undermines its pro-Civil Rights agenda through its portrayal of black life under segregation. Yes, there are the standard indignities of separate toilets and drinking fountains. But blacks are portrayed as well-dressed and well-mannered, with mostly intact families—a far cry from liberated blacks today. For instance, the blushing and decorous courtship of Katherine and her future husband seems like something out of a Jane Austen novel. It bears absolutely no resemblance to the booty-twerking, muh-diking Negroes of today.

But what of the fate of talented blacks languishing under segregation? Well, all the events of the movie took place before the Civil Rights Act, didn't they?

Let's focus on the central character, Katherine, played by Taraji Henson. Katherine Coleman was a genuine mathematical prodigy. She also has so much white ancestry that she has blue eyes (meaning white ancestors on both sides) and a fair enough complexion to pass as white. Katherine's intellectual gifts were recognized at an early age, and she was given an appropriate education. She graduated from high school at the age of 14 and from college at age 18. Because of her talent, she was the first black woman admitted to the graduate school of West Virginia University in 1939, which she quit to start a family. In 1953, she was hired by the precursor of NASA and worked there the rest of her career.

Segregation did not impede the rise of these women, provided they were plucky enough to persevere. But segregation did impede the fall of the vast majority of blacks, who through the subtle and not-so-subtle pressure to conform to white behavioral norms (the hated "white supremacy" system) were far more decent, decorous, and law-abiding than blacks today. They were probably even happier.

But they were not "free." Specifically, they were not free to be themselves, to create a society that felt natural to them. They were being oppressed by white cultural norms. And when all that oppression was relaxed, the vast majority of black America went straight to hell.

Hidden Figures is a feast for the fantasies of white liberals, who somehow overlook the fact that the black community portrayed in the movie was the product of segregation, not Civil Rights, and the blacks who terrify them today are the products of Civil Rights, not white racism. To the extent that black viewers of *Hidden Figures* feel nostalgia for the communal life it portrays, they too are experiencing nostalgia for segregation.

Hidden Figures isn't a particularly good movie, even as pro-black propaganda. But that has not stopped mostly white and Jewish liberals from hailing it as a work of genius, setting off a virtue-signaling spiral that is as hard to stop as an ovation for Comrade Stalin. There's actually a whole Wikipedia page for the accolades. It is even in the running for an Academy Awards Best Picture nomination. Surely, the Nobel Peace Prize cannot be far behind.

If *Hidden Figures* sounds like your kind of movie, you have blundered into the wrong website. But no need to spend your time and money seeing it in the theater, as you are going to spend the rest of your life having this dry, insipid turkey of a film served up for free on every channel you flip to. We might have to go back to space, just to escape it.

Counter-Currents, February 6, 2017

JODOROWSKY'S DUNE

Jodorowsky's Dune, Frank Pavich's 2013 documentary, tells the story of the "greatest movie never made," Alejandro Jodorowsky's abortive adaptation of Frank Herbert's *Dune*. Jodorowsky is a Chilean-born Jewish filmmaker and author of graphic novels and books on spirituality, psychology, magic, and divination. (My review of *The Dance of Reality* appears in *Son of Trevor Lynch's White Nationalist Guide to the Movies*.)

In 1974, after the successes of his psychedelic cult films *El Topo* and *The Holy Mountain*, Jodorowsky and his friend Michel Seydoux decided upon an adaptation of *Dune* and began assembling an amazing cast and creative team.

To help create the world of *Dune*, including designs for sets and costumes, Jodorowsky brought in French cartoonist/graphic novelist Jean Giraud (Moebius), English science fiction illustrator Chris Foss, and Swiss surrealist painter H. R. Giger. To realize their designs, he hired Dan O'Bannon to do special effects. For music, Jodorowski settled on Pink Floyd, with Magma to provide the music of the Harkonnens.

Jodorowski's casting decisions were equally inspired. Salvador Dalí was to play Emperor Shaddam IV. Dalí wanted to be the best paid actor in the world. It was agreed he would be paid $100,000 per minute—but not for minutes worked, for minutes on the screen. Dalí also suggested plot elements and set designs, right down to the emperor's toilet. At one point, he asked for a flaming giraffe, which was duly inked into the storyboards by Moebius. Clearly, Dalí was perfect for the role of a megalomaniac. Dalí's muse Amanda Lear was to play Shaddam's daughter Princess Irulan.

For the Harkonnens, Orson Welles was to play Baron Harkonnen; Mick Jagger was cast as Feyd-Rautha; and Udo Kier was to play Piter De Vries.

David Carradine was cast as Duke Leto Atreides, and Jodorowski's son Brontis was to play Paul.

Although not mentioned in the film, Gloria Swanson was also

cast, perhaps as Reverend Mother Mohiam.

Apparently Jodorowsky had not even read *Dune* before suggesting the project. He simply had second-hand reports about a science fiction epic involving a mind-expanding drug and the coming of a messiah. But he wanted to suggest a highly ambitious project, and *Dune* popped into his head. Later, when he read the book, he came to regard it highly, "like great literature," comparing Herbert to Proust.

Jodorowsky decided to make *Dune* into a vehicle for his own LSD-fueled version of Vedanta, much like his classic *The Holy Mountain*. Thus, his vision departed from the novel in crucial ways. Like David Lynch after him, he wanted to emphasize the genuinely magical and messianic elements of Herbert's more ambiguous story. He wanted to make a movie that would give people a unitative mystical experience analogous to a psychedelic trip. His goal was to create something sacred, and he treated his creative team like a band of spiritual warriors.

In Jodorowsky's telling, Duke Leto has been castrated in a bullfight, and Paul is conceived by Bene Gesserit magic from a drop of his blood. This plot device later appeared in Jodorowsky's graphic novel *The Metabarons*. Leto is also tortured and dismembered by Piter De Vries in a scene resembling the Passion of the Christ.

But the most shocking departure is that Paul Atreides dies at the end, his throat slashed by a minor character, Margot Fenring. But Paul cannot really die, for he has transcended his ego and become one with the cosmos. Death simply cuts his final tie with individuality and ego. Jordorowksy's dramatization of this apotheosis is brilliant: everyone begins to speak with Paul's voice. "I am Paul. "I am Paul."

Then, in a miracle far outshining Lynch's rainstorm on Arrakis, the planet too is awakened. It transforms itself into a verdant paradise and begins moving through the galaxy, seeding it with cosmic consciousness. Naturally, none of Herbert's sequels would have been possible. It is not known what Frank Herbert thought of this ending, but he did have a good working relationship with Jodorowsky. In the documentary, Jodorowsky likens his adaptation to rape—but with love.

The first draft of Jodorowsky's *Dune*—the script, the storyboards by Moebius, plus paintings by Foss and Giger—were pulled together into the legendary *Dune Book*, as thick as a major city's telephone directory. If there were ever a project for Taschen to publish, this is it.

Copies of the *Dune Book* were sent to all the major Hollywood studios, including Disney. But nobody wanted to finance a 14-hour movie. So after two years of intensive creative work, the project was canceled.

But the *Dune Book*, like the traveling planet, was still out there, passing from hand to hand, fertilizing the imaginations of many moviemakers to come. As Brontis Jodorowsky points out, when you watch many movies you hear the voice, "I am *Dune*." "I am *Dune*."

For instance, Dan O'Bannon wrote a script and brought together Giger, Moebius, and Foss to make *Alien*. The original *Star Wars* trilogy owes much to *Dune*, specifically to Jodorowsky's *Dune*. The documentary points out borrowings in *The Terminator*, *Raiders of the Lost Ark*, *Masters of the Universe*, *Contact*, and *Prometheus*. I think a case could be made for borrowings in *Akira*. Clearly there were also subtle borrowings—let us call them homages—in Lynch's *Dune*, including a glimpse of a fat face and open mouth on the Harkonnen planet that quotes Giger's original design for the Baron's Castle. If only Lynch had used more.

Pavich's documentary is highly entertaining, and I recommend it without reservations. Pavich interviews Jodorowsky—whose charisma is undimmed even in old age—and as many of the surviving participants as possible. But my favorite sequences were simple slide-show animations of the storyboards. Jodorowsky, of course, went on to produce multiple films and graphic novels. But it is a pity he never revisited *Dune*, for he already had the makings of a brilliant animated series. Quick, somebody translate this review into Japanese.

Counter-Currents, November 7, 2018

JURASSIC WORLD

I was a dinosaur kid, and it does not take much to reawaken the wonder. Thus I enjoyed 1993's *Jurassic Park* a good deal, although I thought it much inferior to Michael Crichton's book. The best thing about it, frankly, is John Williams' wonderful music. That, and a droll little detail: "Objects in mirror are closer than they appear." I never saw the first sequel, *The Lost World* (1997), but for some reason I saw *Jurassic Park III* (2001). I guess I found it forgettable, because I have entirely forgotten it.

But the franchise reboot, *Jurassic World*, is a genuinely excellent movie: wondrous and exciting for kids and engaging for adults. The main characters are highly attractive and admirable whites. The story is imaginative, the script is tight, the music effective, the special effects awe-inspiring, and the pacing admirable. Just when you feel exhausted, there are poetic lulls, for instance in a lab where the characters contemplate actual reptiles, made all the more beautiful by the fact that they are too tiny to eat us.

It is also a surprisingly healthy movie. Apparently the filmmakers felt that they had fulfilled their liberal propaganda quota with a multiracial cast and some moralizing about the commercialization and weaponization of living things. As a New Rightist, I have no real objections to the latter message anyway. Thus when it came to the treatment of the sexes and the family, a very wholesome message somehow slipped through, to the displeasure of the sick minds of the chattering classes.

First, *Jurassic World* is pro-masculine, indeed paleomasculine. The hero, Owen Grady (played by Chris Pratt), is a natural alpha male. Even the velociraptors recognize it. One of the best scenes is when two brothers, Zach and Gray, ask who the alpha of the velociraptor pack is, and Grady replies—in a totally matter-of-fact manner, without a hint of vanity or apology—"You're lookin' at him." Grady is a classic Nordic hero. He is strong, taciturn, brave, and gallant. He dresses and talks somewhat like an American frontiersman. He demonstrates mastery of animals and machines, and he is pretty good with women too. Admit it:

you wanted to see this movie the second you saw Chris Pratt on a motorcycle leading his pack of velociraptors into battle.

Zach, who is 16, and Gray, who is around 10, are also old-school boys. Gray is obsessed with dinosaurs, Zach with girls. But the wonders of the park soon reactivate the kid in Zach. The brothers are adventurous, which gets them into trouble, and brave and resourceful in getting themselves out of it, at one point fixing a jeep left over from the old Jurassic Park. They naturally admire Grady as the "bad-ass" that he is. Faustian little men, the both of them.

Second, *Jurassic World* is anti-feminist. The main female character, Claire Dearing, is played by the beautiful Bryce Dallas Howard (Ron Howard's daughter). Claire is a stressed-out career woman running the Jurassic World theme park. She and Grady have a mutual attraction and dated once, but things did not work out. She was too wrapped up in her job. Also, she clearly disdains him for living modestly and working with his hands. She is wrapped up in artifice, and Grady teases her for being unable to relate to the dinosaurs' simple needs to hunt, eat, and mate. In the course of the film, however, she comes to appreciate Grady's mastery of animals and machines. She pitches in and helps, like a good frontier woman, but she is following his lead. I saw a matinee on a weekday, with a lot of young women with children in a *very* liberal area. I had a strong impression that by the end of the film, a good number of them wanted to breed with Chris Pratt—although their husbands would do in a pinch.

Which brings us to my third point: *Jurassic World* is a pro-natal movie. Zach and Gray are Claire's nephews. When they come to visit, she is too busy with work and fobs them off on an assistant. She does not even know how old they are. When she speaks to her sister Judy, she says "if" she has kids, and the sister responds firmly "when." When Claire chides her for talking like their mother, Judy shoots back that their mother was right. When dinosaurs overrun the park, endangering her nephews, Claire gets in touch with her nurturing side. Indeed, she is willing to risk her life for her nephews, the next generation of her family (so far).

Fourth, *Jurassic World* is pro-family. Zach and Gray's parents are estranged, and Gray fears divorce. Zach is a bit too old to relate to his kid brother. Claire is too busy for her existing family, much less to create one of her own. By the end of the film, Claire, Owen, and the two boys work together like a family. And when the boys are reunited with their real parents, we see that danger has taught them all what is really important: ties of blood and kinship, sticking together in the face of adversity.

Once the danger is past and their virtual family dissolves, it is quite natural for Claire and Owen to think of starting their own. At the very end of the movie, Claire asks Owen what he thinks they should do. His answer is classic, and it is something all the feminists and MGTOWs need to hear: "I think we should stick together—for survival." Because this is a date movie, I predict that nine months from now, there will be a measurable increase in the white birthrate.

Finally, underlying it all, *Jurassic World* is pro-nature, thus it is for masculine men, feminine women, reproduction, and family life. And dinosaurs. But *Jurassic World* is not anti-science. It is profoundly pro-science, because science has brought back wondrous creatures from extinction. But the movie does warn us that commerce and warfare can distort nature—our nature, and the nature that we have brought back from extinction—which is true.

The error that drives the plot forward is the decision to create a genetically modified dinosaur—a super-predator—to draw new visitors to the park. Of course such a creature has military potential as well. One could take this as a cautionary anti-biotechnology even anti-eugenics message. But it was biotechnology that brought the dinosaurs back. And one technique they used was splicing in missing DNA from similar creatures.

But one could argue that there is an essential difference here. It is one thing to use biotechnology to bring back—and even perfect—natural species. It is quite another to create entirely new species for commerce or warfare. Of course, the latter is really no different from the ancient practice of animal domestication. Is there any real difference between breeding dogs for war and breeding dinosaurs?

In the end, the message is not to junk biotech, but merely to proceed with caution. Given that there is massive opposition to biotechnology on stupid, ignorant, and superstitious grounds (including egalitarian race denial), I am frankly glad that it is sustained by sheer greed and even the search for bioweapons. I am also very grateful to Michael Crichton for giving the masses a much more appealing reason for supporting biotechnology: bringing back the dinosaurs.

Naturally, as a member of a dying race, I find the idea that technology might resurrect extinct species rather comforting. Perhaps someday the Chinese will bring white people back for inscrutable purposes, although I would prefer to be resurrected by highly intelligent lizards for their own amusement parks.

But the best option is to avoid extinction entirely, which is why we need white men and women to stick together—for survival.

Counter-Currents, February 2, 2019

JURASSIC WORLD: FALLEN KINGDOM

I loved 2015's *Jurassic World*, the reboot of the *Jurassic Park* "franchise" starring Chris Pratt and Bryce Dallas Howard, directed by Colin Trevorrow, and co-authored by Trevorrow and Derek Connolly. *Jurassic World* blew away the *Jurassic Park* films. It is highly entertaining and also surprisingly wholesome. Along with the main attractions, the dinosaurs, *Jurassic World* is pro-masculine, anti-feminist, and pro-family, with an overwhelmingly white cast and virtually no political correctness. White audiences loved it since it was not calculated to offend them—and everyone else loved it too. It as close to a perfect movie as one can expect from Hollywood, and a very tough act to follow. But a movie that popular was bound to have a sequel.

That sequel is the runaway global blockbuster *Jurassic World: Fallen Kingdom,* which I am delighted to announce is a superb, flawlessly entertaining film. Chris Pratt and Bryce Dallas Howard return as the leads, Owen Grady and Claire Dearing. The script is again by Trevorrow and Connolly. But this time Spanish director J. A. Bayona is at the helm. *Fallen Kingdom* is thrilling and scary (but not terrifying and gross). The special effects are on such a high plane that one no longer sees CGI dinosaurs. One simply sees dinosaurs. The movie is well-paced, with lyrical and touching interludes that allow you to catch your breath between the action sequences. The diversity consists of two likable and white-presenting minorities. There are a number of extremely funny scenes. The cinematography is stunning, delivering the sublimity of nature with enormous impact. And there are sequences of pure visual magic, such as when a dinosaur transforms into a storybook dragon menacing a damsel in a tower.

As in the first movie, Claire Dearing is a stressed-out career woman. In the first film, she was running the Jurassic World park. In the new film, she is lobbying the US government to DO SOMETHING to save the dinosaurs now roaming free on Isla Nublar, who are threatened by extinction yet again by the imminent eruption of the Island's long dormant volcano. As in the first film, she turns for help to her ex-, Owen Grady, a paleo-masculine frontiersman type. The reason they are no longer together is that Owen's unpretentious, nature-centered lifestyle does not accord well with Claire's feminist-urbanite idea of the good life. But Owen's courage, mastery of machines, and literal alpha-maleness—he's the alpha of a pack of velociraptors—prove indispensable. As in the first movie, human greed and hubris are no match for dinosaurs. All hell breaks loose, and Claire and Owen team up for survival, forming a surrogate family by protecting two boys in the first film, a girl in the new one.

When the film began, I was sad that Owen and Claire's on-again, off-again romance was off again, as it was at the beginning of the first movie. There's a huge amount of wholesome sexual chemistry between Owen and Claire, and we really thought it was going somewhere. Fortunately, there will be a third film. So no more on-again, off-again. No more surrogate families. We want the real thing. People this good-looking need to breed. And if Trevorrow knows what's good for him, he needs to deliver in the third installment, which he will direct and which is due in 2021.

In truth, *Fallen Kingdom* is a very close and calculated remake of *Jurassic World*, with the same larger themes, dramatic conflicts, and dinosaur antics. But *Fallen Kingdom* is not a cynical, clumsy, mechanical remake, like *The Force Awakens* or *The Last Jedi*. In fact, I found the movie so captivating that the similarities didn't even occur to me until the next day. And that really is a testament to what a virtuoso team Bayona, Trevorrow, and Connolly are.

Then again, every sequel is a highly calculated affair. Very few sequels surpass the originals, because directors and studios are afraid to take risks and cover new ground. (*The Empire Strikes Back* is a significant exception to this.) If you want to assure success, you repeat what came before. But there are two kinds of repetition. The Disney *Star Wars* formula is to behave like 70-IQ cargo cultists, who have no idea of what is essential, so they just copy everything. The other approach, exemplified in *Fallen*

Kingdom, is to understand what was essential to the success of the previous film, to preserve that, and to make the rest as new as possible.

Just as a virtuoso pianist can take the same dots on paper that he has played and you have heard a thousand times before, and enthrall you with something that seems entirely new, spontaneous, and effortless, *Fallen Kingdom* recaptures everything we loved about *Jurassic World* and brings the story forward, ending on a very serious and sublime note, and setting us up for another sequel that I can't wait to see.

Counter-Currents, July 13, 2018

JUSTICE LEAGUE

Watchmen is the greatest superhero movie of all time, and when it was released, its director Zack Snyder was poised to follow Christopher Nolan into the first rank of directors working today. But instead, he has directed an ever-worsening series of turkeys: *Sucker Punch, Man of Steel, Batman v Superman,* and now *Justice League,* which is one of the worst movies I have ever seen: derivative, dumb, and dull. An assault on the senses and an insult to the intellect. It is also one of the most expensive movies ever made, costing an astonishing $300 million. It is really rather amazing that a director of Snyder's proven talent, with a solid cast and a $300 million budget, could not have turned in a better movie. Clearly, there's a lot of rot and a lot of ruin still left in Hollywood, and the sex scandals are just the beginning.

Justice League is a critical and commercial flop. Some people are trying to deflect the blame onto Warner Bros. and Joss Whedon. It turns out that in 2017, Snyder's 20-year-old Chinese adopted daughter, Autumn, committed suicide. (Snyder had eight children, four natural and four adopted.) Snyder took some time off to be with his family, and Warner Bros., which deemed the movie too long and too dark, brought in Joss Whedon for rewrites and reshoots. The problem, however, is not with Whedon's superficial changes but with the basic script, which is utterly derivative, and with the characterization, which is laughably shallow.

Stop me if you've heard this one before. In remotest antiquity, a dark lord from another world named Steppenwolf (hold your laughter) tried to conquer the world with the aid of three magical "Mother Boxes" and an army of zombie-cyborgs called parademons. However, the races of the earth—the Olympian gods, Amazons, Atlanteans, and men—came together in an alliance to defeat him. The Mother Boxes were wrested away from Steppenwolf, who vanished. The Mother Boxes, which only worked in tandem, were then separated and placed in the care of the Atlanteans, the Amazons, and the kings of men.

After untold thousands of years, however, the death of Superman somehow reactivated the mother boxes, which called Steppenwolf back to earth. Of course, this is a ridiculously arbitrary plot turn, since Superman was only a recent arrival on earth, which raises the question of what kept the Mother Boxes "sleeping" for the untold millennia before his arrival. But never mind. The dark lord Steppenwolf is back with his parademons searching for the magic Mother Boxes that will allow him to conquer the world. To stop him, a league must be created, bringing together an Atlantean (Aquaman), an Amazon (Wonder Woman), and several humans, including Bruce Wayne/Batman, Barry Allen/Flash, and Victor Stone/Cyborg.

Yes, thus far, it is just a retelling of *The Fellowship of the Ring*.

But the combined efforts of the Justice League are still not enough to defeat Steppenwolf, so a *deus ex machina* is required. Thus they use one of the Mother Boxes to resurrect Superman, who whooshes in to save the day. There are lots of CGI battles, which basically feel like being trapped inside a pinball machine, and finally Steppenwolf is sent packing, no doubt to return some day when bidden by the dark lords of Hollywood to harvest more shekels from the *goyim*.

Okay, okay. But aren't there are only so many plots? And can't a derivative plot still be salvaged by interesting characters and dialogue? This is true, but *Justice League* fails there as well. We have already been introduced to Batman, Superman, and Wonder Woman. Thus all Snyder really needed to do was breathe some life into Aquaman, Cyborg, and Flash. And what a lousy job he does. Aquaman is the most one-dimensional character of all. He is covered with tattoos, has long hair, and swigs whiskey from a bottle. So we know he's badass. He's angry at his mommy. He likes to help people for some reason, but thinks he does it best alone. Cyborg is a black man with a stratospherically high IQ which he inherited from his black scientist father. No regression to the mean in this universe. And Flash, just like Lex Luthor in the last movie, is a shrimpy, neurotic, fast-talking, cowardly Jewboy. (What's Zack Snyder trying to tell us?) There's no depth, nuance, subtlety, or humanity in *Justice League*, just plastic robots, batteries not included. The established characters also seem hollowed out and flattened. But with no human beings at its core, the movie's CGI battle scenes become a tedious, emotionally uninvolving assault on the senses.

One of the running theses of my career as a movie reviewer is that someone in Hollywood is reading anti-modern, Traditionalist Rightists and recognizes that we represent the most fundamental negation of liberal humanism and thus the perfect supervillains. *Justice League* nods in this direction at the beginning when Wonder Woman foils a group of white "reactionary" terrorists who want to blow up the Old Bailey in London. Also, under the opening credits, which are a montage of social chaos after the death of Superman to a cover of Leonard Cohen's "Everybody Knows," we see a white man with shaved head menacing a shopkeeper in a hijab and her child. But like everything else in this film, even this feels perfunctory, phoned-in, and fake.

I hope the failure of this movie and the suicide of his daughter will cause Zack Snyder to take some time away from Hollywood to rethink his career. The great weaknesses of his recent films have been plot and characterization. His best films, *300* and *Watchmen*, were based on classic graphic novels, and from that high starting point, he actually improved upon them, both in terms of visualization and plot. But Snyder's career since then seems almost like a controlled experiment to establish that all the directorial and technical wizardry in the world can't make a compelling movie if the plot and characterization are lacking, nor can brand-loyalty and PR-puffery turn it into a success.

The fact that *Justice League* has bombed is proof that there is still some justice in the world.

Counter-Currents, November 28, 2017

THE LOVED ONE

The Loved One (1965) is my all-time favorite comedy. Based on a 1948 novel of the same nameby Evelyn Waugh, *The Loved One* stands alongside Flannery O'Connor's *Wise Blood* (the book and the movie) as a savagely on-target, dark comic satire on American Protestant civilization.

Both Waugh and O'Connor, of course, were Catholic. But much to my surprise, the movie of *The Loved One* measurably deepens Waugh's Christian satire of the spiritual emptiness of American religion and capitalism, even though that could have been no part of the intentions of director Tony Richardson and screenwriters Terry Southern and Christopher Isherwood.

Henceforth, I will be speaking of the movie of *The Loved One*, and side references to the book will be clearly identified.

The setting is Los Angeles at the dawn of the Space Age, i.e., about 1965. A young Englishman, Dennis Barlow (Robert Morse), has won a free airline ticket and decides to visit his uncle, Sir Francis Hinsley (John Gielgud), who works as a painter at Megalopolitan Pictures in Hollywood. The opening of the movie is thus a very droll satire of Hollywood, where, as Sir Francis says, people "talk entirely for their own pleasure, and they don't expect you to listen." Remembering that, he tells Dennis, is "the secret of social ease."

The comedy turns a bit darker, however, when Sir Francis is fired from the studio and commits suicide, which provides the segue from the prologue to the main part of the picture, which is a satire on the American way of life—and death. The leader of the British expatriate community in Los Angeles, Sir Ambrose Abercrombie, a character actor who plays Prime Ministers and butlers (Robert Morley), believes that Sir Francis has let down the team. He persuades Dennis that the best way to ease Sir Francis' disgrace is to sell his uncle's house to pay for an expensive burial at Whispering Glades Cemetery (based on Forest Lawn).

A necropolis by way of an amusement park, the best word for Whispering Glades is "kitsch," meaning the prostitution of beauty to sentimentality and commerce. Whispering Glades is the creation of the Blessed Reverend Wilbur Glenworthy (Jonathan Winters in his greatest role). Like William Randolph Hearst, Glenworthy plundered the whole world of European high culture, meticulously re-creating buildings and monuments, but larger and in concrete and steel. It was perfectly pitched to the sentimentality and social insecurity of its middle-brow, high-dollar clientele.

Both Waugh and Richardson were anti-American snobs, as is Dennis Barlow. But Barlow soon follows in the footsteps of his uncle, Sir Ambrose, and the Blessed Reverend when he realizes that the social prestige and objective worth of European culture can be used to profitably bilk American Philistines out of some of the nation's embarrassing riches. Although in Dennis' case, he merely passes off English Romantic poetry as his own to woo Miss Aimée Thanatogenous, whom he meets at Whispering Glades. (She is the cosmetician of the Gothic Slumber Room. Her name, by the way, means "loved one generated by death.")

Aimée Thanatogenous, beautifully played by Anjanette Comer, who perfectly captures the "glint of lunacy" Waugh ascribes to her in the novel, is the central character of *The Loved One*. She is the tragic portrait of a cultureless, almost feral American whose moral, religious, and aesthetic longings are cruelly betrayed by the soulless American void.

The novel fleshes out her back story a bit. She was named for Aimée Semple Macpherson. Her father lost all his money in religion. Her mother was an alcoholic who abandoned her. She studied art, psychology, and Chinese for a semester or two, then was forced to leave college and earn a trade as a cosmetician and hairdresser. She is not religious, but she regards herself as "progressive" and "ethical." Her ethics regarding sex, however, are more prudish than progressive.

She has a strong but uncultivated aesthetic sensibility, which does not, however, provide her with sufficient foundations for life. (In the movie, she assembles a magnificent collection of kitsch—in a condemned house, hanging over a void in a slide zone—a metaphor as majestic as the *Titanic*.) As her substitute for religion, she writes regularly for advice to the Guru Brahmin, a local newspaper columnist. She also has total faith in the Blessed Reverend Glenworthy and the "eternity" of Whispering Glades.

Dennis' chief rival for Aimée's affections is Lafayette Joyboy (Rod Steiger), the Chief Embalmer of Whispering Glades, an unctuous, effeminate mama's boy and company man who shares Aimée's absolute faith in the Blessed Reverend.

The Blessed Reverend is merely mentioned in the book, but he is one of the film's best-realized characters. A narcissistic egomaniac, he runs Whispering Glade as a cult of personality. But the Blessed Reverend does not run a religious cult, because in reality he is a cold and cynical businessman in pastoral vestments.

Winters plays Glenworthy with a magnificent voice, capable of conferring cant and heresy with the aura of holy writ. (His characterization may have been inspired by the novel's description of Mr. Joyboy's authoritative, radio-announcer voice.) The movie masterfully captures how yesterday's resonantly intoned con-artist's spiel becomes tomorrow's earnestly (or desperately) repeated pieties of the little people (particularly when the Blessed Reverend's words are repeated in the breathy, panicky voice of his brother Henry, also played by Winters).

One of the drollest subplots is the Blessed Reverend's scheme to turn Whispering Glades to more profitable use as a retirement community for undignified American old people. There's only one problem: how to "get those stiffs off of my property." This being the Space Age, he naturally takes inspiration from a tow-headed boy-genius named Gunther (Paul Williams) and tries to create a trend of blasting bodies into "an orbit of eternal grace" using US government surplus rockets, a scheme he dubs "Resurrection Now!" (It all seems much more plausible when Glenworthy voices it.)

Although the "loved one" of the title is Glenworthy's euphemism for the stiffs he inters, it also refers to Aimée Thanatogenous, who is the central character not as an agent, but as the object of the affections of several men. She is charmed by Dennis' poetry but irritated by his unethical interest in sex, so the Guru Brahmin advises her to marry Mr. Joyboy.

She is impressed by Mr. Joyboy's status and professionalism, but she finds his obese, gluttonous (and unforgettably hilarious) mother unaesthetic, so the Guru Brahmin advises her to marry Dennis. Then the jilted Mr. Joyboy avenges himself by revealing that Dennis' poetry is plagiarized and that he works at the Happier Hunting Grounds, a pet cemetery that Aimée finds unaesthetic (and perhaps unethical as well).

The movie reaches its climax when Aimée turns in her hour of crisis to her two spiritual authorities, the Guru Brahmin and the Blessed Reverend, and discovers both are frauds. The Guru Brahmin turns out to be a cynical, malevolent old drunk named Hump (Lionel Stander) who tells her to jump out a window.

Then she goes to the Blessed Reverend for reassurance after Dennis tells her of the plan to close Whispering Glades. When he admits its truth, she protests, in her cartoon mouse voice, that Whispering Glades is "eternal!" To which he thunders, like a prophet of the true American religion, "Nothing is eternal! All must change!" Then he tries to seduce her.

Her world shattered, Aimée takes Hump's advice, and, in a shocking sequence, commits suicide by embalming herself alive, thus joining the rest of Glenworthy's "loved ones."

A cultureless void is great for clearing away all impediments to the strivers and achievers and go-getters among us as they rocket toward their goals. But as Aimée shows, when one stumbles, one falls, for there is nothing to brace oneself against.

Joyboy finds Aimée's body and, fearing disgrace, bribes Dennis to cremate her at the Happier Hunting Grounds. The movie's addition of the "Resurrection Now!" project makes possible a less distasteful dénouement: Aimée is substituted for the corpse of a washed-up astronaut and fired into space, while the astronaut is consigned to the ash heap, and Dennis departs for England courtesy of Mr. Joyboy, to a rousing chorus of "America the Beautiful."

The movie strikes only one false note. While the novel makes it clear that Jews and gentiles alike were buried in Whispering Glades, the movie features a scene in which a Mr. and Mrs. Bernstein are politely rebuffed. You know, to show just how evil the Blessed Reverend really is.

With brilliant performances by the lead actors; bit parts and cameos by Roddy McDowell, Tab Hunter, Milton Berle, James Coburn, and Liberace; and some achingly beautiful late Romantic music by John Addison, *The Loved One* is a philosophically profound and deeply disturbing dark-comic masterpiece. It is also one of the most anti-modernist and anti-American films of all time.

Counter-Currents, February 2, 2019

Mad Max: Fury Road

Mad Max: Fury Road is the fourth—and the best—Mad Max movie directed by George Miller. Miller was born George Miliotis—the son of Greek refugees from Turkish ethnic cleansing in Anatolia—and is also the creator of two other, and very different, film franchises, the *Babe* the talking pig movies and the *Happy Feet* animated penguin movies.

In *Fury Road*, the title character, which heretofore has been played by Mel Gibson, is played by Tom Hardy (Bane—with another grill thing on his face, no less). Charlize Theron is the female lead as Imperator Furiosa, who has a prosthetic Terminator arm attached to an amputation stump.

Theron's character is the focus of a media kerfuffle about her allegedly "badass" superfeminist character, but it is entirely baseless and manufactured to sell tickets.

James Bond movies have a formula, and so does their advertising. Every few Bond films, we are told that *this time* Bond will be paired up with a "strong woman"—presumably unlike all the other Bond women. Bond aficionados laugh because of course few Bond women ever match Ursula Andress' formidable heroine in the very first Bond movie, *Dr. No*.

Of course Bond movies appeal overwhelmingly to men, so the publicity people probably concoct the "strong woman" pitch to persuade potential female ticket buyers that it will not be too much of a sausage fest. And they figure that a strong woman won't deter male viewers, as long as she is hot. Of course, this is a risky proposition, because there is a well-documented tendency for men to abandon social spaces and activities once they have become too feminized.

I think that pretty much the same reasoning was behind promoting Theron as the strong woman in *Fury Road*—unlike the shrinking violet Tina Turner in *Beyond Thunderdome*, I suppose. But these are the days of Peak Feminism, and this time, there has been a backlash, with many young men swearing off *Fury Road* in disgust.

They'll come round, though, because the feminist elements of this movie, such as they are, would only offend Oriental advocates of purdah and footbinding. Indeed, the society they rebel against is profoundly un-white and un-Western, despite the fact that it is ruled by and predominantly populated by whites.

The Citadel—a set of towering rock formations—is the headquarters of cult leader Immortan Joe. Joe, like the despots of neighboring Gas Town and Bullet Farm, is hideously malformed and debauched. His government is a form of oriental hydraulic despotism—literally, for he hoards water and food and releases them in dribs and drabs to the starving wretches below.

Joe also uses brute force to maintain power, filling the citadel with War Boys, who look like skinheads on chemo. To control the war boys and motivate them to sacrifice themselves, Joe has manufactured a religion which promises Valhalla to the War Boys and some sort of redemption to the rest of his people.

Aside from Joe, everyone is basically a slave. Huge fat women are milked like cows, and the milk seems to be consumed as food and even exported. When Max is captured, he is turned into a "blood bag" to offer transfusions to a sickly War Boy, Nux. (Radiation has made many people sickly. Their abbreviated existence is ironically called a Half Life.)

Another oriental trait of the Citadel is Joe's harem. Healthy and fertile young women are in short supply, so naturally Joe monopolizes them.

The Citadel's combination of polygamy, slavery, militarism, religion, and rule by a prophet/priest/despot actually brings to mind one of history's greatest practitioners of the gangsta/pimp lifestyle, namely the Prophet of Islam.

At this point, I will "spoil" the story by giving away a few plot elements. Furiosa is a trusted driver of one of Joe's armored War Rigs, a tanker that appears to be loaded with water and mother's milk, which Furiosa will drive to Gas Town to barter for gasoline.

At a certain point, however, she turns off road into the desert. Furiosa, it seems, is defecting. Joe discovers that his harem has disappeared. They want something better than being the brood slaves of a bloated tyrant, so Furiosa has promised to deliver them to the Green Place, where she was born and from which she had been kidnapped 20 years before by Joe's people.

Joe sends his army to recover them, and Max is brought along as a blood bag. Max escapes, teams up with Furiosa, and they battle their way across the desert, to discover that all that remains of her people are a few old crones wandering the desert, one of whom carries a treasure: seeds. If only she can find water and soil for them.

The crones team up with Furiosa, Max, and Nux, who has changed sides. Their mission is to preserve life. To find a suitable home for the fertile young women, so the race can live on, and to find fertile ground for the seeds. It is a mission important enough to kill and die for, and they do. But life triumphs in the end.

Feminism has created a false consciousness in women. They imagine that women never exercised agency, never protected themselves against abusers, and never exercised political power until feminism came along and started white, Western women bitching as if they were in purdah. Of course if they really had been in purdah, all the complaining in the world would not have made any difference.

It does not take feminism or Marxism to make white people rebel against the oriental despotism of the Citadel. Such government has never sat well with us. It is not in our nature.

Real feminism is neurotic man-hatred, anti-life nihilism, and sexual separatism. Real feminism is ball-busting posturing and pointless oneupmanship. None are present in *Fury Road*. After overcoming mutual distrust (which is reasonable in the circumstances), Max and Nux team up well with Furiosa, the brides, and the crones *because that is the natural way*.

There is no sense that the crones in the desert are a viable society, only the remnants of one, and the crones are willing to sacrifice their lives to find safety for the brides and fertile ground for the seeds. As the crones charge into battle, one says to another, "One man, one bullet," but this does not apply to all men, of course, and it delightfully tweaks "One man, one vote."

The primary role of women in this movie is nurturers, and it is only because the world has been turned upside down that women are forced to kill to further life. In the end though, they could not have done it without Max and Nux. But the women also provided them something real to fight for.

When our race awakens and begins to fight for its survival, it is not pre-Raphaelite damsels and oriental lotus foots who will be our helpmeets, but women like Furiosa.

I found the opening few minutes of *Fury Road* distasteful, and I almost walked out. I am glad I stayed, though, because it is an excellent movie. Yes, there are lots of chases and fights—thrilling and spectacular ones—but Miller understands pacing, so there are meditative and poetic moments as well, and a number of deeply touching ones.

The world Miller creates is a remarkable work of the imagination, with a stunning steampunk/biker mag aesthetic, and scenes of desolation and horror worthy of Bruegel, Bosch, and Dalí. (I made the mistake of seeing the movie in 3-D, but after a few minutes I went next door to a conventional screening, and I am glad I did. One simply sees more detail.) Thank God there was no *symbolism*.

The performances of Hardy and Theron are excellent. They have real chemistry. You can *feel* that they complete one another: she has found a protector, and he has found a purpose. But for me, Miller's artistry was best displayed when I realized that plot and character, tension and respite, words and silences, had been orchestrated into a deeply moving climax, created with the simplest of means. Hardy simply says, "Max, my name is Max."

I loved this movie.

Counter-Currents, May 19, 2015

THE MARTIAN

Ridley Scott's *The Martian* is a superb movie: suspenseful, inspiring, and deeply moving, with an excellent plot, fine performances, compelling pacing, and completely believable special effects. *The Martian* in set in the near future when space exploration is once again a national priority and manned Mars missions are regular undertakings.

On one such mission a powerful storm forces a six-man team to evacuate the planet and return to their orbiting base ship while they still have a chance. Unfortunately, botanist Mark Watney (Matt Damon) is swept away in the storm and apparently killed, so his crewmates depart without him. Watney, however, survived and is marooned on Mars with a limited food supply and no way to communicate with Earth. His only chance of rescue, moreover, is years in the future, long after he will have starved.

So, after stitching up the wound he suffered in the storm, Watney coolly takes stock of his resources—food supplies, a Martian habitat, a Martian rover, a collection of '70s disco, freeze-dried human excrement, rocket fuel, etc.—and comes up with a survival and rescue plan. He learns to grow potatoes in human excrement and Martian soil. He modifies the rover to extend its range, then uses it to find an old Martian lander that he can use to communicate with NASA.

At this point you realize that this fairly straightforward and jocular narrative has been sneaking up on you to deliver an unexpected and powerful emotional catharsis. When Watney finally communicates with Earth, we are flooded with his fear and loneliness and relief. You'd need a heart of stone not to shed a tear in this scene, and there are more like it to come.

A rescue plan is set in motion, and although the suspense is often quite intense, there is never really any doubt that the Martian Mark Watney will return home to Earth.

The Martian is a very white, very American movie. Matt Damon is basically a high-tech frontiersman—a final frontiersman—who triumphs over adversity using science, technology, and courage. It is also a very Faustian movie, a movie about the exploration of the cosmos, a movie about dedicating one's life to something bigger than oneself, namely mankind's ongoing conquest of nature.

But *The Martian* is a product of today's film industry, which means that its real virtues are accompanied by two serious flaws. First, the movie advances the false worldview of racial and sexual egalitarianism. Second, the morally and metaphysically elevating themes of the movie are undercut by vulgar colloquialism.

The American space program was the product almost exclusively of white men, with our mastery of science and technology, longing for new frontiers, and rivalry with our enemies. America dropped the torch of space exploration when Jewish and Leftist values became dominant. We now have better things to do than explore space, like giving free cell phones to Negroes and a media megaphone to witches exercised about a scientist's sinful shirt.

The most false and offensive aspect of *The Martian* is that it postulates that the US space program will somehow revive in a society in which racial and sexual egalitarianism are the dominant values. The main character, Matt Damon's Mark Watney, is of course white. But his six-man crew has two female members, including the captain, and although five crewmembers are white, the pilot is Hispanic. NASA's director of Mars missions is supposedly an African-Hindu hybrid played by a black actor. The genius who figures out the rescue plan is also played by a black. (Remember, this is science fiction.) An important scientist is played by an Asian, and when NASA needs help, he kindly intercedes with his uncle who runs the Red Chinese space agency. (In the real world, of course, such a scientist would likely be one of the many Chinese-American spies passing intelligence and technology to the Chinese.) The Red Chinese gallantly offer one of their rockets after the Americans prove that they can't perform the rescue on their own. A couple important characters in NASA are white women, and so on.

Although *The Martian* is pro-diversity, one cannot really call it anti-white. The hero and the majority of the cast are highly attractive, serious, and competent white people. No race-mixing is portrayed. And there is a subtle pro-natalism to the film, for one of the astronauts, the German Vogel, has at least four beautiful white children, and two of the astronauts on the mission later marry and have a child at the very end.

Another aspect of egalitarian rot is the pervasive vulgarity of the script. This is a movie about heroism, with a plot worthy of a classic 19th-century novel. But the language and music do not measure up. Lest we idolize Mark Watney too much, he has to be "humanized," with vulgar language and tastes. At one point he vows to "science the shit" out of one of his problems, which he proceeds to do to a medley of '70s pop songs. At a certain point, I felt a tightness in my gut and feared that we would soon be treated to a dance montage like in *Tootsie* or its ripoff *Mrs. Doubtfire*. Ayn Rand brilliantly satirized this kind of anti-Romanticism as the "I'm sorry I can't take you to the pizza joint tonight baby, I've got to go back to the lab and split the atom" approach to science fiction. The sets of *The Martian* are clearly inspired by *2001: A Space Odyssey*. One wishes the soundtrack was as well. Heroic deeds require elevated words and music.

One wonders how more dignified ages have dawned. The Victorian age, for instance, followed the decadence of the Regency era. Thus those "stuffy" early Victorians were not unacquainted with degeneracy. But at a certain point they took themselves seriously enough to regard their little indulgences as contemptible, as childish, as beneath them. And then they just put them away.

These flaws aside, *The Martian* is an excellent movie that will speak especially to whites. It is a reminder that White Nationalists are not only working to save our race from the mud but to put us back on the path to the stars.

Counter-Currents, April 26, 2016

MILLER'S CROSSING

Miller's Crossing (1990) is the third Coen brothers movie, and in my eyes, it remains their best. *Miller's Crossing* is set in an unnamed Midwestern city during the 1920s. (It was primarily filmed in New Orleans.) It tells the story of Tom Reagan (Gabriel Byrne), who serves as advisor to two warring gangsters, Leo O'Bannon (Albert Finney) and Johnny Caspar (Jon Polito).

Miller's Crossing has a superb script, excellent casting and performances, lush cinematography, bravura directing (particularly in the famous "Danny Boy" scene), and effective music. The wide, low-angle panoramas of interiors and the woodland scenes bring to mind similar settings similarly treated in Bertolucci's *The Conformist*.

But the most remarkable thing about *Miller's Crossing* is its message. Actually, there are two of them.

First, from start to finish, the movie deals explicitly with the virtue of rationality. Tom Reagan may be a criminal. He may drink and gamble too much. But his most salient trait is his rationality. He is a thinker. He uses his head and keeps his emotions in check.

The only mistakes he makes come from listening to his heart. He is a natural follower, not a leader, which makes him too deferential to his boss, Leo, even when Leo makes mistakes. He also has a strong distaste for violence. He has to master these tendencies to do the right thing.

Tom's rationality is governed by an honor code. He pays his own debts, and he is loyal to Leo. Leo, however, does not listen to Tom's advice, basing his decisions on his passions, which leads to a disastrous gang war.

Second, *Miller's Crossing* features the most loathsome Jewish villain since Shylock, the bookie Bernie Bernbaum (played by John Turturro, who also played the title role in *Barton Fink*). Being a small-time grifter, Bernie is also a thinker, but unlike Tom, he has no moral compass whatsoever. Everything to him is just about "angles." Bernie does, however, have some loyalty to his sister Verna (Marcia Gay Harden), who is similarly sociopathic, prostituting herself both to Leo and to Tom because Bernie sees an angle in it. Verna is so depraved, she even tried to seduce her brother, a homosexual, to "rescue him from his friends."

Remarkably, the characters of Bernie and Verna Bernbaum provide object lessons in how Jews have hacked the Aryan mind — and how we can defend ourselves from them.

The movie begins with Johnny Caspar and his henchman Eddie Dane (J. E. Freeman — Marcellos Santos from David Lynch's *Wild at Heart*) paying a visit to Leo and Tom. Leo is the head crime-boss in the city; Caspar is an independent operator who is subordinate to Leo. Both Caspar and Bernie Bernbaum pay Leo for "protection." Bernbaum, however, is cheating Caspar on fixed fights, and Caspar is asking Leo for permission to kill the "*shamatte*" (Yiddish for "rag").

It is a reasonable request, given the rules of their trade. Caspar is following the rules, Bernbaum breaking them. Caspar pays Leo a lot, Bernbaum a little. Caspar is too big to anger, but Bernbaum is not too big to kill. Leo glances at Tom, hoping for advice, but then arrogantly refuses Caspar's request, enraging him. It is a mistake that will soon prove disastrous.

When Caspar leaves, Tom says, "Bad play, Leo." To which Leo replies, "Tom, you know I don't like to think." Tom shoots back, "Think about whether you should start."

Tom knows why Leo has decided to protect Bernie: Verna is sleeping with Leo. Tom suspects that Verna is also sleeping with him for the same reason. Verna is a grifter who plays men's hearts. In one scene, she prods Tom to admit that he has a heart. In another scene, she claims that Leo defends Bernie because he has "a big heart." Verna is another Queen Esther, the archetype of the Jewess who whores her way into positions of influence over powerful *goyim* in order to help her people. And as in the case of Esther, Verna's influence leads the *goyim* to massacre one another, Purim-style, although with bullets and bombs, not gallows.

Lesson number one: Never have sex with Jews.

The mob war starts when Leo tasks a henchman, Rug Daniels, to keep an eye on Verna. When Daniels turns up dead, Leo blames Caspar, and the war commences. But Caspar had nothing to do with it. Tom suspects Verna killed Daniels to prevent him from discovering that she was sleeping with Tom as well as Leo. In fact, he was killed by Mink Larouie (Steve Buscemi), one of Verna's drinking buddies that night, who is also in on Bernie's scheme. (Mink is Eddie Dane's butt boy, who relays information about Caspar's fixes to Bernie.)

Tom is so loyal to Leo that he is willing to sacrifice himself to break Verna's spell. He tells Leo that Verna and he are also sleeping together. Leo beats up Tom and expels him from his office. Tom then goes to work for Caspar. He tells Caspar Bernie's location, and Caspar sends Tom and two henchmen to take Bernie on a ride out to Miller's Crossing and kill him in the woods. When they arrive, one of the henchmen hands Tom a gun and tells him that *he* has been ordered to kill Bernie.

The scene is unforgettable. Tom marches Bernie into the woods. Bernie is hysterical, effeminate, and undignified — shrieking, sobbing, and begging for his life. Bernie recognizes that Tom is a kindred soul: they are not "muscle." They commit crimes with their minds. He is a swindler. "It's my nature, Tom," he blubbers. They have no taste for killing. They are not like "those animals" waiting back at the car. Four times, he says that he can't die in these woods like a "dumb animal."

For "animal" here, read "*goy.*" In *Barton Fink*, the title character, also played by Turturro, shrieks at a bunch of soldiers and sailors that they are "animals" who have no appreciation for the mind.

Bernie falls to his knees, sobbing, "I'm praying to you. I'm praying to you. Look in your heart. Look in your heart."

And lo: Tom Reagan has a heart after all. He fires a couple of shots in the air and tells Bernie to leave town. Bernie speeds away, his limbs windmilling spastically.

There is a similar scene in *Barton Fink*. When Karl "Madman" Mundt, who has just blasted two police detectives with a shotgun, accuses Barton of being a stuck-up elitist who doesn't listen, Barton fears that he is next. If Mundt doesn't kill him, the burning hotel will. He breaks down and offers a tearful apology, piercing the heart and deflecting the wrath of the big sentimental *schmuck*, who then frees him from being handcuffed to a bed in a burning building.

Both films, in short, portray how Jews turn our big hearts, our sentimentality, and our willingness to give people the benefit of the doubt against us.

Turturro's performance is utterly riveting. Everything about Bernie is calculated to induce loathing, from his round-shouldered posture (also displayed in *Barton Fink*) to his undignified hyper-emotionality, oily insincerity, and physical cowardice.

John Turturro may be Italian-American, but he looks Jewish and excels at playing Jews, particularly negatively characterized Jews: Bernie Bernbaum, Barton Fink, and Herb Stempel in *Quiz Show*. Turturro certainly has had ample exposure to the tribe. He grew up in Brooklyn and Queens and is married to actress Katherine Borowitz.

A couple nights later, Tom has reason to regret listening to his heart. Bernie Bernbaum breaks into his apartment. He has decided not to leave town after all. He has been brooding over his humiliation in the woods. "It's a painful memory." He is grateful to Tom for sparing his life, but angrier that Tom put him in that position to begin with.

"You didn't see the play you gave me," he tells Tom. By sparing Bernie's life, Tom has betrayed Caspar, and Bernie is now going to use that fact to blackmail him. And, he adds, he is also going to enjoy watching Tom "squirm." It is an utter moral obscenity to blackmail the man who spared your life *with the very fact that he spared your life*.

When Bernie leaves, Tom grabs his gun and exits by a different door, hoping to intercept and kill him. But Bernie anticipates the move, trips Tom, kicks him in the face, then taunts him: "What were you going to do if you caught me? I'd just squirt a few, and you'd let me go."

Later we learn that Bernie has killed his own friend Mink, mutilated his face, and dumped his corpse at Miller's Crossing in case Caspar decides to confirm the kill.

Tom hatches a plan to get Caspar and Bernie in the same place, each looking to ambush the other. Tom plans to kill off the survivor, if any. This plan bothered me a bit, because although Johnny Caspar is brutal and grotesque (almost ruined by the Coens' penchant for cartoonish caricature), he is still a likeable character: slightly less rational than Tom, but slightly more ethical. Tom, however, values peace, and maybe he sees Caspar's death as the only way to end the war.

Bernie kills Caspar. Tom arrives on the scene and coolly offers to dispose of Bernie's gun. Once Bernie has disarmed himself, Tom takes Caspar's gun and points it at Bernie. He plans to shoot Bernie and make it look like Caspar did it.

Bernie is incredulous. "What's in it for you? There's no angle!" Because, of course, nobody would ever wish to rid the world of a Bernie Bernbaum for the common good, as a matter of general principle or simple hygiene.

Then Bernie starts in with the weeping and the praying: "Look in your heart! Look in your heart!"

"What heart?" replies Tom, who then puts a bullet in Bernie's head.

This is lesson number two: Harden your heart; don't be fooled by the tears. The Coen brothers, in short, have done something utterly astonishing — something that is, by all reigning standards, simply obscene. They have created a movie about how to kill Jews.

It is one thing for the Coens to portray how Jews manipulate whites. That could be interpreted as merely a Jewish in-joke. But it is quite another thing for them to show how we can protect ourselves from their manipulations. Thus *Miller's Crossing* is a profoundly anti-Semitic film. Watch it, and ask yourself: Would Joseph Goebbels have changed a single frame?

Counter-Currents, June 22, 2015

PASSENGERS

Passengers, directed by the Norwegian Morten Tyldum, is the best science fiction movie of the current season, so if you have seen *Rogue One* or are simply skipping it, you have an even better option. *Passengers* is something quite rare: a science fiction film that is entirely fresh and new, not part of a series, and not a reboot, remake, or rip-off of other films. *Passengers* has a unique and gorgeous visual style, interesting music, and first rate acting—and it tells a fascinating story.

Passengers is set on the starship *Avalon*, which is transporting 5000 colonists to a new planet, Homestead II. The passengers and crew are in hibernation for the 120-year journey, but one of them, Jim Preston (Chris Pratt) wakes up after only 30 years and has no way of getting back to sleep. At first, he decides to enjoy the luxurious lifestyle offered by the starship. But after a year, he is going mad with loneliness, so he awakens Aurora (Jennifer Lawrence), a sleeping beauty with whom he has fallen in love.

I found *Passengers* to be engrossing because, despite all the sci-fi trappings, it is essentially mythic. First of all, it calls to mind Adam and Eve. Then it folds in elements of *Sleeping Beauty* and *Robinson Crusoe*. But the most subversive and unsettling myth it recapitulates is the rape of the Sabines and similar stories about men in a state of nature kidnapping brides. Aurora falls in love with Jim, but she is also outraged by in effect being abducted by him. In the end, though, they have to stick together "for survival" (as Pratt's character says in *Jurassic World*).

Passengers is also a recapitulation of European emigration and the American frontier in space, including the tensions between old world and new, or "back East" vs. the "wild West." The *Avalon* is the epitome of technological civilization, including some Titanic (or RMS *Titanic*) hubris. Aurora also epitomizes civilization. She is a writer from New York City. Jim, however, is a mechanic from Denver. On the *Avalon*, Jim is in the equivalent of steerage, and in her old world, Aurora would have never noticed him. Jim, however, is needed on the frontier—he wants to live in a world in which his abilities to fix and build things matter—whereas Aurora is only going as a tourist. The frontier, however, subjects civilization to crises that can be mastered only by a rougher breed of men, like Jim, whose heroism and technological mastery save the day.

Passengers, in short, is a deeply paleomasculine film, and Chris Pratt again plays the heroic alpha male to perfection. Jennifer Lawrence's Aurora, by contrast, is largely passive. First, she is a princess being wooed. Then she is a princess in a snit. But then the frontier comes crashing in, and she no longer has the luxury of lounging about. So, like many generations of frontier women before her, she finds it in herself to fight like a fury for survival.

Passengers is an overwhelmingly white film, both in its story and lead actors. (There is a brief appearance by Laurence Fishburne.) Its Faustian, man-against-adversity in space theme reminded me of *The Martian*. The spareness of a movie with such a small cast, its careful lingering over motives and moral questions, and its occasionally leisurely pace might annoy some viewers, but I found it completely engrossing. Some might feel that the action sequences near the end are pat and manipulative, but they had me on the edge of my seat. Because this is a fairy tale, of course they live happily ever after.

The reviews from the lying press have not been good, and *Rogue One* is hogging the spotlight. *Passengers* must be seen on the big screen, so see it while you can. Drag the normies to it after Christmas. Then recommend it far and wide. A movie this good deserves to do well.

Counter-Currents, December 22, 2016

Princess Mononoke

I feel like the skinhead who went to see *Cats* because he'd heard that T. S. Eliot was a fascist.

Japanese cartoons are very popular in our circles. They have even been reviewed at *Counter-Currents*. The closest thing I had seen to a Japanese cartoon is *Twilight of the Cockroaches*. But that mixed animation and live action, and it was more than 25 years ago, so I remember almost nothing about it.

But I like a lot of Japanese cinema, literature, and visual art, and I figured that some experience with anime should be part of my education as both a film critic and New Right thinker, so I asked several friends to recommend a first movie, and *Princess Mononoke* (1997) was highly praised, so I decided to watch it.

Princess Mononoke is set in Japan in the early modern period (the late Muromachi period), before the banning of firearms. But the story has many timeless fantasy elements to it. Indeed, the theme of the movie is the clash between modernity and the pre-modern traditional-magical vision of the world.

"Mononoke" is not a proper name, it is the term for a possessing spirit or demon. It was never clear to me, though, just who the titular princess is, since the only clearly possessed characters in the movie are giant pigs. The princess may be San, the girl raised by wolves, or, more intriguingly, the mysterious Lady Eboshi.

The protagonist of the story, however, is Prince Ashitaka, who *has* been infected by a demon. (Why not call it *Prince Mononoke*, then?) Ashitaka is the last prince of the Emishi, an Ainu-like tribal people driven to the margins of Japan by the Emperors in the distant past and thought to be extinct.

I liked some things about *Princess Mononoke*. Like a lot of Japanese literature and cinema, *Princess Mononoke* gives us a glimpse into the pagan-polytheistic mentality Europeans had before the coming of the desert monotheisms. I also found the portrayal of the great Forest Spirit/Nightwalker to be imaginative and genuinely magical. Finally, I found Lady Eboshi and

Irontown to be a rather brilliant portrait of bourgeois, technological civilization.

Lady Eboshi is clearly a renegade aristocrat. A woman of great ambition without outlet in traditional society, she has created a new society, named Irontown, in which she is the ruler. The people of Irontown are recruited from the dregs and outcasts of society: bumptious peasants, brothel girls, and lepers. (In one amusing scene, the prostitutes confess that they have never heard of an Emperor.) Lady Eboshi has welded them into an efficient military and technological machine by offering them the inclusion and upward mobility denied them in the larger society.

Irontown is devoted to increasing Lady Eboshi's power through the conquest of nature and the creation of technology, including weapons. Irontown clear-cuts the forests, mines iron ore, and turns it into steel. Nature, however, strikes back. The great Forest Spirit sends wolves and wild boars to harry the woodcutters and miners. Irontown is also under attack by the samurai, who wish to plunder its wealth. To protect Irontown, Lady Eboshi needs to make her peasants, prostitutes, and lepers the equals of samurai, which she does by assiduously pursuing superior technology to quell man and beast alike. If anyone is a candidate for demon princess, it is Lady Eboshi.

Lady Eboshi also seeks to literally decapitate nature's resistance by killing the Forest Spirit. To do this, she allies with Jigo, an ugly, vulgar, ignoble, but cunning adventurer who seems to be a defrocked monk. Jigo is very much in the spirit of the wisecracking denizens of the lower orders that populate Japanese cinema and gave us R2-D2 and C-3PO. Jigo has assembled some mysterious mercenaries who seem unbound by any code of honor to help him kill the forest spirit, for whose head the Emperor has offered a large reward. (The Emperor has been told that the head can yield an elixir of immortality. Such Oriental superstitions are driving rare animals to extinction even today.)

I won't say anything about how the plot ultimately plays out, in case you still want to see the movie for yourself after I list its faults, which are significant.

First, *Princess Mononoke* is shockingly "adult" and violent for a cartoon. You would not want to show it to children. Second, the American version also uses a host of extremely annoying American-accented voice actors. Third, I found the animation to be pretty crude throughout. Fourth, the plot was overlong and often draggy. Fifth, there was a lot that seemed frankly arbitrary, but if it had been handled just a bit differently, it would have seemed magical.

My core objection to this movie, however, is the moral confusion at the heart of it. The cause of the Forest Spirit is just. Irontown is simply evil. But our hero Ashitaka does not see it that way. He spends the whole movie speeding around in his earnest-but-dumb fashion trying to prevent conflict rather than taking the right side. His motive seems to be an absolute injunction against "hate," which is a shockingly stupid value system. Is this an outgrowth of Buddhism or a sign of Christian or Western liberal influence? Whatever the answer, it made it impossible for me to regard Ashitaka as a hero. Frankly, I expected better from the Japanese.

Counter-Currents, August 11, 2017

THE PROMISE

When the Young Turk government dragged the Ottoman Empire into the First World War on the side of the Central Powers, their aim was to create a pan-Turkic empire incorporating Turkic lands that were part of the Russian Empire. A major impediment to these plans were the Christian minorities of Eastern Anatolia: the Armenians, Greeks, and Assyrians, who naturally looked to Russia as a potential ally and protector. Thus the Young Turks hatched a plan to exterminate these groups.

The Promise, helmed by Irish director Terry George, is a story from the Armenian genocide, which began with the arrest of the leaders of the Armenian community in Constantinople on April 24, 1915. Most of them were later murdered. Young Armenian men were inducted into the Turkish military, where they were put to work as slave laborers building roads and railroads, then massacred. Older and infirm men, as well as women and children, were marched out of their towns and villages, ostensibly to be relocated to Syria, then massacred. Those who actually made it to relocation camps, died of hunger, disease, and violence. All told, 1.5 million Armenians were killed, as well as 450,000 to 750,000 Greeks and 150,000 to 300,000 Assyrians. Most survivors fled abroad, essentially ridding the heartland of the Empire, which is now modern-day Turkey, of Christians.

The Promise is an excellent movie: a visually sumptuous, old-fashioned period film—a story of love, family, and survival set against the backdrop of a decadent and crumbling empire, the First World War, and the 20th century's first genocide. In terms of visual grandeur and emotional power, *The Promise* brought to mind David Lean's *Doctor Zhivago*. Although some have criticized *The Promise* for making the Armenian genocide the backdrop of a love triangle, what did they expect? A documentary? Besides, *The Promise* is no mere chick flick. It is a genuinely moving film, with a host of excellent performances, not just a predictable, cardboard melodrama—as fun as those can be. And although the comparison actually cheapens this film, if you like historical soaps like *Masterpiece Theatre*, *Downton Abbey*, and

Merchant-Ivory films—or high-order chick flicks like Anthony Minghella's *The English Patient*—you will love *The Promise*.

Another delightful, old-fashioned feature of *The Promise* is its original orchestral score by Lebanese composer Gabriel Yared, who incorporates Armenian music. There is also gorgeous music in a church scene in which the great Armenian composer and musicologist Father Komitas is portrayed singing on the eve of his arrest along with the other leading Armenians of Constantinople. (He survived but was driven mad by his ordeal and never composed again.)

The Promise focuses on Mikael Boghosian (Oscar Isaac), a young Armenian from a small village in southern Turkey who takes the dowry from his betrothal (the promise of the title) to Marak (Angela Sarafyan) to enroll in the Imperial Medical Academy in Constantinople. There he meets and falls in love with Ana Khesarian (Charlotte Le Bon), the French-educated daughter of a famous Armenian violinist, who is the lover of American journalist Chris Myers (Christian Bale). When the genocide begins, Mikael's wealthy uncle is arrested, Mikael is conscripted as a slave laborer, and Ana and Chris work to document the atrocities and save lives. Eventually Mikael makes his way back to his village, finds his family, and marries his betrothed. He then encounters Ana and Chris and joins forces with them to try to save his family, his village, and other Armenians.

All the leading characters in *The Promise* are convincingly three-dimensional and well-performed. Oscar Isaac is excellent as Mikael, as is Charlotte Le Bon in the role of Ana. Every Christian Bale fan, of course, will want to see this film. Although this is not his most compelling character, it is an enjoyable performance nonetheless. My favorite minor character was Mikael's mother Marta, played by the charismatic, husky-voiced Persian actress Shohreh Aghdashloo.

I recommend that all my readers see *The Promise*. It is worth seeing simply as a film, but it is also worth seeing to send a message. For powerful forces are working together to make sure that you do not see this film. A movie about the Armenian genocide is viewed as a threat by the Turkish government and the organized Jewish community, both of which oppose designating the

Armenian tragedy a genocide. The Turks wish to evade responsibility, and the Jews fear any encroachment on their profitable status as the world's biggest victims. Before the film's release, Turkish internet trolls spammed IMDb with bogus one-star reviews. Since the film's release, the Jewish-dominated media has given the film tepid to negative reviews. Given the film's obvious quality, I suspect an organized campaign to stifle this film. Don't let the bastards win.

For many years, I illustrated the Jewish will-to-power compared to other market-dominant minorities with the story of Kirk Kerkorian's purchase of MGM Studios. Kirk Kerkorian was a self-made Armenian-American billionaire. At his peak, he was worth $16 billion and was the richest man in California. In 1969, Kerkorian bought MGM, and instead of seeing it as an opportunity to influence the culture by making movies and television shows, he sold off a lot of its properties and basically turned it into a hotel company. Before he died at the age of 98, however, Kerkorian realized the cultural value of movies and bankrolled *The Promise* with $100 million.

Over his lifetime, Kerkorian gave away more than $1 billion, spending most of it on helping the Republic of Armenia. If only white American billionaires had a shred of this sort of ethnic consciousness, White Nationalism would be flourishing. Until such figures emerge and start taking media power seriously, the Western mind will be nothing more than a battleground over which highly-organized Levantines fight for control. From a White Nationalist point of view, of course, this is an intolerable situation. But anything that challenges Jewish media hegemony is in the long-term interests of whites. White Nationalism, moreover, has many Armenian allies and well-wishers. So I regard *The Promise* not just as an excellent film, but as a positive cultural and political development. Thus we should wish it every success.

I can hardly wait for a movie about Operation Nemesis.[1]

Counter-Currents, February 2, 2019

---

[1] See Greg Johnson, "Operation Nemesis," in *Toward a New Nationalism*.

Rashomon & Realism

Akira Kurosawa's *Rashomon* (1950) is commonly found on lists of the world's greatest movies, and deservedly so. *Rashomon* features avant-garde narrative techniques (flashbacks, multiple points of view), dynamic black-and-white cinematography by Kazuo Miyagawa, compelling Ravel-like music by Fumio Hayasaka, subtle and intensely dramatic performances, and a complex but tightly edited script, all combined into a fast-paced 88-minute masterpiece with an emotionally devastating climax. *Rashomon* is also distinguished by featuring one of the most loathsome and twisted female villains in all of cinema ("Let's you and he fight, and I'll go with the survivor").

When *Rashomon* won the Golden Lion at the 1951 Venice International Film Festival, it did more than lay the foundations for the enduring world-wide fame of Kurosawa and his star, Toshiro Mifune; it opened the eyes of the world toward Japanese cinema as a whole.

Rashomon is the story of a rape and murder committed in 12th-century Japan. Or, rather, it is four radically divergent stories of the same rape and murder. *Rashomon* is constantly trotted out by coffee-house intellectuals as an illustration of the subjectivity of our perceptions and the relativity of truth. But this is a superficial misreading of the film.

The stories in *Rashomon* do not diverge because of the ineluctable subjectivity of all claims about the world. The witnesses are simply *lying*. Furthermore, if we pay attention to their testimony, the characters of the witnesses, and the enduring facts of human psychology, *we can reconstruct what really happened*. Finally, *Rashomon* does not just presuppose that reality is objective and knowable, but that there is a *moral order* that is objective and knowable as well, an objective *ought* as well as an objective *is*. In short, *Rashomon* is not a relativist film but a deeply realist one.

The film opens in a downpour. Two men, a woodcutter and a priest, have taken refuge from the rain in the ruins of the Rashomon gate of Kyoto. It is a time of war, famine, natural disasters, and social breakdown. The woodcutter speaks the first words of the film: "I can't understand it. I can't understand it at all." The two men look at each other and then turn to morosely watch the rain.

Soon they are joined by a third man, who turns out to be a cynic and a thief. Hearing the woodcutter repeating "I just can't understand it," the cynic asks what he is talking about. The woodcutter and the priest both state that they have heard troubling testimonies that day. The cynic asks to hear all about it. When the priest begins to sermonize, though, the cynic cuts him off. He only wants to hear the facts for his amusement. The priest can keep his moralizing to himself.

The Woodcutter's First Story

According to the woodcutter, three days before, he went to the forest to gather wood. Walking along a forest path, he first encounters a woman's hat with a veil hanging on a bush, then a samurai's hat trampled in the leaves, then a length of rope, then an amulet case, then the dead body of a man. Horrified, he rushes off to tell the police. Next we see the woodcutter testifying in court. When asked by the judge if he saw a sword, he answers no.

The Priest's Testimony

Next, we see the testimony of the priest, who passed the murdered man on the road on the afternoon of his death. The murdered man was a samurai, carrying a sword and a bow and arrows. His young wife was on horseback. The priest, who does love to sermonize, then begins to speak of the fragility and fleetingness of human life.

The Policeman's Testimony

Next we see a policeman sitting next to the bound bandit, Tajomaru (Toshiro Mifune). The policeman claims that he captured the bandit after he had been thrown from a horse, which turns out to be the horse of the samurai's wife. The policeman also found the samurai's bow and arrows.

Tajomaru's Testimony

Tajomaru scoffs at the policeman's claim that the great bandit Tajomaru had been thrown from a horse. Instead, he claims, he had been sick with dysentery from drinking polluted water. He then admits that he killed the samurai and tells how it happened.

It was a hot day, and Tajomaru was resting alongside the road. The samurai and his wife passed by, and a breeze momentarily lifted her veil. Struck by her beauty, the bandit decided that he would have her, even if he had to kill her husband. (This sort of contingency brings to mind Camus' *The Stranger*, in which the protagonist Patrice Meursault ends up killing an Arab because it is an especially hot day on the beach.)

Tajomaru quickly hatches a plan. He approaches the samurai and tells him that he found a treasure of swords and mirrors buried in the woods. He offers to sell them to him at a good price. The samurai follows the bandit down a forest path and into a grove, where the bandit springs on him and ties him up. The bandit returns to the wife and tells him her husband has taken sick. Her childlike concern made him feel jealous of her husband. He wanted to show her his disgrace and led her into the grove.

When she sees that her husband has been captured, her expression goes cold. Then she pulls out a dagger and attacks the bandit fiercely. He evades her blows, and as she tires, he seizes her. She breaks down in tears as he rapes her, dropping the knife as she gives in.

After the rape, the bandit prepares to leave and allow them to continue on their journey, but the wife stops him with a shocking proposal. She has been shamed. Two men cannot know of her shame. One of them must die. The two must fight, and she will go with the survivor. The bandit is horrified by this proposal. He cuts the husband's bonds. The husband seizes his sword and attacks. There is an epic swordfight, and the samurai is killed. It is an honorable death, but it was not what the bandit intended.

When the fight was over, the bandit discovered that the woman had run off. So he took the husband's sword and bow and arrows. Then he found the wife's horse and left. He sold the samurai's sword. But he forgot to collect the dagger, which he calls his "biggest mistake."

Throughout his testimony, and in the flashbacks as well, Tajomaru's testimony is filled with bravado, boasting, boyish hijinks, and loud, hollow laughter. At times, he seem maniacal. Even though he has been captured and will surely die, he pretends that he is in control, speaking haughtily to the policeman and judge. Genuine laughter is an expression of a sense of superiority. Nervous or forced laughter is an expression of feelings of inferiority trying to mask itself as superiority. The same is true of boasting. The bandit has been shamed, and he is trying save face. We must bear this motive in mind.

Japan, like other Far Eastern societies, is a shame culture, not a guilt culture. In shame cultures, one's infractions of morals and manners cause intense shame if seen by others. In guilt cultures, one's infractions of morals and manners cause pangs of conscience, even if nobody else knows about them. In shame cultures, one does not suffer pangs of conscience if one's infractions go unnoticed or can be covered up with a face-saving lie. All the lies in *Rashomon* are motivated by the desire to hide shame and save face. If one bears this motive in mind, one can reconstruct what actually happened from the four widely diverging stories.

After Tajomaru's story, the movie returns us to the Rashomon gate. Much to the cynic's surprise, the wife was found alive, hiding in a temple, and was brought to the court to testify. The woodcutter then declares that both Tajomaru and the wife were lying. How does he know this? It turns out that he saw the whole thing and lied about it to the court.

THE WIFE'S TESTIMONY

In the court, the wife is far from being the virago described by Tajomaru. Instead, she is tearful and submissive. According to the wife, after the bandit raped her, he told her his name and mocked her husband. The husband struggled in his bonds, and the wife ran to his side to help. The bandit laughed and ran away. The wife was frozen by her husband's glance, which was aloof and filled with loathing. She screamed for him to kill her, but not to hold her in contempt. She fetched her dagger, freed her husband, and asked him to kill her. Then she grew hysterical and fainted. When she awoke, she found her husband dead, the dagger in his chest. It is never made clear whether he died at her hand or his. She said that she did not remember leaving the woods. She found herself by a pond and tried to drown herself, but failed. Then she took refuge in a temple. She ends her testimony by asking, "What could a poor, helpless woman like me do?" The whole thrust of her story is to establish her good intentions and to absolve her of all responsibility for what happened. She does not even have the agency to secure the honorable death that she claims she desired.

The movie then returns us to the three men conversing at the Rashomon gate. The cynic doubts the woman's testimony, accusing women of fooling themselves and using tears to manipulate men. Then we learn that the dead samurai also testified in court, though a spirit medium. The woodcutter, however, declares that the dead man's story is a lie as well. Again, he can say this because, as revealed later, he actually witnessed the whole crime.

THE HUSBAND'S TESTIMONY

The medium's testimony is one of the most imaginative sequences in the film. The medium is played by a woman, who engages is some sort of shamanic ritual, then speaks in a raspy, unearthly male voice.

According to the husband, after the rape, the bandit tried to console his wife and persuade her to run away with him. The wife agrees to go with the bandit, but then she implores him to kill her husband, again to hide her shame. The bandit is horrified by this and feels sympathy for the husband. He turns to the husband and says that he will kill her if he wishes it. The husband says that for these words, he almost forgave the bandit. The woman then fled, and the bandit chased her. Later, the bandit returns alone. The woman has escaped. The bandit frees the samurai and leaves. The samurai, sickened by his dishonor, takes up the wife's dagger and stabs himself. As he dies, he feels someone approach and remove the dagger from his chest.

At this point, we return to the gate, and the woodcutter blurts out that the story is untrue, for the samurai was killed by a sword, not a dagger. At this point, the canny cynic realizes that the woodcutter had seen more than he let on and persuades him to tell the whole story.

The Woodcutter's Second Story

As in his original story, the woodcutter first found the woman's hat on a branch. But then he heard a woman weeping. He crept closer and found the samurai tied up and the bandit begging the woman to stop crying. The bandit has just raped her, but now he begs for her forgiveness. He offers to marry her. He even offers to work to support her. He then threatens to kill her if she refuses.

The wife gets to her feet and uses her dagger to free her husband. She does not wish to choose between the two of them. She wants the men to fight to the death, and she will go with the winner. The husband, however, holds her in complete contempt. He will not risk his life for a shameless whore and tells her to kill herself.

The bandit too is repulsed by her. He begins to leave but she begs him to stay. When her husband continues to insult her, however, the bandit stops and sticks up for her. Pressing her new opportunity, the wife manically shames both men, saying that if they were real men, they would fight each other. She says that women can only be won by strength, by the sword.

At this point, both men are still united by loathing for the woman, but they are also shamed by her into a half-hearted battle, a battle that they think will restore their honor but which simply deepens their own feelings of self-loathing. Instead of the epic show of swordsmanship in Tajomaru's story, we witness an utterly degrading farce in which two men, sword hands trembling, advance hesitantly then quickly retreat, rolling in the leaves and dirt. Eventually, almost by accident, the husband—begging for his life—is killed by the bandit who throws his sword at him, almost to renounce responsibility for the killing in the very act. He is utterly sickened by his victory. (This long-drawn, sordid murder brings to mind the killing scene in Hitchcock's *Torn Curtain* some years later.) The woman then flees, dishonoring the bandit still further. The bandit picks up the samurai's weapons, finds his horse, and flees, full of furtiveness and self-loathing.

When the woodcutter finishes his story, the cynic questions the truth of the tale, and the woodcutter bristles and says that he is telling the truth. A bit later, the cynic asks him why he omitted any mention of the dagger, and the woodcutter admits that he stole it and sold it.

WHAT REALLY HAPPENED?

We can determine what really happened in *Rashomon* if we understand that all the lies and omissions in the various tales—save one, which is crucial to the movie's end—spring from the same motive: the desire to conceal shame and save face. I think it is most plausible to work backwards from the woodcutter's second tale. The woodcutter's account is most likely to be accurate because he was merely a witness, not a participant in the events. But even he conceals something out of shame, namely his theft of the dagger. But that was after the rape and murder took place.

If we take the woodcutter's account as basically accurate, then remove everything from it that the bandit, the wife, and the samurai would find shameful, we will arrive at the tales they tell.

The woodcutter did not see how the samurai and his wife ended up in the grove, or how the rape took place, so we simply have to take the bandit's account of those events at face value.

The humiliating events that the bandit omits from the woodcutter's tale are begging the woman to marry him, the woman's verbal abuse and shaming, and the disgraceful duel at the end. Instead, as the bandit told it, he was prepared to leave and let the samurai and his wife to continue their journey, but she begged him to kill her husband. He was horrified by this proposal and released the husband. The husband then attacked. A gallant duel followed, ending with the samurai's honorable death.

The woman's tale omits everything after the rape that casts her in a shameful light. Gone is her proposal to have the two men fight to the death, which is present in all the other accounts. Gone is the bandit's horror at this proposal, which is also present in the other three accounts. As the wife tells it, the bandit simply leaves, the husband treats her contemptuously, she begs him to kill her, then faints. When she comes to, she finds her husband dead with her dagger in his chest—perhaps at his own hand, perhaps at hers. Her story does not account for what happened to the dagger, which was not found at the scene of the crime.

The tale told by the samurai's ghost also omits everything personally shameful to him: his wife goading the men to fight and his death at the end of their degrading duel. Instead, he claims that he committed suicide, but, unlike the wife, he had the presence of mind to explain why he was not found with a knife in his chest.

What remains to be explained is the discrepancy between the woodcutter's first and second accounts . Why did he completely omit the events after the rape leading up to the murder? To answer this question, we need to examine the final scene of the movie.

THE FOUNDLING

After the woodcutter finishes his second story, the priest bemoans the fact that human lies and selfishness create hell on earth, and they are living through it.

The ruined Rashomon gate is not just a place where people take refuge from the rain. It is also a spot where unclaimed corpses and unwanted babies are abandoned. After the priest finishes his lament, they hear the cries of a baby.

The woodcutter and the priest are horrified to find the cynic stealing the baby's clothes and an amulet left for its protection. The cynic defends himself by claiming that if he did not do it, someone else would. The woodcutter accuses him of being evil and selfish. The cynic deflects that by claiming that the parents of the foundling are evil and selfish for abandoning it.

The woodcutter disagrees. The amulet was left for the baby's protection. It must have been hard for the parents to abandon their child. The cynic mocks the woodcutter's compassion for the parents and leaves. The woodcutter then tells the priest that he will adopt the baby. He has six children already. One more won't matter. The priest then tells the woodcutter that he has restored his faith in humanity. The rain stops, sun breaks through the clouds, and the woodcutter departs with the foundling. The End.

How has the great Rashomon gate of Kyoto become a ruin where rotting corpses and unwanted babies are abandoned? How did life on earth become hell?

Rashomon's answer is: because of Japanese honor culture, because of the selfish desire to save face, to construct and propagate an image of oneself, which requires lies, manipulation, and the domination of others. How does one get beyond selfishness, lies, and violence to heal the world? The woodcutter shows us the way: through compassion. I read *Rashomon* as a critique of Japanese honor culture, including the code of the samurai, from the point of view of a Buddhist ethics of compassion.

The woodcutter's compassion even explains why he omitted so much when testifying in court. Granted, he had selfish reasons not to mention the theft of the dagger. But then again, he had six children to feed. However, he did not omit the story of the murder to hide his own shame, but because he felt compassion for the shame of the bandit, the samurai, and his wife. It was painful for him to watch. It is painful for *us* to watch. We want to look away, and we can understand why the woodcutter did not want to compound their shame by revealing it to the world.

If *Rashomon* is a deeply realist work, presupposing that both facts and morality are objective and knowable, why has it become the favorite film of relativists? Why has such a superficial reading become the dominant one? What sort of bovine mind could view four completely contradictory accounts of what the rest of us naïvely call "the same events" and conclude that there's nothing more to the film than that? How can one watch *Rashomon* all the way to the end and never advance beyond the opening words, "I can't understand it. I can't understand it at all"? What sort of mind would wish to repeat and recommend such an experience? And what do such viewers make of the ending of the film, which I interpret as a repudiation of everything that the relativists praise?

I believe that the relativist reading of *Rashomon* is popular because we today are living in the same kind of world depicted by the film: a Dark Age of selfishness and lies. Relativism is just a philosophical rationalization of the egocentrism and dishonesty that turned the world of *Rashomon* into a hell. Which means that today we face the same problem explored in the film itself: how can we awaken the forces of compassion and solidarity, forces that can free us from the deep solitude of spirit to which this Dark Age confines us, allowing us to redeem this hellish fallen world and make it a place we can all call home?

Counter-Currents, October 16, 2017

ROGUE ONE:
A STAR WARS STORY

Rogue One is quite simply one of the best *Star Wars* movies ever. It has an interesting plot, a tight script, good pacing, uniformly good acting, excellent special effects, amazing sets, spectacular new worlds, and dazzling battle scenes. I really loved this movie.

When I first saw the teaser trailer I groaned. I thought it was going to be just a remake of *The Force Awakens*: a Mary Sue female lead, a multiracial cast, and another plot centering around the god-damned Death Star! Can't these pathetic shekel-grubbing cynics at Disney come up with a single original idea?

My jaundiced reading was well-grounded, based on the last *Star Wars* movie, Jar Jar Abrams' absolutely abysmal *The Force Awakens*, which was a cynical, mechanical, character-by-character, scene-by-scene, sometimes shot-by-shot remake of *A New Hope* and *The Empire Strikes Back*, maximally pozzed with feminism and diversity, and completely lacking in the magic and humanity of the Lucas films. (See my review in this volume.) The idea that Disney would follow this wretched remake with a remake of it seemed like a bad idea whose time had come.

But I was delighted to be proven wrong. *Rogue One* is set in the *Star Wars* universe right before *A New Hope*. A few characters are present from the other films, but they all have minor roles. Instead, *Rogue One* adds a whole cast of new characters and a novel plot to the larger *Star Wars* saga, rather than remaking other films in the series or dining out on nostalgia for the cast of the original trilogy, as Abrams did.

The female lead, Jyn Erso (Felicity Jones) is not a Mary Sue like Rey in *The Force Awakens*. Jyn was raised in part by Jedi rebel Saw Gerrera (Forrest Whitaker), who taught her to fight, and then left to her own devices at the age of 16, when she embarked upon a life of crime. It is a tough life, but Jyn remains a fundamentally feminine character. For instance, Jyn does not think in principles but in terms of personal relationships. She rejected the rebellion because she felt rejected by it. She rejoins it, because she hopes to reconnect with her father. But she is capable of heroism nonetheless. In truth, Jyn is not Mary Sue, but a plucky Frodo Baggins. (You'll see it in the Council of Elrond sequence.)

Yes, the cast is multiracial, with two very appealing Asian characters among the principals. But this is an Empire, after all, and set a long time ago, in a galaxy far, far away. It also seems dumb to complain about Asians and blacks on the screen when there are far more exotic races. In short, casting non-whites in *Star Wars* is not the same as putting them in stories like King Arthur or Robin Hood. And there was no attempt to match up the white female lead with a black, as in *The Force Awakens*.

Rogue One is a movie for grownups. I would not take the younglings. The tone is dark and often quite moving, with touches of genuine humor that are never juvenile or crude. Mercifully, there are no Gungans and Ewoks, and nary a word of Nerf herders.

Rogue One really is a war movie. Basically, it is *The Dirty Dozen* in space. Lucas' droid and clone armies were created to deprive war of real loss, but they deprive it of tragedy and sublimity as well. In *Rogue One*, death is very real, often sudden, and always final.

In the Lucas films, the rebels do nothing wrong. In *Rogue One*, they are every bit as ruthless as the empire. Diego Luna's Cassian Andor is a battle-hardened spy, saboteur, and assassin. And he comes from the moderate faction.

In the Lucas films, the Gungans and Ewoks represent the Third Worldist fantasy that primitives can triumph over technologically advanced war machines with bows, arrows, and slingshots. In *Rogue One*, the rebels meet firepower with firepower, until the Death Star rolls up and vaporizes them.

Of course all that technological terror is no match for the Force, we are told in *A New Hope*. But in *Rogue One*, there is precious little Jedi swordplay, and it is not always superior to a well-aimed blaster.

Some other things I really liked about *Rogue One*:

1. We learn that the Death Star thermal exhaust port was

sabotage.
2. The childish and petulant droid K-2SO, voiced by Alan Tudyk, was one of my favorite characters and provided most of the comic relief.
3. Peter Cushing is digitally resurrected to play Grand Moff Tarkin, and it was uncannily well done.
4. It has the best space battle ever.
5. Director Gareth Edwards, who helmed the 2014 *Godzilla* remake, deserves enormous credit. This is arguably the best-directed *Star Wars* movie ever.
6. The final act of this film is particularly intense, moving, and full of surprises. Where lesser films would have wrapped up, this film keeps pressing on to new heights — then topping them.
7. There's no "crawl" at the beginning, and frankly I did not miss it.
8. Many of the lines and shots in the trailers were not in the movie. So if the trailers put you off, you have been mislead.
9. The Schwartz was not with us. Aside from the casting issues already mentioned, this movie has no obvious Jewish subversion or propaganda, even though the screenwriters claimed it did.
10. The main heavy, Director Krennic (played by Ben Mendelsohn — with distant Prussian-Jewish echoes), had a great visual style with his white cape and black-armored bodyguard, and was an interesting study in sardonic world-weariness and thwarted ambition. (As in *The Dark Knight Rises*, Mendelsohn has a great "Do you feel in charge?" scene, this time with Darth Vader.)
11. Vader's battle scene was incredibly intense and will be endlessly re-watched and analyzed.
12. Forrest Whitaker's Saw Gerrera is fascinatingly realized: a Jedi turned terrorist, he is a wheezing cyborg like Vader, driven by murder and intrigue into gibbering paranoia.

Rogue One has a few flaws:

1. John Williams did not write the score, and he is sorely missed. Honestly, they should have just done a pastiche of his scores from the previous seven movies.
2. I really wish Darth Vader had more screen time. He's the only character from the other films I really wanted to see more of. They should have given him some of Grand Moff Tarkin's lines.
3. If the planetary shield on Scarif could prevent Jyn from transferring the Death Star plans, why did it not prevent Bodhi Rook from contacting the rebel fleet to tell them to expect Jyn's communication?
4. The crystals being removed from Jedah were not really necessary for the Death Star, if it could show up on the heels of the last departing ship to blast the place.
5. A much more plausible cover for the destruction of the holy city would have been an asteroid strike.

Rogue One is so superior to *The Force Awakens* that Disney should seriously consider just scrapping its new trilogy and instead focusing on making more "anthology" films set in the *Star Wars* universe. (But there needs to be an absolute moratorium on Death Stars.) Jar Jar Abrams, of course, should never work in this galaxy again. But, frankly, Gareth Edwards will be writing his own ticket for many years to come.

At the end of *Revenge of the Sith*, one feels a certain knowing pleasure in seeing how familiar things were brought about. One feels the same pleasure at the end of *Rogue One*, as it dovetails perfectly with the beginning of *A New Hope*. But the ferocious battles and fearsome sacrifices of *Rogue One* give the rebellion a new seriousness and sublimity, which will forever change how we view *A New Hope* and its sequels. Thus *Rogue One* is not just a great movie in itself, it will also deepen and elevate Lucas' original trilogy. This is a remarkable achievement.

Post Script

I decided to re-watch the original *Star Wars* (which I hate to call *A New Hope*), to confirm my hypothesis that *Rogue One* will significantly change one's experience of the original trilogy. And

I was correct. One interesting detail that popped out is that, aside from the Emperor himself, Tarkin was apparently the only person in the galaxy who could say "no" to Darth Vader. In *Rogue One*, he sends Vader into battle. In *Star Wars*, he tells Vader to stop choking a subordinate and is "holding Vader's leash," as Leia puts it. In *The Empire Strikes Back*, Vader is unleashed, and his chokings are no longer mere warnings but a method of execution.

I then went on to re-watch *The Empire Strikes Back*, and I must alter one aspect of my review above. (Pray I don't alter it further.) *The Empire Strikes Back* really is the best *Star Wars* movie ever. Yes, the embarrassingly juvenile moments remain. Yes, Carrie Fisher is a princess only in the Jewish sense: spoiled, obnoxious, aggressive, and rude. But on the whole, the script, direction, acting, music, special effects, and overall feeling of darkness and dramatic seriousness are superior to any other *Star Wars* film—especially the third act in the cloud city, and the climactic "I am your father" scene, where Vader offers a proposition that, frankly, Luke should not have refused.

Counter-Currents, December 16, 2016

SILENCE

Martin Scorsese's *Silence* is a very fine film that seems to belong to an entirely different world. Imagine what American movies would be like if our film industry were not controlled by hostile and decadent aliens who have weaponized the medium against European man and culture. *Silence* is such a film. It is wholly untouched by political correctness and white guilt or self-abasement. Instead, *Silence* is the story of self-confident, expansionist whites battling non-white savagery.

Silence is about Portuguese Jesuit Missionaries in 17th-century Japan, who had converted large numbers of Japanese to Christianity before the Japanese government, alarmed at the threat to their culture and sovereignty, launched savage persecutions that extirpated organized Christianity and drove the remnants underground for more than 200 years, until the Meiji restoration established religious tolerance in 1871.

The film follows two young Jesuits (Andrew Garfield and Adam Driver) who are smuggled into Japan to learn the fate of their mentor, Fr. Ferreira (Liam Neeson), who has reportedly renounced the faith and gone native. The young priests and their Japanese converts are movingly portrayed as intensely religious in the face of methodical and cruel persecution and martyrdom.

Yet, as the story unfolds, we come to knew and even respect the Japanese Inquisitor who orchestrated these atrocities. The Inquisitor's interpreter speaks of learning Portuguese from one of the Jesuits, who merely taught his language but never learned Japanese. The Jesuits also, apparently, neglected to learn about Japanese religion, Japanese culture, and the Japanese mind. As the interpreter drily remarks, "Japan already has a religion. Pity you did not notice it."

The Japanese, by contrast, learned all they could from the Jesuits about the doctrines and methods of the Church, then promptly turned them against it, including the creation of an Inquisition complete with executions by crucifixion and burning alive and a whole panoply of tortures to secure confession and apostasy. The Japanese even understood Christian theology well enough to make priests renounce Christianity out of essentially Christian motives. (This is how we get liberalism, by the way.)

But the Japanese understanding of religion as an essentially public and civil affair still left a space for inward Christian belief and private household devotions. Thus, in the end, one could argue the Inquisitor was defeated. The Japanese answer, however, might be that even the private Christianity of the Japanese was more Japanese than Christian. Beyond that, the real threat posed by Christianity was as a tool of Western colonialism, and that was stopped dead in its tracks—basically until 1945.

One small touch that reveals the alienness of the Japanese mind, which accords absolute primacy to social roles over individual identity, is that two apostate priests were simply given the identities of dead Japanese men: their houses, wives, children, even their names. One wonders what the wives and children thought of the arrangement. But that apparently did not matter any more than whether some of them might have prayed in their hearts to Jesus. The first man is said to have been executed, so maybe the whole family was being punished.

There are two debates between the Inquisitor and one of the captive priests. The Japanese clearly think Christianity is false, but they diplomatically declare that it may be true in Portugal, but it is not true in Japan. The priest glibly replies that truth is universal. Of course the Japanese wondered why a universal truth required that converts adopt foreign names and customs. They might have wondered why a universal truth came to them from men of a different race, speaking a different tongue, who told stories of a very particular tribe in the Near East (near to Europe, that is), who answered to a man in Rome, and who worked hand in glove with European conquerors and colonizers. That's a whole lot of particularism, and in its face, who can blame the Japanese for choosing to defend their own culture, religion, and independence—with Christianity's own weapons, if necessary?

Silence is a superb film, largely because of its intelligent script and sensitive acting. The pacing is slow and thoughtful. The camera work is not flashy, focusing on its objects for seconds at a time. There are no American gangsters, kung-fu fighting, CGI monsters, or laser battles. In short, this is a movie for grown-ups. *Silence* is one of Scorsese's best films. The fact that it springs from and portrays intense Christian devotion will rankle and discomfit modern Leftists. But in the end, I predict that it will win great critical acclaim. It will not sell a lot of tickets, though, unless the churches promote it like *The Passion of the Christ*. See *Silence* in the theater, not because "you've got to see it on the big screen," but because we should want this movie to do well, so more movies like it are made.

Although *Silence* was long in the making, there is a kind of symbolic appropriateness about the fact that it was released after the election of Donald Trump. Political Correctness is dying. We're saying "Merry Christmas" again. And movies like *Silence* are being made. Meme it, until the spirits of the enemy completely break, until they trample on their Hope posters and begin to praise Kek.

From an Identitarian point of view, *Silence* is somewhat paradoxical. On the one hand, it is a story about the heroism and suffering of European Christians and their Japanese converts. And for all the film's fair-mindedness toward the Japanese Inquisitor—itself a very white thing—*Silence* remains an essentially Christian film dedicated, at the end, to the greater glory of God. On the other hand, all my sympathies ultimately were with the Japanese, not because white is bad and non-white is good, but because their cunning and ruthless struggle against a colonizing universalism is the struggle of all white men today.

Counter-Currents, January 27, 2017

SOLO:
A STAR WARS STORY

I had a bad feeling about this.

It wasn't just *Solo*'s cursed production history: the original directors were sacked near the end of shooting, and Ron Howard was brought in to finish the movie, reshooting 70 percent of it. It wasn't just the rumors that Alden Ehrenreich was not up to the role of Han Solo. It wasn't just the tepid reviews.

The real problem is making a movie about the young Han Solo in the first place. Because what makes *Star Wars* compelling is not space battles and cantinas full of exotic aliens. It is the presence of Grand Politics—the Empire and the Rebellion—and the Numinous: the Force and its initiates, both good and evil. Han Solo before his involvement in either is just the cynical smuggler we met on Tattooine.

Now, there was nothing to stop Disney from making a great movie about a cynical smuggler with a good heart trying to make his way in a savage universe. But such a movie would be unlike any other *Star Wars* movie, and that would present a problem for the writer and director. They could not dine out on Grand Politics and the Numinous. At best, these could only appear on the margins and in a manner in which Han could not grasp their full significance. Instead, they would have to do a straightforward adventure movie set in the *Star Wars* universe, *but without depending upon the factors that make the franchise unique and compelling.* (To say nothing of sure-fire hits, even when they are bad.)

But there are two kinds of adventure movies: pulp films in which cardboard characters dodge random explosions—and good films, which need to have three things: character development, dramatic conflict connected to deep moral and metaphysical themes, and a story that is not just one accident after another. A good plot needs an element of necessity. The story has to be in some way generated by the characters and the moral and metaphysical themes. Great, involving stories are encounters between what is deep in us and what is deep in the universe.

Solo could have been a good movie, even a great one. But the writers and directors needed to ask themselves at every step: Would this still be a good movie if we dropped all the *Star Wars* crap and set it in any other universe or time period? The answer, unfortunately, is no. I found *Solo* to be a lifeless, uninvolving movie from beginning to end.

Solo is not a calculated, cynical, derivative farce like *The Force Awakens* and *The Last Jedi*. Those films are evil and inept. *Solo* is neither. It has an original plot. It is well-directed. It is competently acted. It is often great to look at. But it is basically just a pulp-level caper film, where the heroes rush from one contrived crisis to another, always saving the day in the nick of time.

At one point, it crossed my mind that maybe Disney had confused Han Solo with Indiana Jones. But the first three of those movies were pretty good, and even they had mystery and magic. (Of course everybody knows that *Star Wars* is based on old pulp space opera serials. But Lucas took them to a higher level.)

Basically, *Solo* makes a list of all the things that we know about the young Han Solo from the original trilogy. He presumably had a childhood. He has a name. He met Chewie. He won the *Millennium Falcon* in a card game with Lando Calrissian. He made something called the Kessel run in 12 parsecs. The movie then resolves to stitch all these together while including other obligatory *Star Wars* tropes: a cantina scene, a wisecracking droid, some space battles and chases. There's nothing about the Jedi and the Force, and the Empire is only present on the edges, and in the most sordid and grimy way possible. (We do, however, discover why Storm Troopers can't shoot, for the application procedure is hardly rigorous.)

But this is not how you create a great story. At best, these are just side dishes and trimmings. The main course should have been an original plot. The back story stuff should have been worked in as asides or surprises. One of the best things about *Revenge of the Sith* and *Rogue One* is how neatly and pleasurably they slotted into what we already knew happened from the first trilogy. But they weren't just back stories. They had self-contained plots.

Furthermore, the underlying plot of *Solo* is stupid. Han and Qi'ra are in love. Han and Qi'ra are on the run from gangsters. Han escapes, but Qi'ra is captured. Han then spends the next three years in the Imperial Army, hoping for an opportunity to get a ship, return home, and find Qi'ra. But why does he need *his own* ship to return home? Couldn't he book passage on another vessel? And why does he even need to return home to learn about her fate? Are we to believe that in a universe with faster-than-light travel, people don't have email?

I can't recommend *Solo*. It simply left me cold. It is not a bad movie, but it is not good either. It did not make me angry like *The Force Awakens* and *The Last Jedi*. It just made me bored. It is a waste of time and money. I never thought much of Han Solo to begin with. And I still don't. The character has no magic or grandeur. He was never quite up to the *Star Wars* universe, and he is nothing without it. Ron Howard is a talented director, but there may have been nothing he could do. *Solo*'s fate may have been sealed before he stepped in.

Solo has plenty to irritate racially conscious whites. Alden Ehrenreich is twice as Jewish as Harrison Ford. Woody Harrelson's character has a black squeeze. Space pimp Lando is supposed to be pansexual, but that is simply to say he is an actor. His droid has a sassy black Communist woman trapped inside it. Emilia Clarke's Qi'ra is supposed to be something completely new: a strong, badass woman. But she's actually no MaRey Sue. She's simply treacherous and backstabbing. The leader of the marauders has a face from the *National Geographic* miscegenation issue. And so forth.

Like I said, I had a bad feeling about *Solo* going in. And as the movie unfolded, I definitely felt the absence of grandeur and mystery. But at the end, the source of my dissatisfaction was confirmed when the hologram of Darth Maul appeared to summon his servant to Dathomir. This only makes sense if one has watched the animated series *Star Wars: The Clone Wars*.

After *The Last Jedi*, I gave up hope for theatrical *Star Wars* movies and decided to explore the two animated series, *The Clone Wars* and *Star Wars: Rebels*. After all, *Star Wars* movies are mostly cartoons anyway.

I was pleasantly surprised. These animated series, under the guidance of director and producer Dave Filoni, are simultaneously true to the spirit of the original Lucas films while being highly imaginative and original—and often quite deep and emotionally powerful. They are infinitely superior to all of Disney's movies and the true heirs and guardians of George Lucas' legacy.

NOTE

Here's my current ranking of the *Star Wars* movies and animated series (*Rogue One* sank considerably after I viewed it on BluRay):

The Empire Strikes Back
Star Wars (A New Hope)
Star Wars: Rebels
Revenge of the Sith
Star Wars: The Clone Wars
Return of the Jedi
Rogue One
Attack of the Clones
Solo
The Phantom Menace
The Last Jedi
The Force Awakens

Counter-Currents, May 25, 2018

SPECTRE

I'm feeling a quantum of disappointment with the latest James Bond movie *Spectre*. But maybe my expectations were unreasonably high. The last Bond movie, *Skyfall*, was one of the very best. And *Spectre* has two of the most artful and enticing trailers ever made. With such a buildup, maybe I was doomed to disappointment.

What did I like about *Spectre*?

First, and foremost, there is Daniel Craig, who is the best actor to ever to have played Bond. Craig is not a handsome man, but he is highly charismatic. He is pure masculinity untainted with prettiness. He brings a depth and emotional complexity to the character that were well-exploited in *Casino Royale* (2006) and *Skyfall* (2012). Craig was wasted, however, in his second outing, *Quantum of Solace* (2008), which was a frenzied and unmemorable clone of a Jason Bourne movie. I call it *Quantum of Bollocks*. (When Craig retires, he should be replaced by Tom Hardy.)

Second, there is the return of Spectre and Ernst Stavro Blofeld (Christoph Waltz) — *and the cat*.[1]

Third, there are two extremely feminine but formidable Bond girls: the elegant, aristocratic Léa Seydoux as Dr. Madeleine Swann, and Monica Bellucci, still stunning at 51, as Lucia Sciarra, the widow of a Spectre assassin.

Fourth, I very much enjoyed the title song, "Writing's on the Wall" by Sam Smith. Also good was Adele's "Skyfall" song. But there's a long list of pretty forgettable Bond songs before them. Thomas Newman's score is quite good. And the tentacle porn title sequence is also pretty over the top.

Finally, this film has all the Bond touches: exotic locations; beautiful buildings, interiors, people, clothes, and cars; and spectacular fights, chases, and stunts, all of them stylishly directed by Sam Mendes.

---

[1] See Jef Costello, "The Cat is Back! The Spectre Behind S.P.E.C.T.R.E.," in *The Importance of James Bond & Other Essays* (San Francisco: Counter-Currents, 2017).

What didn't I like about *Spectre*?

The main problem was the plot, specifically the plot in the last 30 minutes. *Skyfall* was such a powerful movie because in the last half hour it shifted from being just another Bond thriller into something mythic. Bond realizes that his nemesis, Silva, can use any computerized technology against him. So he decides to go back to the old ways. He loads M into a classic Aston Martin from the 1960s and heads to his family home, Skyfall, on the blasted heath of Scotland. There he meets his family gamekeeper, played by Albert Finney. Both he and M are about the age that Bond's parents would have been, had he not been orphaned in childhood. Thus not only is Bond going back in time to his family seat, he is recreating his family. Then the family pulls together to defend their fortress from attackers. It is emotionally powerful because it is mythic and primal.

In *Spectre*, similar expectations are set up. Bond again goes back into his past. After he was orphaned, a guardian was appointed by the court. The guardian had a son, who was jealous of his father's affection for Bond. He felt cuckolded, and he says so. Later, he murders his father, fakes his death, and takes on his mother's name. This is the origin of Ernst Stavro Blofeld. It is the stuff of Greek tragedy.

But once this back story is revealed, the rest of the movie is just a bunch of fights and chases, including the equivalent of Blofeld tying a woman to the train tracks, which is the stuff of Dudley Doright, not Greek tragedy. In short, the enormous dramatic and emotional potential of the back story and the plot so far is simply dissipated in farce.

What should have happened? They should have recapitulated the primal scene of cuckoldry, this time Blofeld trying to cuckold Bond with Dr. Swann as the object of affection. Instead, we have a pointless torture scene followed by a ridiculously easy escape, followed by fights and chases and escapes with helicopters and speedboats and some other things I probably missed as I was glancing at my watch.

Spectre is a good Bond movie. But it could have been a great one.

Counter-Currents, November 9, 2015

STAR TREK: BEYOND

I have seen a lot of *Star Trek* on the big and small screens, and from the perspective of middle age, it seems like an appalling waste of time. Recently, I watched a number of episodes from the original series, which I had not seen since childhood, and found them quite creaky and often laughable. My feelings about the original cast surfaced when I saw Walter Koening appear on an episode of *Babylon Five* (yes, it was awful, but I gave it a chance!), and I blurted out, "Science fiction will not be safe until all these people are dead."

Yes, I liked *The Next Generation* beginning in season three. But my favorite series was *Voyager*. Despite the ludicrously PC casting, *Voyager* simply had excellent stories. I found the Borg, which featured prominently in both series, to be one of the *Star Trek* universe's most imaginative creations. *Deep Space Nine* was worth a single run through, but *Enterprise* was a major disappointment, although the season three story arc was interesting. I doubt that I will bother to watch a new series, should one appear.

As for the movies, the best part of the first movie was Jerry Goldsmith's wonderful music. Only *The Wrath of Khan* and *The Undiscovered Country* play like something more than padded-out TV episodes. The fourth and fifth movies were ludicrous. None of *The Next Generation* movies made much of an impression. In fact, I think I missed one or two of them entirely. Then came Jar Jar Abrams' incompetent big-screen reboot of the original series, including his totally needless remake of *The Wrath of Khan*. And now we have the thirteenth movie in the franchise, *Star Trek: Beyond*, helmed by Chinese director Justin Lin.

Beyond is the most visually impressive *Star Trek* movie ever. But the dazzling spectacle only underscores the hollowness of the plot. The villain, Krall, is a Star Fleet captain marooned for 100 years on a desert planet who has for some reason morphed into an alien, and then just as inexplicably morphs back to being human.

During his exile, he has prolonged his existence by draining the life forces of sentient beings; he has conjured up a vast alien army; and he has nursed a plot to wreak havoc on the Federation because they stand for peace and unity (what, no diversity?), whereas he stands for struggle and stuff. He is a former soldier, you see, whereas Star Fleet is basically an interstellar Peace Corps.

He acquires an ancient Macguffin, a bioweapon that can destroy all life within its reach, and sets out to extinguish the millions of souls on Starbase Yorktown. I guess that'll show 'em. (Of course his vast fleet of ships could do the same thing without the weapon, but never mind.) Naturally, though, he is stopped by the plucky crew of the *Enterprise* under the command of Captain Kirk (played by the handsome Chris Pine, who is 75% less Jewish than William Shatner).

As spectacle, it was dazzling, but as drama it left me cold. With all the money and technical skill at the director's command, you'd think he would have secured a good script, with characterization and drama and a couple of twists to glue all the action sequences together. Hell, he could have stolen a better story from Shakespeare or Melville or countless *Star Trek* fan novels. But no.

This being *Star Trek*, I of course expected *Beyond* to be pozzed with liberalism and multiculturalism. Of course, the cast is just one giant *Star Wars* cantina of diversity, but instead of a wretched hive of scum and villainy, we have physically superior specimens of all races idealistically devoted to the higher good.

We do learn that Mr. Sulu is a homo with a partner (perhaps even a husband) and adopted daughter, both of whom are also Oriental. But the real surprise is that Spock's relationship with Uhuru was on the rocks because in light of the destruction of Vulcan, it seemed logical to him to be making pure Vulcan babies rather than Vulcan-human half-breeds. Seems logical to me too and not a bad meme to propagate.

About 15 minutes before the end of *Beyond*, I started thinking of the shortness of life and contemplated leaving. But I came to write a review, so I stayed to the end. I wonder, though, what I was hoping to find in this movie. What has sustained millions of fans through five mostly bad TV series and 13 overwhelmingly bad movies?

Star Trek combines two incompatible worldviews, both of which appeal to large numbers of people.

First, there is the Faustian quest for exploration and adventure, the desire to see mankind ascend to space and explore the universe. Part and parcel of Faustianism is the economic utopianism of *Star Trek*, in which unlimited clean energy and "the replicator" have basically abolished scarcity. Machines have put us all out of work, so mankind is free to perfect itself and explore the cosmos. (For more on this, see the essay "Money for Nothing."[1]) Faustianism is primarily a white thing, as whites for better and worse are largely responsible for the scientific and technological progress that we call modernization. This is what appeals to me about *Star Trek*. This is what kept me coming back.

Second, there is liberalism, multiculturalism, and (literal) universalism, which assume that everybody in the universe (except the bad people who wish to cling to their eccentric identities), no matter how apparently different, is basically the same insofar as they can become part of a United Federation of Planets.

Unfortunately, as we have discovered since *Star Trek* first debuted in 1966, Faustianism and multiculturalism are not compatible. The Apollo program was ferociously attacked by the Left, which wanted the money to go to uplift programs for non-whites. Trillions have been spent on such programs, to no real effect, whereas the same trillions of dollars could have taken us to Mars by now.

One of the main spurs to technological progress is high labor costs. Only by keeping labor expensive will we arrive at a world in which machines put us all out of work. Thus economic globalization and open borders are undermining technological progress by creating a global plantation economy, in which "productivity" and profits rise simply by cutting labor costs rather than by technological improvements that actually make labor more productive.

---

[1] Greg Johnson, "Money for Nothing," in *Truth, Justice, & a Nice White Country* (San Francisco: Counter-Currents, 2015).

Globalization also inevitably causes First World living standards to plunge towards equalization with the Third World, destroying the white human and social capital that made progress possible in the first place.[2] If present trends continue, it will be homogeneous high-IQ Asian societies that rise to the stars while the white world descends into the mud of Third Worldization.

Thus if you want to make *Star Trek*'s Faustian utopia real, you need to put away liberalism, multiculturalism, and other childish things and devote yourself to the most serious cause of all: fighting for White Nationalism. Silly movies like *Star Trek: Beyond* have nothing to contribute to progress. They are just ways of amusing ourselves as we decline.

Counter-Currents, August 24, 2016

---

[2] See Greg Johnson, "The End of Globalization," in *Truth, Justice, & a Nice White Country*

STAR WARS: THE FORCE AWAKENS

The new *Star Wars* movie is exactly what I deduced it would be from the trailers and the fact that it was directed by J. J. Abrams, a filmmaker so vulgar and artless that he makes Jerry Bruckheimer seem like Ingmar Bergman. *The Force Awakens* is not an homage but a ripoff. It is not a reboot but simply a remake of *Star Wars* with a bit of *The Empire Strikes Back* thrown in.

I saw it coming: Abrams, after all, badly bungled the reboot of the *Star Trek* movies. And instead of coming up with a new plot for the second one, he did a totally botched remake of *The Wrath of Khan*. The absurdity, of course, is that there are whole universes of *Star Trek* and *Star Wars* fan fiction out there that he could have ripped off. So mere lack of imagination and originality did not force him to remake existing movies.

My plot summary borrows from, corrects, and augments a rather droll meme floating around the web. Yes, it contains spoilers. The movie begins on the desert planet of ~~Tatooine~~ Jakku, where an orphaned ~~boy~~ girl named ~~Luke~~ Rey scratches out a living on the margins of society. Also in the desert of ~~Tatooine~~ Jakku lives an old robed and bearded hermit who possesses arcane knowledge of the Force named ~~Obi-Wan Kenobi~~ Lor San Tekka, played by prominent ~~English~~ Swedish actor ~~Alec Guiness~~ Max von Sydow. ~~Kenobi~~ Tekka is later killed by his apprentice ~~Darth Vader~~ Kylo Ren, who has gone over to the Dark Side.

A cute beeping, burbling droid named ~~R2-D2~~ BB-8 lands on ~~Tatooine~~ Jakku entrusted with secret information essential to the ~~Rebellion~~ Resistance against the ~~Empire~~ First Order, a totalitarian state led by ~~Emperor~~ Supreme Leader ~~Palpatine~~ Snoke, who is an initiate of the Dark Side of the Force. Pursuing the droid is ~~Palpatine's~~ Snoke's right hand, ~~Darth Vader~~ Kylo Ren, his apprentice in exploring the secrets of the Dark Side.

~~Luke~~ Rey finds the droid and is drawn into the ~~Rebellion~~ Resistance when the ~~Empire~~ First Order destroys ~~his~~ her ~~home~~ hometown in search of ~~R2-D2~~ BB-8. ~~Luke~~ Rey and ~~R2-D2~~ BB-8 narrowly escape ~~Tattooine~~ Jakku on the *Millennium Falcon* with the help of its captain Han Solo and first mate Chewbacca. ~~Darth Vader~~ Kylo Ren pursues them. ~~Luke's~~ Rey's helper ~~Han Solo~~ Finn is a bit of a rogue and coward, but he eventually comes around and joins the fight against the ~~Empire~~ First Order.

~~Luke~~ Rey and companions learn that the ~~Empire~~ First Order has created a super-weapon, the ~~Death Star~~ Star-Killer Base, a space station the size of a ~~moon~~ planet that can blow up an entire ~~planet~~ solar system.

~~Luke~~ Rey also learns that ~~he~~ she has the ability to tap into the Force. This ability runs in families, and ~~Luke~~ Rey has inherited it from ~~his~~ her father ~~Darth Vader~~ Luke Skywalker. On a jungle planet, ~~Luke~~ Rey encounters a long-lived little ~~green~~ yellow rubber creature who imparts wisdom. Also on the jungle planet, ~~Luke~~ Rey descends into a ~~cave~~ cellar and has a vision of his ~~her~~ father and the Dark Force initiate ~~Darth Vader~~ Kylo Ren.

Ren isn't Rey's father, though, he's her cousin. His mom is princess Leia, and his dad is Han Solo. ~~Darth Vader~~ Kylo Ren meets his ~~son~~ father ~~Luke Skywalker~~ Han Solo on a gangway over an abyss in the ~~Cloud City~~ Star-Killer Base. But Ren doesn't chop off his father's hand, because that would be derivative, and J. J. Abrams is an artist with integrity. Instead, Ren kills his father.

The ~~Rebellion~~ Resistance discovers a weakness in the ~~Death Star~~ Star-Killer Base: the ~~thermal exhaust port~~ thermal something or other. The ~~Rebellion~~ Resistance attacks with its X-wing fighters, led by crack pilot ~~Luke Skywalker~~ Poe Dameron, who hits the target, causing the whole ~~Death Star~~ Star-Killer Base to explode. Luckily, ~~Darth Vader~~ Kylo Ren gets clear of the exploding ~~Death Star~~ Star-Killer Base, so we can expect him to return for at least two more wretched movies, perhaps followed by another wretched trilogy about his childhood.

At the end of the movie, ~~Luke~~ Rey goes off to a remote planet to learn the ways of the Force from the last living Jedi master, ~~Yoda~~ Luke Skywalker.

I knew going in that *The Force Awakens* would be derivative.

The trailers also made it clear that it would be visually striking in places. But I was genuinely surprised by the pedestrian dialogue, flatline drama, and total lack of magic. Even as pure spectacle it is far inferior to the earlier films.

Daisey Ridley was a pretty good choice for Rey, even though I am very tired of "strong woman" leads in action movies. Feminism teaches values that lead young women to be less happy and self-actualized than more traditional women.

John Boyega was a bad choice for Finn. It is not just that I dislike black actors in leading man roles, which give the false impression that blacks are just as capable as whites in positions of authority. It is not just that pairing black males with white females on screen encourages white girls to make bad romantic choices, exposing themselves to dramatically increased risks of rape, battery, murder, STDs, drug abuse, and single motherhood. It is not just that African midi-chorlian counts are two standard deviations lower than whites.

No, I just don't like this fellow's face. He's very African looking: prognathous jaw, big lips and teeth, flat nose with huge nostrils, etc. He sweats a lot, his mouth is always gaping open, and the camera practically dives into his nostrils. Finn is also a liar and a bit of a coward (the Han Solo character of the remake). It is little wonder that after all his efforts to impress and save Rey, he finally ends up in the friend zone. Let's hope he stays there.

Adam Driver plays Kylo Ren, the ludicrous Darth Vader knockoff, complete with black helmet. Ren has zero gravitas. He is as spindly as Barack Obama and tries just as hard. He has tantrums like a teenager. He is supposed to be emotionally conflicted. Or so the script says. But it does not come to life on the screen. His best scene is the final duel in the forest with Rey. But I thought that one needed long training to wield a light saber, and Rey has had none.

Another reason I thought this movie would be bad was the choice to dine out on nostalgia by bringing back cast members from the first three films. Harrison Ford as Han Solo wheezes though the action sequences and delivers his lines with no conviction. Carrie Fisher's performance as Leia is as stiff as her botoxed face. Her vocal chords seem partly paralyzed as well. She should be warm and maternal, but she's so reptilian I expected a forked tongue to flick out between her little croaks of dialogue. There is zero chemistry between Ford and Fisher. Mark Hamill's Luke Skywalker came off best, perhaps in virtue of the fact that he had no lines. Chewbacca, Admiral Ackbar, and the droids are looking good though. They haven't aged a bit.

The low point of the movie was General Hux (played by the blonde-haired, blue-eyed Domhnall Gleeson) giving a Hitleresque speech to a Nuremberg-style rally, to which the Stormtroopers responded with a Roman salute. This stuff makes George Lucas seem subtle. (Lucas, of course, paid homage to *Triumph of the Will* in the finale of the first *Star Wars* movie, and of course Stormtroopers remind us of Stormtroopers, and the Grand Moff reminds me, at least, of the Grand Mufti.)

The best part of *The Force Awakens* is John Williams' music, but I listened closely, and what is great is not new, and what is new is not that great.

Many racially-conscious whites have boycotted *The Force Awakens* because of its politically-correct elements (a feminist heroine, a black hero). But in truth, these are no worse than most movies today, and they certainly do not approach *The Girl with the Dragon Tattoo* levels of evil. This movie is not so much evil as it is cynical, greedy, and incompetent. I found it completely emotionally uninvolving.

I have never been a big *Star Wars* fan, but I collected all the soundtracks, and for some reason *The Empire Strikes Back* has always been a "comfort" film that I pull out about once a year, usually on a miserable rainy day. A few years ago, I received a Blu-ray player for Christmas, and I watched all six Lucas films. I had not seen *Star Wars* (I do not call it *A New Hope*) since childhood, and despite the juvenile elements, there is real magic there. Lucas taps into primal Indo-European pagan themes: a Force that lies beyond the duality of Light and Dark, initiatic orders of warrior ascetics who attain superpowers by tapping into the Force, the cremation of the dead, and so forth.

Comparing *The Force Awakens* to the original has given me a new appreciation of Lucas as a director. Lucas may have been terrible at casting, but he knew how to pace scenes and get dramatically compelling performances from so-so actors, something Abrams fails at repeatedly.

I think the key difference is sincerity. Lucas takes *Star Wars* seriously, whereas Abrams poisons it with Jewish cultural ironism, creating a "product" that rings hollow and plays like a farce. There are times when this movie is two clicks from *Spaceballs*. The Schwartz is definitely with him.

The prequels, moreover, had highly intricate and fascinating plots and created visually dazzling worlds. If anything, *The Force Awakens* will make us appreciate the prequels more. Even *The Phantom Menace* now looks better by comparison. In fact, I was hoping all along it was Jar Jar's snout hiding under Kylo Ren's mask.

Counter-Currents, December 18, 2015

STAR WARS: THE LAST JEDI

The Last Jedi isn't an awful film. Not *Force Awakens* awful. But it is pretty bad. Down there at the bottom of the scrap heap, with *The Force Awakens* and *The Phantom Menace*. The question on my mind was whether *The Force Awakens* was just a *Phantom Menace* moment, a rocky start to a trilogy that redeemed itself with two pretty good films. (Yes, I like *Attack of the Clones* and *Revenge of the Sith*. Fight me.) But no, it was not to be. It was not hard, of course, for *The Last Jedi* to improve upon *The Force Awakens*. But it still isn't a very good film, and no amount of directorial and technological wizardry can redeem this wretched trilogy now.

So is it time for the *Star Wars* franchise to die?

No. Last year's *Rogue One* proved that Disney can turn out a good *Star Wars* film. *Rogue One* took elements from the established *mythos* and populated it with new characters and an original story. There is literally no end to the possibilities of such films, especially if they have good scripts and good directors. I am actually looking forward to next year's Han Solo film, directed by Ron Howard. That, Disney, is the way to go forward. But the scripts have to be original and good, and why not get the best possible directorial talent? Why not get Christopher Nolan to direct a *Star Wars* film? Why not David Lynch, who was actually discussed as director for *Return of the Jedi*? (Imagine what he would have done with Jabba and the Ewoks.)

The problem with the new trilogy is that it is a calculated remake (a "soft reboot") of the original one. Given that there is a whole universe of fan fiction as well as countless authorized *Star Wars* novels to steal from, the cynicism and complete poverty of imagination revealed by the decision to do an ill-concealed, sometimes shot-by-shot, remake is truly breath-taking. I have already detailed how *The Force Awakens* is a shameless remake of *A New Hope* and elements of *The Empire Strikes Back*. Let's look at how *The Last Jedi* rips off *The Empire Strikes Back* and *Return of the Jedi*.

At the end of *Awakens*, the ~~Death Star~~ Star Killer Base has been destroyed. But the ~~Rebellion~~ Resistance is put to flight, and the ~~Imperial~~ First Order fleet commanded by Dark Side adept ~~Darth Vader~~ Kylo Ren is hunting them down.

The pursuit of the ~~Rebels~~ Resistance is intercut with the story of aspiring Jedi ~~Luke Skywalker~~ Rey going to a remote sanctuary to learn the ways of the Force from cantankerous old Jedi Master ~~Yoda~~ Luke Skywalker.

Midway through the film, we are diverted to the ~~cloud city of Bespin~~ casino planet of Canto Bight (an upscale Mos Eisley cantina scene) where the fleeing ~~Rebels~~ Resistance seek the aid of an off-white rogue named ~~Lando Calrissian~~ DJ, who later betrays them to the ~~Empire~~ First Order.

The third act takes place on ~~Emperor Palpatine's~~ Supreme Leader Snoke's command ship, where the ~~Emperor~~ Supreme Leader tortures Jedi adept ~~Luke Skywalker~~ Rey, who watches the destruction of the ~~Rebellion~~ Resistance fleet, until ~~Darth Vader~~ Kylo Ren has a change of heart and kills his master. Then ~~Vader~~ Ren reaches out to ~~Luke~~ Rey with the offer of a lifetime: to join him and help rule the galaxy. ~~Vader~~ Ren even offers ~~Luke~~ Rey information about ~~his~~ her parents. No, ~~Vader~~ Ren is not ~~Luke's~~ Rey's father, because that would be derivative, and Rian Johnson is a director with artistic integrity.

The fourth act of the movie, which feels tacked on, is on an ice planet called ~~Hoth~~ Crait, where the ~~Rebellion~~ Resistance has taken refuge in an underground base protected from space bombardment by a shield, so that it must be taken by ground assault by ~~Imperial~~ First Order Walkers.

Yes, it really is that derivative.

Of course, even with a derivative plot, *The Last Jedi* might still have been redeemed with interesting characters and good dialogue, especially if well-performed and directed. There are some witty exchanges ("Can you put on a cowl, or something?"), some cute details (Luke Skywalker's island is swarming with Pokémons), some neat product tie ins (all I want for Christmas is a crystal fox), etc. Supreme Leader Snoke was astonishingly well realized. Some of the scenes between Kylo and Rey worked quite well, even though they were a pale imitation of the Vader-Skywalker relationship. Kylo and Rey's battle with Snoke's guards was highly entertaining, although why they just didn't shoot them down with blasters is beyond me. Mark Hamill was surprisingly good throughout and, along with Adam Driver (Kylo Ren), really carried the movie, but Yoda's scene stole the show. The music by John Williams is truly magnificent. His score for *The Force Awakens*, although the best part of the movie, had a phoned-in feel. The score for *The Last Jedi* is truly riveting.

But there's just not enough that's good here.

I hated Carrie Fisher's Princess Leia from the first trilogy, where she was a rude, abrasive bitch. Here, she is practically a corpse, with the croaking voice and decrepit movements of a woman of 90. (Fisher died this year at the age of 60, worn out from a lifetime of mental illness and drug abuse.) It is just as well that she spent most of the movie in a drug-induced coma. That, at least, was convincing. I love how she flew through space like a witch, but that was mostly CGI. If they bring her back for the third movie in CGI form, it might actually breathe some life into the role. Obviously, given that Carrie Fisher is dead, the best thing they could have done is killed her off when she was sucked into the void, and then reshot her subsequent scenes without her. Or dropped them altogether. Instead, they weighted the movie down with a ridiculous resurrection scene and passed the buck on explaining her demise to the next director, who has a lot bigger problems to worry about.

Aside from Admiral Akbar, who dies, practically the whole leadership of the Resistance is a collection of cat ladies, including Laura Dern's Admiral Holdo, whose locks are Tumblrite purple and whose idea of communicating authority and inspiring confidence is to wear an evening dress and tiara into battle. It is perhaps unsurprising that Oscar Isaac's Poe Dameron mutinies twice, but the cat ladies think he's just too adorable to dump out an airlock.

The First Order's officers include Domhnall Gleeson's General Hux, who is ludicrous, and Gwendolyn Christie's Captain Phasma, who is useless. Their posh British accents are supposed to symbolize the acme of aristocratic European civilization, which is to be brought low by the Resistance, which consists of a rabble of Americans and non-whites.

The ugly and charmless John Boyega returns as Findu, joined

by an ugly and charmless Vietnamese girl named Rose, to appeal to the vast Asian market. Although he is a sanitation worker and she a humble technician, both of them turn out to be competent speeder pilots in the final battle, because diversity is magic. Just when we think that Findu might sacrifice his life for the common good of the Resistance and the Franchise, Rose deflects him—out of love. We don't win, she says, by killing the people we hate but by saving the people we love. Then she plants a kiss on Findu's huge lips, causing the stomachs of all Asia to flip. Is this an argument against love? Because the other interpretation—that it is okay to endanger everything and everyone one is fighting for on a romantic whim—is surely too disgusting a meme even for Leftists. Finn was just about to save all the people he loves by killing some of the people he hates. But apparently that is too nuanced for Tumblristas. Really, it is just the sort of morally confused rubbish one would expect from an army led by cat ladies.

The whole Canto Bight sequence seemed to have been invented just to give Findu and Rose something to do, but it was ridiculously arbitrary. First, we have to accept that the First Order fleet cannot catch up with the Resistance in conventional space, and the Resistance cannot jump into hyperspace, so the only thing the First Order can do is pursue the Resistance ships until they run out of fuel. This premise gives us enough time for Findu and Rose to race across the galaxy to Canto Bight to find the one guy who can solve their problem, a code breaker named DJ (Benicio del Toro, for added diversity), who can get them on the First Order flagship and enable the Resistance to escape. Basically, another thermal exhaust port.

Beyond that, there is a massive incoherence in the timelines, for Rey's period of training with Luke seems to last much longer than the events taking place with the two fleets in space. But that is a problem with *The Empire Strikes Back* as well, for Luke's time with Yoda seems to have been much longer than the timeline connected with the *Millennium Falcon*.

Yes, they spent 200 million dollars on a movie, and this plot was deemed good enough for the *goyim*.

The opening battle features space bombers which open their

bomb-bay doors and drop bombs into space. Apparently, the designers of these ships never heard of cabin depressurization or gravity. And when the witch Leia opened the door to re-enter the ship, why didn't everyone else get sucked out into space?

Given all the genuinely terrible things in this movie, it strikes me as odd that many viewers had especially negative reactions to Luke Skywalker's dismissive and brusque attitude toward Rey. For instance, quite a few fans were upset that Luke tossed away his lightsaber as soon as Rey presented it to him. But the Jedi are in part modeled after Zen monks, and it is standard Zen practice to test seekers by discouraging them as much as possible. The same can be said of Luke's claim that he simply came to his planet to die. Obviously, that was a lie, since the last movie was all about getting ahold of the map he left so people could find him in case of emergency. The complainers are just snowflakes who would wash out the first day.

Still, there seems to be something more than just a test to Luke's insistence that the Jedi order needs to die—namely, guilt and bitterness over his failure with Kylo Ren. Yes, it seems a little implausible that Luke would wish the destruction of an ancient initiatic order that has upheld goodness across the galaxy for millennia simply because he can't forgive himself for his greatest failure—but then one remembers that millions of whites actively support policies that are leading to the destruction of our race to expiate spurious and unearned guilt for racism, colonialism, and slavery.

Whether Luke was sincere or not about claiming that the Jedi order should end, he ultimately passes his teachings and torch on to Rey, who remains the same absurd "Mary Sue" character from the first film, a girrrl who can effortlessly do anything a man can do only through arduous training and hard work. Luke Skywalker may not be the last Jedi, but if Disney has its way, he will be the last white male one.

Others were outraged at Luke's death. But of course he will just reappear in the next film more powerful than ever, with a glow.

Why is Disney hell-bent on making such a botched and derivative reboot of *Star Wars*?

One possible explanation is a complete lack of any understanding of the essence of what made the original films so appealing, which would necessitate the imitation of all sorts of inessential details, hoping that they might luck out and find the formula.

This would make sense if Disney were run by 70-IQ cargo cultists. But Disney is run by cynical, predatory, but intelligent Jews and their ilk.

Were they just motivated by greed? No, that is not enough. Making new *Star Wars* movies with original plots is not exactly a financially risky proposition.

Which forces us to consider another possibility: Disney chose the "soft reboot" route because they want to make as much money as possible from *Star Wars* nostalgia while simultaneously degrading the originals and packing them full of Left-wing rubbish. This interpretation is supported by two plot details that strike me as calculated swipes at hard-core fans: killing off Snoke without telling us anything about his back story, and revealing that Rey's parents were nobodies. There are countless fan articles and videos spinning out theories about Snoke and Rey. But the truth is that these characters were not to be taken seriously. They are just one-dimensional, disposable ciphers in a giant cash grab based on the calculated exploitation of nostalgia for Lucas's genuinely heroic and inspiring films.

Disney is spitting on the Star Wars mythos and its fans. It is time for the fans to strike back.

Counter-Currents, December 19, 2017

THREE IDENTICAL STRANGERS

Three Identical Strangers is a 2018 documentary directed by Tim Wardle. It premiered at the 2018 Sundance Film Festival, where it won the US Documentary Special Jury Award for Storytelling. You can now watch it online.

The documentary tells the story of Edward Galland, David Kellman, and Robert Shafran, identical triplets who were separated shortly after birth. (There was actually a fourth brother, who died at birth.) Born to an unwed Jewish mother, the brothers were placed by the Louise Wise Adoption Agency—which specialized in Jewish adoptions—into three rather different Jewish homes, the Shafrans, headed by a doctor; the Gallands, headed by a school teacher; and the Kellmans, headed by a shopkeeper, all of whom had different levels of education and income.

The boys were reunited by accident when they were 19 and became a media sensation. The story of their reunion is quite touching. The boys had never experienced blood kin before. And beyond that, they were genetically identical, so they were not just meeting their brothers, they were meeting other selves. Naturally, they shared a lot in common: their expressions, their gestures, their reactions to the same events. They knew their brothers' thoughts and could complete their sentences. They all wrestled in high school. They had same tastes—in colors, cigarettes, drugs, alcohol, and women.

To make up for lost time, the triplets got an apartment together in New York City. (One image shows them sleeping in the same huge bed.) Later, they opened a very successful restaurant called Triplets.

This segment of the movie is quite entertaining and heartwarming, and it is an excellent way to introduce normies to biological determinism and Genetic Similarity Theory.

If one wants to study the role of heredity versus environment—nature vs. nurture—in the formation of personality and shaping the course of human lives, one naturally looks for identical siblings (who share the exact same genes) who are separated at birth and raised in very different environments. If the children's personalities and lives more closely resemble those of their adoptive parents and siblings, then we can conclude that nurture is more powerful than nature. If, however, identical siblings raised apart more closely resemble one another (and their birth parents) than they do their adoptive parents and siblings, then we can conclude that heredity is stronger than environment. Note: this conclusion follows irrespective of the particular *theory* of heredity that you hold.

Of course this particular story is not the only case of identical siblings raised apart. There is now a quite vast literature on the subject. The best summary of these studies is Nancy Segal's *Born Together—Reared Apart: The Landmark Minnesota Twin Study* (2012). I also recommend her highly entertaining popular books, *Entwined Lives: Twins and What They Tell Us About Human Behavior* (2013) and *Indivisible by Two: Lives of Extraordinary Twins* (2007). These studies provide crushingly persuasive evidence of fine-grained hereditary determinism, which refutes the "blank slate" theory of environmental determinism.

Blank slatism, of course, is the foundation of a host of modern political ideologies and social engineering projects. If people basically have the same potential, then different group outcomes—for instance, low black IQ and high black crime—must be due to inherently discriminatory social environments, which can be identified by social science and corrected by social engineering, so outcomes will be equalized. The failure of generations of egalitarian uplift programs is simply attributed to increasingly occult forms of social discrimination.

But if heredity is more important than environment in determining factors like intelligence and criminality, then modern egalitarianism is a fool's errand. Multiracial societies will inevitably be unequal societies, with all the disharmonies inequality entails.

Identical siblings not only destroy the foundations of modern multiracial egalitarian social engineering, they also point to a better alternative. For if the most egalitarian and harmonious human relationships are between identical siblings, this means that the foundation of social equality and harmony is genetic similarity. This is the genetic foundation of ethnonationalism.[1]

After about 30 minutes covering the triplets' reunion, the media sensation, and their early life together, the documentary takes a dark turn, or actually two of them. The themes are entwined in the film, but it is best to review them separately.

Naturally, the triplets shared negative traits as well as positive ones. They all suffered from depression; at least two of them spent time in mental hospitals; and one of them, Eddie Galland, killed himself in 1995. All three boys had different experiences growing up in households with different sets of adopted parents and siblings. But apparently Eddie had been the most alienated.

The other dark theme is far more pronounced. Naturally, the adoptive parents wondered why the triplets were separated, so they went as a group to the Louise Wise Agency and were told by its directors that the boys were separated because it was hard to place a set of triplets. It seemed plausible enough.

But when Dr. Shafran returned to retrieve his umbrella, he saw the board uncorking a bottle of champagne and toasting, as if they had just dodged a bullet. The whole "Gentlemen, here's to evil" quality of the toast led the families to conclude that the agency was hiding something. So they contacted lawyers with the intent of getting to the truth.

But after initial interest, various New York law firms declined to represent them, citing conflicts of interest. It was claimed that associates at the firms were seeking to adopt children from the Louise Wise Agency. It seems plausible, given that we are talking about law firms in New York City. But it was not unreasonable to suspect that very powerful people might be engaged in a coverup. Eventually the families dropped the issue.

---

[1] On the connection between Genetic Similarity Theory and ethnonationalism, see J. Philippe Rushton, "Ethnic Nationalism, Evolutionary Psychology, and Genetic Similarity Theory," *Nations and Nationalism* 11 (2005): 489–507 and Frank Salter, *On Genetic Interests: Family, Ethnicity, & Humanity in an Age of Mass Migration* (New Brunswick, N.J.: Transaction Publishers, 2006).

Then investigative reporter Lawrence Wright discovered that primarily in the 1960s, the Louise Wise Agency, working in tandem with the Jewish Board of Family and Children's Services, had been engaged in a study of identical siblings, who were adopted into different home environments, then carefully observed over the years as they matured. The parents of the cildren agreed to this. They were told that it was a policy of the agency to study the development of the children, but they were not told that they had identical siblings. All told, five sets of identical twins in addition to the triplets were part of the study.

The study was overseen by two psychiatrists, Viola W. Bernard and Peter B. Neubauer. Neubauer seemed to be the principal psychiatrist. Only he is discussed in the documentary. Neubauer was an Austrian Jew who fled from the Nazis. Neubauer studied medicine in Vienna and Bern, emigrated to the US in 1941, and worked as a child psychiatrist. He was a Freudian and worked closely with Freud's daughter Anna.

Judging from the documentary, everyone involved in the study was Jewish: Neubauer and his staff, the agencies that made it possible, the adopted children, and the adoptive families. Nevertheless, the experiment was likened to something done by the Nazis. Apparently, we are supposed to think that Dr. Neubauer was the Jewish Dr. Mengele, who also took an interest in identical siblings.

The children and their parents were of course scandalized. But it is really not clear if anything unethical took place. First of all, a crucial piece of information is lacking: was the policy of separating identical siblings and not telling the adoptive parents *dictated by the study*? Or did the policy already exist—because it really was difficult to place sets of twins and triplets—so that all Neubauer did was to collect data that would otherwise have gone unknown?

The latter seems far more likely, given that "separated at birth" stories are widespread, but the Neubauer study was apparently unique. I would, of course, argue that we should prefer not to separate identical siblings. Most people probably feel the same way. But that preference may have to be sacrificed to the higher necessity of finding adoptive parents for such children. Given that separation was an accepted practice at the time—and may have been necessary—was there anything unethical about collecting potentially valuable scientific data?

The strangest thing about the Neubauer study is that the findings were never published. Neubauer did publish a book, *Nature's Thumbprint: The New Genetics of Personality* (Reading, Mass.: Addison Wesley, 1990), co-authored with Alexander Neubauer, which surely drew on his studies. But Neubauer's research papers were presented to Yale University and placed under seal until 2065.

These papers surely do not record Mengele-like enormities. So why put them under lock and key? One of Neubauer's assistants speculates that maybe people aren't ready to learn just how much of their lives and choices are controlled by heredity. This seems quite reasonable, but the massive literature on other identical siblings "separated at birth" already establishes that point quite well. (The assistant, by the way, is a colossal liberal. She herself is probably not ready to grapple with the political implications of refuting blank slatism, given that the blank slate ideology is the foundation of the modern Left.)

Neubauer's sample size was not large, but as far as I know, nobody else followed the development of identical siblings in different environments from birth. Interestingly enough, Neubauer had his subjects filmed, and one of the reasons this documentary is so striking is simply *seeing* the triplets on film. So perhaps his studies reveal something profoundly disconcerting, something worth covering up.

Neubauer came from the Freudian school, and Freudian psychology has little place for heredity. But this would not really explain why Neubauer would cover up his findings, because if he were an orthodox Freudian, he never would have embarked upon the studies in the first place.

A similar coverup takes place at the end of *Three Identical Strangers*. For despite the massive evidence of hereditary determinism presented by the triplets, they and members of their own family are not comfortable with the idea that nature is so powerful. One family member claims that she thinks that nurture is powerful enough to overcome anything. They believe this, of course, because they want to believe that Eddie could have been saved from suicide.

Of course, different contingencies made a mark on the three boys. They grew up in different families. They married different women. One had appendicitis. One killed himself. But in a very real sense, they were the *same* person living three different lives, which diverged in countless ways. But if they had switched places, they probably would have reacted in pretty much the same ways to the contingencies that separated them. Today, one of the brothers is heavier than the other. They wear their thinning hair differently. But because they so bitterly regret Eddie's suicide, they cling to the faith that if he had just been *nurtured a bit differently*, he would still be alive. They seem blame his death on his father, who was known as a disciplinarian. It strikes me as grotesque, but they might even be right. If Eddie were alive, chances are he'd think the very same thing.

I highly recommend *Three Identical Strangers*. It is an ideal way to introduce people to hereditary determinism and Genetic Similarity Theory—as well as the motives that make people shy away from their ultimate political implications.

The Unz Review, January 23, 2019

TO LIVE & DIE IN L.A.

James O'Meara's article on "Essential Films . . . & Others"[1] was inspired by my "Ten Favorite Films,"[2] but it inspired me in turn to reflect on my own list of *essential* films, essential defined by Coleridge as "that to which with the greatest pleasure the reader returns." For many of my favorite films are not works to which I return with pleasure. *Vertigo* and *Blue Velvet*, for instance, are too emotionally harrowing to just pop in on a rainy afternoon. So this spurred me to reflect on the movies I watch, again and again, simply for pleasure: if I am under the weather, too tired to work, or just want to savor my solitude.

It is a very different list, heavy on sci-fi, spectacle, spycraft, and silliness: *The Empire Strikes Back, The Two Towers, The Fifth Element, Flash Gordon, Hudson Hawk, Goldfinger, Octopussy, Bram Stoker's Dracula, Blade Runner,* and *To Live and Die in L.A.*

To Live and Die in L.A. is my equivalent to James' *Manhunter*, an '80s time-capsule with a captivating visual style, excellent period music (Wang Chung), and real—though often overlooked—substance. I became an adult in the 1980s, so it is natural for me to feel a certain amount of nostalgia for the music, movies, styles, and politics of the era. I know Reagan was not really a good President, but he would have made a great king: the embodiment of everything wholesome in American culture. Even with all I know, the sound of his voice in the film still comforts me, and it has nothing to do with the paroxysms he induces in the Left (although those are fun too).

To *Live and Die in L.A.* was released in 1985. It stars William Petersen and Willem Dafoe as well as Dean Stockwell and John Turturro. It is the only movie that I actually like by Jewish director William Friedkin (*The Exorcist, The French Connection*). The movie is filled with striking images—Willem Dafoe burning a painting, the shadows of palm trees on a plaza in late af-

---

[1] James J. O'Meara, "Essential Films . . . & Others," *Counter-Currents*, February 13, 2015.

[2] In *Son of Trevor Lynch's White Nationalist Guide to the Movies*.

ternoon, a money-printing montage, a presidential motorcade, all captured in a fluid, dynamic visual style. Although at the time, some critics compared the aesthetic to *Miami Vice*, in truth the movie focuses on the least glamorous parts of Los Angeles: docks, rail yards, freeways, refineries, junk yards, the "river," dive bars, etc., but manages to aestheticize them with bravura directing and camera work.

The core of the film is a character study in corruption. The main antagonists are a Secret Service agent named Richie Chance (Petersen) and a counterfeiter named Rick Masters (Dafoe). Although they are on opposite sides of the law, they have a lot in common: They are cold-blooded and have nerves of steel. Men like this actually have low resting pulse rates. This makes them cool in tense situations, but it also leads them to *seek out* tense situations to stimulate themselves, lest they sink into the torpor of inaction. They are restless, always getting into things. They are prone to take risks, cut corners, and cross lines. If they lack conscience, they can easily become criminals — or they become cops or soldiers and *then* commit crimes.

The cold-bloodedness of Chance and Masters is highlighted by their associates, who lack nerve. A couple of them even possesses a bit of conscience. Masters' contrast is his "mule" Cody played by John Turturro, a twitchy fellow who suffers from an ulcer and whose bravado comes off as brittle and false. When Cody is arrested, Masters realizes that he lacks the strength to do jail time. He will turn against him. Thus he has to be killed.

We first meet Chance in the pre-credit sequence, when he coolly deals with a suicide bomber who is trying to kill President Reagan. I first saw *To Live and Die in L.A.* at a midnight movie in a college town, early in 1986, shortly after the terrorist attacks at the Rome and Vienna airports. When the terrorist, who vows to "bomb myself on you and all the enemies of Islam," is foiled and explodes as he falls from a building, the audience burst into applause. Chance's partner, Jimmy Hart, who is a few days from retirement, is far more shaken up than Chance. "I'm too old for this, Richie," he pants. The next time we see Richie, he is base jumping from a bridge.

Chance's other contrasts are his informant Ruth and his new partner John Vukovich. Ruth is tormented by anxiety and conscience. She fears the criminals she informs on and thinks the stars are "God's eyes" watching her (a notion that Chance, who lacks conscience, casually dismisses). In one scene, where Chance is high on adrenaline and Ruth is melting down from anxiety, she shrieks "What's the matter with you?" (It's that low resting pulse.) Like Ruth, Vukovich lacks nerve and has a conscience, but in the course of the movie, Chance corrupts him, until he is framing suspects and stealing to catch Masters. In the end, Vukovich even dresses like Chance. But he will never *be* a Chance, because both danger and morality stir him too deeply. To Chance, that just makes him a "pussy."

When I first saw this film, Chance and Masters seemed very grown up and manly. (Both Dafoe and Petersen were about 30 at the time.) Both characters are capable of violence and daring, but in retrospect, they seem more like lost boys than grown men. The only really mature, centered, manly character is the older agent, Jimmy Hart.

Interestingly, Chance's manner around Hart is boyish, submissive, and slightly effeminate. Petersen has a well-developed, masculine body, but his combination of tight faded jeans plus dark shirts and jackets accentuates his hips, giving him a womanish aspect. His curly hair is tinged with gray, but his face is unlined and heart-shaped, which adds to the unsettling aspect of androgyny and eternal boyhood.

Dafoe's Masters is more manly than Chance because he is more ruthless, more in control, more of a mastermind. (The names Chance and Masters are not exactly subtle.) Perhaps to set Masters' ruthlessness in relief, he is portrayed as an artist, with well-developed tastes and a somewhat fruity wardrobe. He has a hot girlfriend, a modern dancer who is much taller than him. But Friedkin has Masters whine womanishly about working with rubber gloves on and even treats us to a fake "gay kiss." (Masters actually begins kissing a male body double, then Friedkin cuts to him kissing his girlfriend.) Thus Masters is a strange combination of decadent aesthete and ruthless criminal, the Gabriele D'Annunzio of crime.

I enjoy *To Live and Die in L.A.* I return to it again and again. I highly recommend it. But I would never be comfortable calling it a great film. Yet it is highly entertaining, with images and characters and music that will stay with you. The main cast is white. Blacks are portrayed as no-account criminals and braggarts. The there is no offensive anti-white propaganda. Even the fact that everyone smokes (filthy habit) gives the movie a pre-PC feel. Every time I watch it, the present day seems more "dated," and the '80s look better and better.

Counter-Currents, March 2, 2015

Unbreakable

Unbreakable (2000) is many people's least favorite M. Night Shyamalan film, but I think it is his best: brilliantly conceived and scripted, beautifully acted and filmed, and quite moving. Since the film is almost two decades old, I trust nobody will complain about spoilers.

Unbreakable is a superhero film, but it does not contain any computer animation, strobe-fast editing, or deafening crashes and booms. Instead, *Unbreakable* has the pacing and style of an art film. It is highly realistic, but in a glossy rather than gritty fashion. Shyamalan's camera imbues mundane objects and scenes with a luster that blunts any desire to look beyond their surfaces. His goal—which is communicated even in his use of low camera angles—is to conjure up a world in which the fantastic and heroic exist only in the imagination.

As Elijah Price—Samuel L. Jackson in one of his most emotionally powerful roles—says, this is "a mediocre time." "People are starting to lose hope. It's hard for many to believe that extraordinary things live inside themselves as well as others." The "surprise ending" of the film is the discovery that extraordinary possibilities really do exist in the comfortably superficial world Shyamalan's camera has created.

Unbreakable may be a superhero film, but the key to its emotional power is that it is an allegory about the fate of everyman—literally every man, and manliness itself—in an overly feminized and bourgeois society that prizes the long and inglorious life over the riskier, more glorious path.

The hero of *Unbreakable* is David Dunn, played by Bruce Willis. Dunn is a bald, middle-aged, unassuming everyman. He works as a security guard, while his wife Audrey (Robin Gayle Wright) is a physical therapist. The Dunns have one child, their eleven-year-old son Joseph. Of course, "Dunn" has the connotation of dull, and Audrey's maiden name "Inverso" is an omen of their relationship, since she is the dominant partner in the marriage. She has a profession, whereas David is blue-collar. David also defers to Audrey in all matters connected with their son, including discipline. Joseph wants to look up to his father and spend time with him doing man things, like playing football and working out, but Audrey thinks they are unsafe. Unsurprisingly, the Dunns are both unhappy in their marriage. They sleep in separate beds while they plan their separation and divorce.

Every morning, David Dunn awakens to a feeling of sadness. Later we learn why. In college, David Dunn was not a soft-spoken schlub. He was the star quarterback on his football team, winning games and adulation, perhaps in the very stadium where he is now merely a security guard. David and Audrey were dating in college, and they were in a terrible car accident. David quit playing football after the accident, claiming injury. But it turns out that was just an excuse. Although David had been thrown clear of the car, he was not injured at all, and he had the strength to save Audrey from the burning wreckage.

The real reason David quit playing was Audrey's moral opposition to football. As an aspiring physical therapist, her purpose was to fix broken bodies, whereas football broke bodies in the pursuit of glory. Thus Audrey domesticated David, getting him to quit football. They both thought it would make them happy, but it didn't. Domesticity is emasculating. Men can't be happy without taking risks, and women aren't really attracted to emasculated men. Modern bourgeois society programs couples to make marriages equal and risk free, even though that is not really what people want, and getting it doesn't satisfy them.

At the beginning of the movie, David is returning home to Philadelphia from a job interview in New York. His train derails and is struck by a freight train. Everyone is killed except for David, who is not even scratched. After a memorial service for the victims, David finds a note on his windshield asking him if he has ever been ill. The card reads Limited Edition, the name of a comic book art gallery owned by Elijah Price.

Elijah is the only child of an unwed black mother in a Philadelphia slum. He was born with a rare genetic disease, osteogenesis imperfecta, which makes his bones highly brittle. Because of this he spent most of his life indoors, avoiding injury, when not actually in hospital beds. Elijah is highly "breakable." The children in his neighborhood mocked him as "Mr. Glass."

Elijah spent a great deal of his life reading comic books, and when he grew up, he turned his expertise into a business. Elijah is convinced that comics communicate truth in symbolic form. Specifically, he thinks that superheroes and supervillains may actually be real. Thus when he heard that David had survived the train crash "miraculously unharmed," he reached out to him, thinking that he might be an extraordinary person, chosen for a special destiny.

Elijah's quest is sustained by a metaphysical conviction: "If there is someone like me in the world, and I'm at one end of the spectrum . . . Couldn't there be someone the opposite of me, at the other end?" Elijah is quite certain this is the case. This conviction is known as the "principle of plenitude," which holds that all possibilities are actual, or will be actualized in the fullness of time. If Elijah is Mr. Glass, Mr. Breakable, doesn't that mean there is a Mr. Unbreakable somewhere in the universe? If such a person exists, then Elijah wants to find him. If he does not know his own powers, Elijah wants to help him discover them.

Elijah has at least two motives for his search. First, he thinks the world is in need of heroes to free it from flatness and mediocrity and give it meaning. Second, Elijah believes that discovering his counterpart would give his own life meaning. It would allow him to make something good of his suffering and alienation.

This brings us to a second classical philosophical principle: the actualization of potentiality. For humans, becoming who we really are is the path to well-being or happiness. Each human being has an ideal self, which needs to be actualized. If we actualize ourselves, we feel happy. If we fail to actualize ourselves, we suffer. But whether we flourish or fail, we are the same persons in either case.

David Dunn is unhappy, because he has failed to actualize himself. He fails because he does not know himself, and he does not know himself because his wife convinced him not to test his limits. *Unbreakable* is a moving film, because self-discovery and self-actualization are necessary for the well-being of every one of us. David, urged on by Elijah and his son Joseph, discovers that he has extraordinary powers: He can intuit crimes by touching people. He is enormously strong. And he is almost invulnerable. Water is his only weakness. It is his kryptonite.

As David begins to understand and actualize his powers, he shakes off the sadness that has haunted his life and ruined his family. He bonds with his son but also feels comfortable disciplining him authoritatively. After his first major rescue, when he saves two children from a home invader who has killed their parents, he carries his wife upstairs to his bed. It is a primal, paleo-masculine gesture, and Audrey loves it. The next morning, the family is united around the breakfast table, and Audrey is cooking for them.

Unbreakable does not merely celebrate paleomasculinity but also specifically *white* athleticism—contrasted with black fragility. In one scene, we are introduced to a Temple University cornerback who is mentioned early on as being destined to go professional. Every other director would cast a black. But instead, Shyamalan casts a magnificent blond, idolized by white schoolboys who leap up to hang off his flexed biceps. Shyamalan handles it without a touch of irony.

David goes to visit Elijah and tells him what has happened. Elijah asks him if the sadness is still there, and David answers "No." Then Elijah says, "I think this is where we shake hands." When David takes Elijah's hand, he intuits what Elijah has done. Elijah has caused an airplane to crash, burned down a hotel, and derailed David's train, killing hundreds of people in the process—all in search of a man who could survive miraculously unharmed. Elijah always wondered why he suffered. What his place and purpose were in this world. Finding David gave him an answer. It gives new depth to one of the Joker's lines to Batman in *The Dark Knight*: "You complete me." It is terrifying but logical. Surprising but necessary. For if David is Elijah's opposite, that makes Elijah a supervillain. If Elijah's body was so breakable, then of course his mind and character were breakable as well.

But the kids knew it all along. They called him Mr. Glass.

It is an unforgettable scene, brilliantly played by Jackson, whose powerfully expressive voice makes him compelling despite his grotesque appearance and evil deeds. David Dunn walks out of the store, and a caption informs us that he led police to evidence of three acts of terrorism, for which Elijah Price was confined to an institution for the criminally insane.

I loved this ending. You realize with a start that you have just been drawn into a classic "origin story." But because of Shyamalan's art-film style, it sneaks up on you. Once you get to the end, of course, you realize there were signs all around you. For instance, Elijah dresses in a quasi-Empire style, carries a cane made of glass, drives a vintage car whose interior is padded with black foam eggs, and runs a high-end art gallery. Aside from black, his colors are purples and dark blues. In his wheelchair, he looks like a cross between Stephen Hawking and Prince. But I never thought Elijah was actually a comic book supervillain. I just thought that he had spent a bit too much time reading about them. James Newton Howard's understated Holst-like score also intimates genuine heroism and magic without going full *Star Wars*.

The end of *Unbreakable* of course sets you up for a sequel. You want a sequel, because Elijah Price is a psychologically interesting villain. He is obviously not maliciously or sadistically evil. He does not kill because he thinks it is bad. He kills because he believes it is good, that it is necessary to find his counterpart. And once he finds him, helps him discover who he is, and sets him on the path to heroism, he feels it is time to confess his crimes. For the sole purpose of Elijah's supervillainy is to be the midwife to the birth of a superhero, a hero who will eventually save far more people than were sacrificed to bring about his birth.

One wonders what would happen to such a generous but twisted soul if left to stew long enough in the inevitable bitterness of being confined to the equivalent of Arkham Asylum while David Dunn is out saving people.

But I was certain that *Unbreakable* was just a one-off stunt, and even if Shymalan had considered a sequel, he would have been deterred by the film's generally unfavorable reception. Much to my delight, however, as I searched for an online version of the *Unbreakable* script, I learned that in 2019, Shyamalan, Willis, and Jackson will return to the big screen with *Glass*.

Counter-Currents, May 14, 2018

VALERIAN & THE CITY OF A THOUSAND PLANETS

Valerian? Isn't that a root one chews to fall asleep?

I saw Luc Besson's *The Fifth Element* near the end of its run in the theaters, and it was love at first frame. I loved its Manichean/ancient astronauts plot, unique and dazzling visual style (imagine the Coen brothers remaking *Barbarella*), the madcap action, blond Bruce Willis, Gary Oldman's Zorg (an evil Ross Perot with slightly displaced Hitler hair and Fu Manchu's wardrobe), Milla Jovovich's Leeloo ("perfect"), the blue diva, and of course THE SCREEEEEEEEAM.

Ever since, *The Fifth Element* in its screen, VHS, DVD, and Blu-ray incarnations has been on my short list of "comfort films": movies that I watch at least once a year when I am home alone for a holiday or feeling out of sorts.

I never got into Besson's other films, and for 20 years now, I have been wishing that he would do another film like *The Fifth Element*. What I got was *Valerian and the City of a Thousand Planets*. Careful what you wish for.

I really wanted to like this movie and saw the first non-3D screening in my neighborhood. *Valerian* has the imaginative visual style and thrilling action of *The Fifth Element*, but the plot is unoriginal, politically correct, and often quite boring: basically a mashup of *Zootopia* and *Avatar*.

Zootopia is the ludicrous "city of a thousand planets," a vast space station that looks like a garbage dump on the outside and is basically one large *Star Wars* cantina on the inside, i.e., a terrifying mass of seething diversity and vibrancy and decadence—replete with filth, corruption, slavery, and cannibalism.

The other setting is basically *Avatar*'s Pandora, populated by opalescent androgynous primitives who—they tell us twice in the same dialogue bubble—lived in "harmony" with nature until evil colonialist types came along and spoiled things. There's also a dash of holocaust sanctimony (six million dead, a diaspora of miraculous survivors, etc.) to trigger the tear ducts of the college educated and signal that the movie is now *serious* for a sec.

If there's a message to this movie, it is that the denizens of the *Star Wars* cantina need to feel guilty of colonialism and genocide and perhaps atone with some more diversity. That, and that one should not trust authority or keep oaths, but one should trust one's girlfriend, and don't even think of breaking promises to her.

The lead roles of Valerian and Laureline are absurdly miscast. Dane DeHaan is the most uncharismatic leading man in movie history. Action heroes should look like Ryan Gosling, Chris Evans, or Ryan Reynolds, not a prepubescent Leonardo DiCaprio with bags under his eyes. Cara Delevingne is beautiful, but as an actress . . . well, she makes Milla Jovovich and even Natalie Portman look like RADA graduates. Their love affair would have been appealingly wholesome if there were any chemistry between them at all.

I will say nothing of the plot, save that involves good guys and bad guys, both of which are trying to find something *really important*. There's also a boy and a girl who have a somewhat stormy mutual attraction. There are lots of chases and fights, then a pretty happy ending with a pop song over the closing credits.

My favorite bits were the trio of fast-talking Jew birds and the scene with the new blue diva, this one a dancer.

Valerian is a huge disappointment, but I will probably watch it again, and with any luck it will someday settle into the so-bad-it's-good category, along with *Barbarella* and *Flash Gordon*. It might even make back its 209-million-dollar budget with midnight movie showings, sometime well into the 23rd century.

Counter-Currents, July 22, 2017

WATCHMEN

Watchmen is one of the most thoroughly Right-wing, even fascistic works of recent popular culture, despite the right-thinking Leftism of the creators of the original graphic novel, Alan Moore, who wrote the story, and Dave Gibbons, who illustrated it—and of Zack Snyder, who directed the movie adaptation, which to my mind is the greatest superhero movie of all time, a movie that not only does justice to the original novel but actually improves upon it in fundamental ways.

Watchmen was not a Leftist parody of the Right that went off mark. Moore is too good a writer to fail in a big way. When Moore engages in parody, such as his sendup of far-Right Cold War journalism in *The New Frontiersman*, he hits the mark nicely.

Snyder also introduces elements of satire into the movie's treatment of Richard Nixon. In the graphic novel, Nixon is portrayed as a lonely, dignified, and thoughtful figure who rejects rash decisions. (This is quite telling in itself.) The movie takes us into *Dr. Strangelove* territory, but it gives Nixon some great lines—contemplating the nuclear destruction of the Eastern Seaboard: "The last gasp of the Harvard establishment. Let's see them debate their way out of nuclear fission"—that we find ourselves laughing with him, not at him. But Snyder's treatment of the main characters follows Moore in being serious, not satirical.

Thus the Right-wing flavor of *Watchmen* is a product of design, not accident. At heart, it is a gallery, not of Right-wing caricatures, but of complex and compelling characters with a range of far-Right outlooks. These characters are placed in an extraordinary plot driven by fundamental moral and political, and even metaphysical and religious, conflicts. With its archetypal characters and high-stakes plot, *Watchmen* is a 19th-century Romantic novel disguised as a comic book.

THE SETTING & BACK STORY

The main events of *Watchmen* take place in October and November 1985. They are set primarily in New York City, in Antarctica, and on Mars, within an alternative history in which

Richard Nixon has been President since 1968 and superheroes, called "Watchmen," actually exist.

There are two generations of Watchmen.

The First Generation

The Watchmen began in 1938 as eight individual costumed crime-fighters, six men and two women. In 1939, they teamed up and were referred to collectively as "Minutemen," after the rapid-response partisan militia of the American Revolutionary War. These superheroes were physically fit and public-spirited but otherwise ordinary individuals who donned masks and costumes to fight crime.

Five of them play little or no part in the graphic novel and movie: Silhouette (a lesbian who was murdered with her lover), Captain Metropolis (Nelson Gardner), Hooded Justice (missing in 1955, presumed dead), Dollar Bill (killed by bank robbers when his cape got caught in a revolving door), and Mothman (confined to a mental hospital). (Zack Snyder, who is a brilliant silent movie director, shows these stories under the opening credits of the film.)

Three first-generation Watchmen play important roles in the graphic novel/movie: Nite Owl (Hollis Mason), Silk Spectre (Sally Jupiter), and The Comedian (Edward Blake), all of them in their late 60s at the time.

The Minutemen rapidly fell apart. The Comedian was expelled in 1940 for trying to rape Silk Spectre. He went on to fight in the Second World War and after the war became a government "black ops" specialist who, among other things, assassinated John F. Kennedy from the grassy knoll near Dealey Plaza. Silhouette was murdered in 1946; Dollar Bill was gunned down around the same time; then, in 1947, Silk Spectre quit to have a family. In 1949, the Minutemen officially disbanded as a group, although some members continued to fight crime on their own.

The Second Generation

Despite their failure, the Minutemen did inspire a second generation of Watchmen, which formed in the late 1960s under the name Crimebusters. In the novel, they are called together by

Captain Metropolis (Nelson Gardner), thus establishing a link with the first generation. (Gardner was to die in a car accident in 1974.) In the movie, they are convened by Ozymandias (Adrian Veidt). The Comedian also returned to costumed crime-fighting. Silk Spectre's daughter Laurie took over her mother's identity. Dan Driberg replaced Hollis Mason as Nite Owl. And three new personas emerged: Ozymandias, Rorschach (Walter Kovacs), and Dr. Manhattan (Dr. Jon Osterman).

The second generation of Watchmen includes some genuine superheroes. Although the Comedian, Rorschach, and Silk Spectre are all-too-human vigilantes dependent on will and athleticism, Ozymandias and Nite Owl have to some extent transcended human limitations, Veidt through physical and mental exercises which made him the smartest man alive and fast enough to catch a bullet, and Dreiberg primarily through technology which he could afford to develop because of the money left to him by his father, a wealthy banker. (Nite Owl, therefore, resembles Batman in more than just the costume.)

Dr. Manhattan, however, is a true superman. He is virtually indestructible and can see the future, mold matter with the power of thought, and transport himself and anything else instantaneously over great distances.

The second generation of Watchmen operated for about a decade, and they were more than just crime-fighters. The Comedian walked out of the initial meeting because he saw little point in fighting crime in a world menaced by nuclear war. But he involved himself anyway, because his objections were taken seriously by both Dr. Manhattan and Ozymandias. Instead of being mere vigilantes trying to save New York, they began to think geopolitically about saving the whole world. The high point of their operations came when Dr. Manhattan intervened to win the Vietnam War for the United States. (The Comedian came along for laughs.)

But only a few years later, in 1977, public opinion had sufficiently turned against the Watchmen that the US Congress passed the Keene Act banning costumed vigilantes, and Nixon signed it.

In the eight years from the Keene Act to the opening of the

story in 1985, Adrian Veidt (whose true identity was already known before the Keene Act) focused on building up a multi-billion-dollar business empire. Dr. Manhattan and the Comedian returned to doing secret work for the government, the former in research and development, the latter in black ops, knocking over Marxist republics in Latin America. (Nixon also has the Comedian keep tabs on the former Watchmen.) Laurie Jupiter went on the government payroll as Manhattan's lover. Dan Dreiberg went into retirement, never revealing his true identity. Rorschach, however, remained active, but entirely outside the law.

THE PLOT

My primary focus is on the cast of *Watchmen* as a gallery of Right-wing archetypes. But before I deal with the characters in greater depth, I must sketch out the plot.

Both the novel and the movie open with the murder of Edward Blake by an unknown assailant. Rorschach investigates and discovers that Blake was the Comedian. Rorschach then breaks the news to the other members of his fraternity—first Dreiberg, then Veidt, then Jupiter and Manhattan—warning them, also, that they might be targets. (In the movie, Dreiberg warns Veidt.)

When Rorschach observes the former supervillain Moloch paying his respects at the grave of the Comedian, he tails him to his apartment and forces him to talk. Moloch reveals that he has terminal cancer. He also reveals that Blake broke into Moloch's apartment, drunk and weeping, and told Moloch that he had discovered a terrible conspiracy involving Dr. Manhattan, his ex-girlfriend Janey Slater, and Moloch himself. But Blake never mentioned the details or who was behind the conspiracy. A week later, he was dead, apparently silenced by the conspirators before he could talk.

Meanwhile, Dr. Manhattan's relationship with Laurie is fraying as he becomes increasingly detached from the human condition. Laurie walks out and goes to Dan Dreiberg, Nite Owl II, for company. Reminiscing about their crime-fighting days, they walk through a dangerous area looking for trouble and end up in a fight with members of a gang, the Knot Tops, whom they trounce.

That same evening, Dr. Manhattan goes on *Nightline* and is accused on live television of giving cancer to Janey Slater, his friend Wally Weaver, and other associates. Enraged, Manhattan teleports himself to Mars. The Soviets take advantage of the absence of America's ultimate deterrent to launch an invasion of Afghanistan, setting the United States and the USSR on the path to nuclear war.

Rorschach's theory that someone is targeting the Watchmen receives further confirmation when a gunman tries to kill Adrian Veidt. The gunman, however, swallowed a cyanide capsule before he could be compelled to reveal who was pulling his strings. Then Moloch was murdered. Rorschach was framed for the crime and arrested, but he is rescued in the middle of a prison riot by Nite Owl II and Silk Spectre II, who have grown closer, begun a sexual relationship, and returned to crime-fighting.

After the prison break, Manhattan teleports Laurie to Mars, where she tries to persuade him to return to Earth to prevent an imminent nuclear war. Meanwhile, Nite Owl and Rorschach investigate Roy Chess, the gunman who attempted to kill Veidt. They eventually discover that Chess, Moloch, and Janey Slater all worked for Pyramid Transnational, and that Pyramid was secretly owned by Adrian Veidt himself. They also discover a psychological profile on Manhattan that makes clear that Veidt was behind an elaborate plot to drive Dr. Manhattan to sever his ties with humanity, the success of which had brought the world to the brink of nuclear annihilation. They immediately depart for Veidt's Antarctic research center (a kind of Fortress of Solitude) to get some answers.

Veidt reveals that he has engineered Manhattan's exile not to start a nuclear war but because Manhattan is the only person who could foil Veidt's plans to *stop* it. At this point, the plots of the graphic novel and the movie diverge significantly. In the graphic novel, Veidt destroys New York City by faking an attack by a huge squid-like monster of apparent extraterrestrial origin. In the movie, he destroys a number of cities with explosions that bear the energy signature of Dr. Manhattan. In both cases, the result is that the United States and the Soviet Union call off their war and unite to face a greater threat: extraterrestrial invasion in one case, Dr. Manhattan in the other. In both the novel and the movie, Manhattan and Laurie return to Earth too late for him to do anything to stop it.

As a Lovecraftian, I am, of course, a sucker for tentacles. But I have to admit that the climax of the movie is far more elegant.

First, it provides a more plausible motive for driving Dr. Manhattan off the planet. Veidt had already successfully prevented Manhattan from seeing through his plot by creating tachyons, which obscured his vision of the future. Thus Veidt had no need to send Manhattan to Mars—as if such a piddling distance would matter to Manhattan anyway.

Second, the movie's climax heightens Manhattan's heroism. In the novel, Manhattan, Dreiberg, and Laurie agree not to reveal what Veidt has done, because to bring Veidt to justice would undo the unity he created and set the world back on the path to war. In the movie, however, Manhattan does more than just keep Veidt's secret. He also *takes the blame* for Veidt's crimes. Thus he plays a unique and supreme role in saving humanity by accepting, like Christ, the role of the scapegoat for the sins of others.

The dénouement of both the book and the movie are essentially the same: Rorschach refuses to keep Veidt's secret, so Manhattan is forced to kill him. Manhattan then leaves Earth forever, perhaps to create life on another planet. The threat of nuclear war having passed, New York rebuilds (with Veidt Industries profiting handsomely). Dreiberg and Laurie decide to marry. And Rorschach's diary, which tells the whole story up to his departure to Antarctica, when he dropped it in the mail, is fished out of the crank file at his favorite Right-wing periodical, *New Frontiersman*, bringing the story back to its beginning.

PRINCIPAL CHARACTERS: FIRST GENERATION

NITE OWL I (HOLLIS MASON)

Hollis Mason's primary role is as chronicler of the first generation of Watchmen and as a murder victim.

According to Mason's memoirs, which are excerpted in the graphic novel, the Minutemen were called "fascists" and "perverts," and there was an "element of truth in both those accusations," although "neither of them are big enough to take in the whole picture." In particular, Hooded Justice was heard "openly expressing approval for the activities of Hitler's Third Reich," while Captain Metropolis "has gone on record making statements about black and Hispanic Americans that have been viewed as both racially prejudiced and inflammatory." As Mason sums it up, "Yes, we were crazy, we were kinky, we were Nazis, all those things people say."

But, he adds significantly, "We were also doing something because we believed in it. We were attempting, through our personal efforts, to make our country a safer and better place to live in."

This is an important point to bear in mind, for in mainstream comics, Right-wing political views are not the mark of superheroes, but of supervillains. Even the most macho vigilante scofflaw, like Batman, still has to pay lip-service to humanistic, egalitarian morals. But in the *Watchmen* universe, Right-wing superheroes are still superheroes. Indeed, as we shall see, they are the only kind.

Mason is killed by a gang known as the Knot Tops in retaliation for a beating meted out to their members by Nite Owl II (Dreiberg) and Silk Spectre II (Laurie Jupiter). (The gang members either don't know or don't care that there are two Nite Owls.) Dreiberg feels great guilt for Mason's death, because he and Jupiter sought out the confrontation as they edged themselves toward resuming crime-fighting.

Silk Spectre I (Sally Jupiter)

Sally Jupiter (born Juspeczyk) was a model turned crime-fighter. As one might suspect, she was no demure little flower. She drank and cussed with the guys, and also slept with some of them. Sally's principal role in the plot is not, however, as a crime-fighter, but as a mother. The Comedian was drummed out of the Minutemen for trying to rape her. But later they had consensual sex (while she was married to her agent), producing Laurie (Silk Spectre II).

The Comedian (Edward Blake)

Edward Blake is one of the most enigmatic characters in *Watchmen*. He is called the Comedian because he wears a mask of cynicism and irreverence. He is capable of cold-blooded brutality and sadism. At first glance, he seems to be a sociopath. Ozymandias characterized him as "practically a Nazi." But the Comedian is no Joker. Blake has a conscience. When he discovers that Ozymandias is committing crimes far more terrible than anything he has done, he is horrified and distraught and tries to confess to Moloch, one of his old foes.

Blake, moreover, is not just a cynic. He is best understood as a disillusioned idealist. Blake loves America. But he is a political realist enough to know that America has enemies, foreign and domestic, who must be killed. He knows that maintaining law and order sometimes requires going outside the law. Thus he is capable of assassinating President Kennedy and killing countless Communists in Vietnam and Latin America, and probably a lot of innocents who just got in the way.

But at some point, Blake lost his faith in America. Since he began as a conservative American, Blake surely saw liberalism as a decadent deviation from American ideals. But Blake had changed his views by the time of the police strike and riots of 1977, which were followed by the Keene Act, all of which sprung from a Left-liberal rejection of vigilantism.

The Comedian realized that liberal decadence was not a deviation from American principles, but their fulfillment. Exasperated by the ingratitude of the rioters, Nite Owl II asked the Comedian, "Whatever happened to the American dream?" To which the Comedian responded: "It came true." America had been a giant joke after all, and the joke was on him.

Principal Characters: Second Generation

Rorschach (Walter Kovacs)

Rorschach is the narrator of *Watchmen*. We see the story through his eyes. Veidt creates the conspiracy, and Rorschach's investigation creates the plot. Rorschach also has the best lines in *Watchmen* and is by far the most popular character.

But he is also deeply problematic, for as his origin story makes clear, he is a hero out of the most unheroic of motives: *ressentiment*. The son of a prostitute, young Walter Kovacs suffered from abuse, neglect, and scorn. He was placed in a juvenile home at the age of 11, after savagely attacking two older bullies. Walter's anger and embitterment give rise to a powerful desire to punish, both others and himself. Thus he adopts an absolutist, objective, black-and-white moral code which he applies without mercy or compromise.

Rorschach became a masked vigilante in 1964. He teamed up with Nite Owl II to fight crime. In the late '60s, he joined the "Crimebusters" group. Rorschach was known for roughing up criminals, but he delivered them to the police alive. But America's increasingly soft and liberal criminal justice system could no longer be trusted to mete out justice, so in 1975 Rorschach began killing criminals, starting with Gerald Grice, who had kidnapped a little girl, Blair Roche, butchered her, and fed her to his dogs.

Rorschach's excesses were surely a factor that led to the Keene Act, banning masked vigilantes altogether. The other Watchmen retired or went to work for the government, but true to his uncompromising code, Rorschach remained in the fight. Thus Rorschach was on the scene after the Comedian's murder, and his investigation brought the other Watchmen back into action.

But this same uncompromising character leads to Rorschach's death in the end. After Ozymandias has used mass murder and trickery to pull the world back from the brink of nuclear war, Rorschach vows to tell the world. He is so wedded to punitive moral absolutism that he prefers that justice triumph even though the world might very well perish.

When Dr. Manhattan offers Rorschach the choice of silence or death, he chooses death. Rorschach's attachment to principle seems admirable. But the root of his attachment is ultimately a punitive bitterness and spite that turns suicidal when Manhattan blocks him from unleashing it on the world.

NITE OWL II (DAN DREIBERG)

At first glance, there is nothing particularly Right-wing about the character of Dan Dreiberg, who became Nite Owl II. But the mere fact that he is a costumed vigilante in the first place should rate rather high on the F-scale. Thus I would argue that all costumed superheroes should be treated as *de facto* Right-wingers in the absence of any express allegiance to liberal humanism, which is entirely absent in Dreiberg's case.

Dreiberg and Laurie Jupiter are drawn together because they were the only two Watchmen who actually retired into private life after the Keene Act. Rorschach went rogue, the Comedian and Dr. Manhattan went to work for the government, and Ozymandias became a publicly-traded commodity.

Although both of them deny it, they very much miss "the life." Laurie resents being reduced to Manhattan's consort, for which she receives a government paycheck, although it turns out that her principal role in the plot is not as an independent agent but as the object of Manhattan's affections.

If Laurie's retirement reduces her to a sexual companion, Dreiberg's has reduced him to sexual solitude and impotence. Laurie and Dreiberg are first drawn together by loneliness and nostalgia, but they can conquer their discontent only by inching back into crime-fighting. After their dust-up with the Knot-Tops, Laurie moves their relationship in a sexual direction, but Dreiberg is impotent. He only recovers his sexual potency after a full-fledged return to superherodom, right between saving people from a burning tenement and breaking Rorschach out of jail.

The character of Dan Dreiberg is a combination of Bruce Wayne (Batman) and Clark Kent (Superman). Nite Owl II's costume looks like Batman's, more so in the movie. Also, like Batman, Dreiberg is independently wealthy and uses his wealth to create technology that helps him transcend his human weaknesses.

Like Clark Kent, Dreiberg has a bespectacled, nebbishy persona, complete with spit curls. But in the graphic novel, Dreiberg is far more Jewish than Superman. Indeed, with his hook nose, 'berg name, and banker father, he is almost explicitly Jewish, but not quite.

There is, however, nothing distinctly Jewish about Dreiberg's psychology as written by Moore. Dreiberg is earnest, not ironic. His psychological emasculation is not rooted in an overbearing mother or some other mind-twisting childhood trauma, but in the adoption of an emasculating lifestyle. Thus in the movie, Zack Snyder completely Aryanizes the character by casting Patrick Wilson in the role.

As a side note, the graphic novel is filled with Jewish touches. We read an excerpt from Dr. Milton Glass's book on Dr. Manhattan. Mrs. Hirsch is interviewed by the police after her husband kills himself and their two children. Rorschach's mother's maiden name was Glick. Dreiberg is questioned by a detective Fine. Veidt sends a memo to Miss Neuberg. There are also numerous references to the Third Reich, National Socialism, and the Second World War.

Part of this can be explained by the fact that the novel is set mostly in New York City. Another factor, surely, is Moore's desire to fit into the comic book industry, which has an overwhelmingly Jewish culture due to its principal founders. It may also have been calculated by Moore to somewhat counterbalance the political incorrectness of the novel with a little Semitical correctness, in effect giving it a "neoconservative" character.

Snyder, however, scrubs the Jewishness of the novel from the film, except for Veidt's description of the Comedian as "practically a Nazi." Interestingly enough, in *300*, Snyder also mutes the strong Jewish-neoconservative nature of Frank Miller's original graphic novel.[1]

Dr. Manhattan (Jon Osterman)

In 1959, nuclear physicist Jon Osterman was seemingly annihilated in an experiment with an "Intrinsic Field Subtractor." But he managed to reassemble himself into a being who can see past, present, and future simultaneously and bend matter to his will. The birth of Dr. Manhattan was greeted by the news that, "The superman exists, and he is American." But Wally Weaver, who was present at Osterman's death and resurrection, went further,

---

[1] See my review of *300* in *Trevor Lynch's White Nationalist Guide to the Movies*.

declaring that "God exists, and he is American."

And indeed, Dr. Manhattan is portrayed as a god, and not just a god, but a savior. Like Osiris and Dionysus, he was killed through dismemberment, then reassembled and resurrected, showing mankind the way to conquer death. Like Jesus, who also died and was resurrected, Dr. Manhattan appears floating in the air in a halo of light.

He is also portrayed as a Hindu avatar of Vishnu, specifically Krishna: muscular, with glowing blue skin, and a circular "bindi" mark on his forehead, which to a Hindu indicates expanded consciousness. He even appears in a lotus position.

But of course Dr. Manhattan does not just *look* the part of a savior. He actually plays it, saving mankind from nuclear annihilation, by assuming, like Christ, the role of scapegoat for the sins of others, in this case Adrian Veidt. The use of such symbols and myths is part of the emotional power of *Watchmen*.

SILK SPECTRE II (LAURIE JUPITER)

Just as Sally Jupiter's primary role in *Watchmen* is not as a crime-fighter but as the object of the Comedian's lust and mother of his child, Laurie Jupiter, Laurie's primary role is not as a crime-fighter, but as the object of Dr. Manhattan's affections. Needless to say, this is a very traditional and anti-feminist conception of the true power and proper role of women.

When Manhattan learns that Laurie was produced through the sordid union of Sally and the Comedian, he is snapped out of his estrangement with humanity and resolves to save mankind. This is the crucial moment in the plot, marking the emergence of one of its deepest themes: Love for an individual human being can redeem the whole universe.

If you love someone, you are implicitly saying "yes" to his existence. You are glad of his existence and wish it to continue. Logically, you cannot love someone and wish that the causes of his existence were otherwise, for then one's beloved would not exist. And since everything in the universe is causally connected with everything else, if you really love someone, you cannot wish that the universe were otherwise. And this is true even though the universe is filled with many things that, in themselves, are terrible.

At the end of the story, this theme is reprised with great emotional power when Laurie is reconciled with her mother. Laurie can forgive her mother because she loves herself, which entails accepting all the conditions that made her life possible, including the union of her mother and the Comedian. Laurie says, "I love you, mom. You always did right by me." Sally is also reconciled with the Comedian because he gave her Laurie, whom she loves.

OZYMANDIAS (ADRIAN VEIDT)

Ozymandias is the only openly liberal character in *Watchmen*. He is 46 when the story of *Watchmen* begins. The hyper-Nordic child of wealthy German immigrants, Adrian Veidt is a self-made superman. He has used meditation and other physical and mental training techniques to become the smartest and fastest man alive. When he was young, he gave his vast inheritance to charity and pursued the life of a costumed crime-fighter, taking the name Ozymandias, a name for the Egyptian Pharaoh and megalomaniac Rameses II. But when the Keene Act forced Ozymandias into retirement, he went into business and became a billionaire in his own right.

Ozymandias is a vegetarian and a pacifist. He is unmarried, and Rorschach thinks he is a "possible homosexual." In the graphic novel, he is portrayed as beefy and also—despite his gymnastics exhibition—as macho, posturing in victory like a quarterback after a touchdown. In the movie, he is portrayed by the wiry and epicene Matthew Goode, who heightens the character's liberal do-gooder "vibe."

Ozymandias is also a materialist who believes that war is caused by the poor seeking wealth and the rich trying to hold onto it. He believes, therefore, that free, unlimited energy will bring about universal abundance and end the Cold War. He is a utilitarian governed by the principle of the greatest good for the greatest number. He reckons in terms of human quantity rather than quality. (He believes that anybody can become a superman through the Veidt Technique.)

In short, Ozymandias is a quintessential egalitarian humanist, which is the moral code of virtually every superhero outside the

Watchmen universe. But Ozymandias is the only egalitarian humanist in the cast of *Watchmen*. Ozymandias would seem to be a counter-example to my thesis that *Watchmen* is a Right-wing comic, were it not for the fact that he is also the *villain* of the story, the cold-blooded, calculating murderer of millions.

Ozymandias is no less the villain because his scheme worked to prevent nuclear war. Indeed, his scheme to goad Dr. Manhattan into exile brought the world to the brink in the first place. Moreover, he is no less a villain because he in effect uses nuclear blackmail to force the other Watchmen to remain silent, and Dr. Manhattan to kill Rorschach, all in order to keep his secret.

There is a sense in which even Ozymandias is a Right-wing archetype, namely a Right-winger's archetype of a villain: the egalitarian, humanist, pacifist mass murderer.

Although egalitarian humanists like Lenin, Stalin, and Mao are the biggest butchers in world history, within the world of comics, the heroes are always egalitarian humanists, and the villains are always people who reject that morality, e.g., traditionalists, Nazis, fascists, racists, eugenicists, and the like.[2] *Watchmen* neatly and completely inverts this code. That is why it is the supreme masterpiece of pop fascism.

Counter-Currents, February 18, 2014

---

[2] See my reviews of *Batman Begins, The Dark Knight, The Dark Knight Rises, Hellboy,* and *Hellboy II* in *Trevor Lynch's White Nationalist Guide to the Movies.*

WILD AT HEART

Wild at Heart is not David Lynch's best movie, but it is my favorite. I would argue, for instance, that *Blue Velvet*, *The Elephant Man*, and *The Straight Story* are all better films. But for some reason they do not call me back year after year like *Wild at Heart*.

Wild at Heart was released in the summer of 1990, when Lynch was riding high on *Twin Peaks* mania. It won the Palme d'Or at the 1990 Cannes film festival, albeit over vocal protests. Critics had their knives out for this film, most prominently the blockhead Roger Ebert.

I decided to give *Wild at Heart* a pass in the theaters because the film had been characterized to me as a boring exercise in nihilism: a tedious road picture about two sex-crazed pinheads filled with pointless weirdness, exploding heads, and running references to *The Wizard of Oz*. It was the *Oz* thing that did it. It sounded precious and postmodern, the kind of thing that college-age cineastes would self-satisfiedly snigger at in the theatre.

Seeing *Twin Peaks* for the first time that fall, however, whetted my appetite for more Lynch, so I watched *Wild at Heart* as soon as I could obtain a VHS tape. On the surface, *Wild at Heart* is everything its critics complained about: a freakshow of obscenity and violence and *The Wizard of Oz*.

But *Wild at Heart* is emphatically not a pointless exercise in nihilism. Indeed, there is genuine sentiment and humanity in *Wild at Heart*, as well as a deep moral order. It is definitely a road picture, but the road leads through the wasteland, the Kali Yuga, in which the moral order is almost entirely hidden by a fallen and degenerate world and visible only in fleeting glimpses and grotesque guises. But even in this world, what is right by nature still has the power to bring the film to a satisfying conclusion.

Wild at Heart is the story of two almost feral young Americans, Lula Pace Fortune and Sailor Ripley (played by Laura Dern and Nicholas Cage) who fall in love and go on the run from Lula's mother, Marietta Fortune, a "crazy fucking bitch" played by Dern's real-life mother Diane Ladd. At one point, Sailor addresses her as "Miss Fortune," and she is indeed Our Misfortune — in pumps.

Wild at Heart is based on the neo-*noir* novel of the same name by Barry Gifford, who later co-authored the screenplay to Lynch's *Lost Highway*. Comparing the novel of *Wild at Heart* to the movie deepens one's appreciation of Lynch's artistry. Gifford's novel is frankly two-dimensional, and a straightforward adaptation really would have been a pointless exercise in nihilism.

Lynch seems to have responded primarily to Gifford's colorful character names and turns of phrase. There really is something wonderfully vivid about how Southerners of all classes talk.

Lynch takes Gifford's basic road caper plot but imbues it with real moral and psychological depth. He also wrote a much more satisfying happy ending.

Lynch uses two techniques to deepen Gifford's narrative.

First, he intercuts statements from Lula and her mother with flashbacks that indicate that they are lying, deceiving themselves, or both. This adds mystery, suspense, psychological complexity, and the satisfying feeling of being let in on secrets.

For instance, at one point Lula recounts how when she was 15, her mother told her she should learn the facts of life. When Sailor replies, "But I thought you said your uncle Pooch raped you at 13." Lula admits this is correct but denies her mother knew it. The flashback, however, indicates her mother did know. Lula then reports that uncle Pooch — not really an uncle but one of her father's "business associates," i.e., a criminal — died in a car accident a few months later. But there's a strong implication that Marietta had Pooch killed. Later, we learn that he had impregnated Lula, and the child had been aborted. But both Lula and Marietta either are lying about some aspects of these events, or they have edited them out of their memories.

Second, Gifford's characters and the world they inhabit are entirely profane. But Lynch adds a religious dimension to the film — but only the sort of religion that could appear to feral Americans in the dregs of the Kali Yuga: a movie.

Religions use myths to create meaning and bring about moral transformations. In *Wild at Heart*, the overarching myth is *The*

Wizard of Oz. But even though it is merely a profane simulacrum of a religion, it still performs the same functions, helping Sailor and Lula make sense of the world and giving Sailor the courage to do the right thing in the end.

Where does the movie's title come from? At one point, Lula says despairingly, "This whole world's wild at heart and weird on top." What does it mean to be "wild at heart"? Longtime readers will know immediately where I am going with this.

I find Plato's tripartite psychology to be genuinely helpful in understanding this film. In Plato's *Republic*, Socrates argues that the human soul has to be distinguished into three distinct and irreducible faculties: *desire*, which seeks such necessities as food, shelter, sex, and self-preservation; *reason*, which seeks truth; and *spirit* (*thumos*), which seeks honor. Plato associates reason with the head, desire with the belly, and *thumos* with the chest, which is where we feel pride and anger. *Thumos* is wildness of heart.

Thumos is the capacity to passionately identify with and love things that are one's own—one's self-image, one's own family, one's own friends, one's own nation, etc.—and to defend them when they come under attack from people with conflicting partialities.

Thumos is often translated as "spirit," which makes sense if we understand it as "team spirit" or "fighting spirit." The Greeks associated *thumos* with anger, for we are upset when we or those we love are dishonored.

Thumos is also associated with self-sacrifice, since fighting over honor risks death. This is how we know that *thumos* is different from desire. Desire aims at self-preservation. But *thumos* is willing to risk self-preservation for honor.

Socrates suggests that we can differentiate types of men based on which part of the soul wins out when different parts come into conflict. A man ruled by honor follows it, not reason and desire, when they come into conflict. Whenever men fight even though fear or calculation tell them to retreat, they are ruled by *thumos*. The *thumotic* man prefers death to dishonor. The man ruled by desire follows desire rather than *thumos* or reason when they conflict. Drug addicts, for instance, continue to indulge their addictions, even when reason and honor forbid them. The man ruled by reason follows reason whenever it conflicts with desire or *thumos*. *Thumos* may urge one to fight against hopeless odds, but reason can say no. Desire may urge one to excess, but reason can impose measure.

Sailor Ripley has strong appetites for sex, drink, and cigarettes. But he is primarily ruled by *thumos*, which becomes apparent in the first scene. He and Lula are leaving a dance when Sailor is approached by a black man named Bob Ray Lemon, who begins verbally picking a fight with the intent to stab Sailor. When Sailor realizes what is going on, he says "Uh oh." But he's clearly not worried about his own safety. He's signaling that Lemon is crossing a line. When Lemon pulls out his switchblade, Sailor goes into full berserker mode, repeatedly slamming Lemon's head into a rail and then into the floor, finally hurling his corpse against the wall, its brains spilling onto the floor. Sailor's reaction clearly set aside all considerations of self-preservation or likely consequences. Reason and desire were totally overwhelmed by *thumos*.

After spending 22 months in jail for manslaughter, Sailor is released and reunited with Lula. Fearing the interference of Lula's mother, though, the couple decide to break Sailor's parole and head to California by way of New Orleans. One night as the couple are passing through Texas, they encounter an accident scene. Two young men are dead. Suddenly a badly injured girl staggers out of the darkness. Sailor and Lula both rush to her aid. They have to take her to the hospital. It is simply the right thing to do. But doing so ensures an encounter with the police, who might learn that Sailor has broken parole. Sailor sees this immediately, but given the choice between following self-interest and helping a gravely injured human being, he does not hesitate to help. When the girl dies in front of them, there is no point in risking discovery, but at this point, Sailor and Lula have less than $100. Practically every other character in this movie is a sociopath whose first instinct would be to rob the dead, but it does not occur to Sailor or Lula.

Another characteristic of *thumotic* individuals is the value they place on personal loyalty. Sailor speaks fondly of his public defender, who stood by him, but of course the most striking loyalty in the film is between Sailor and Lula. Sailor says that Lula "stood by me after I planted Bob Ray Lemon. A man can't ask for more than that." And the loyalty is mutual, for it is quite risky to resume his affair with Marietta Fortune's daughter.

As the film unfolds, though, it is clear that Lula's loyalty is the stronger, for Sailor is infected with individualism. Sailor's trademark is his snakeskin jacket, which he says is for him "a symbol of my individuality and my belief in personal freedom." Snakes, of course, are low-down, cold-blooded creatures associated with the devil and original sin. Snakeskin is something snakes slough off from time to time, so it is a nice symbol of the individualist who sloughs off relationships and responsibilities in the name of freedom. This is precisely what Sailor tries to do at the end of the movie.

Lula says she has heard the line about the jacket symbolizing individuality and personal freedom "about fifty-thousand times." Perhaps Sailor is just repeating an advertising slogan, in which case he is actually displaying his lack of individuality and personal freedom. Sure enough Sailor repeats the line in the very next scene, where he picks a fight with a punk who started dancing with Lula. (Uh oh—*thumos* again.) The punk looks Sailor over and declares "You look like a clown in that stupid jacket." When Sailor tells him its meaning, the punk simply responds "Asshole."

And although the punk is supposed to be an idiot (he appears in the script as Idiot Punk) he is completely correct. We all look like clowns clad in our symbols of individuality and personal freedom. Individualism makes snakes—and assholes—of us all.

The great moral transformation of *Wild at Heart* is when Sailor finally sloughs off the individualist snakeskin and becomes a loyal, loving family man. A decent society educates its citizens both intellectually and morally, helping them overcome the selfishness and hedonism of childhood and the wildness of adolescence to become responsible and rational adults. But Sailor didn't have much "parental guidance," and the whole of liberal-individualist-capitalist society works to keep him—and us—in a permanent state of adolescence.

Neither Sailor nor Lula is particularly rational. Lula's mind seems to move by association rather than reason. As Sailor puts it "the way your head works is God's own private mystery." When Lula refers to the world as "wild at heart and weird on top," the words "on top" could just mean "in addition." But they could also be in keeping with the physical association of wildness and the heart: wildness is to weirdness as the heart is to the head—"on top." Thus Lula could be referring to her own proud and irrational character as well, for she is very much a citizen of this world.

Sailor himself is not too strong in the reasoning department, either, but he at least recognizes the necessity of making better decisions. At one point he declares, "Lula, I done a few things in my life I ain't too proud of, but I'll tell ya from now on I ain't gonna do nothin' for no good reason. All I know for sure is there's more'n a few bad ideas runnin' around loose out there." (Lynch then cuts to Marietta Fortune, in full-blown psychosis, to the terrifying sounds of Krzysztof Penderecki's *Kosmogona*.)

At another point he promises Lula that he is not going to let things get any worse. Then he promptly lets himself get talked into an armed robbery, which costs him six years in prison and nearly got him killed. When he is released, he returns to Lula and their son, whom he has never met, but then chickens out and leaves. As he returns to the train station, he is surrounded by a multiracial gang of toughs. He stops, lights a cigarette, and asks "What do you faggots want?" It's *thumos* getting the best of him again.

He is duly decked. But in the end, it is not reason that saves him but a vision of Glinda the Good from *The Wizard of Oz*, who tells him, "Lula loves you . . . If you are truly wild at heart, you'll fight for your dreams . . . Don't turn away from love, Sailor . . . Don't turn away from love . . ." If the Sailor Ripleys of the world had only reason to guide them, they'd be pretty much doomed.

The character that sets the whole story of *Wild at Heart* in motion is Marietta Fortune, brilliantly portrayed by Diane Ladd. Everyone else just reacts to her. David Lynch is a master of creating villains with a touch of the diabolical, of superhuman or supernatural evil: Frank Booth, Mr. Eddie, the Mystery Man, Leland Palmer, Killer Bob, etc. And who can forget his version of Baron Harkonnen in *Dune*?

But Marietta Fortune is Lynch's only female Big Bad, and she's just one of *Wild at Heart*'s huge cast of villains: Marcello Santos, Mr. Reindeer, Bobby Peru, Perdita Durango, and the trio of Reggie, Dropshadow, and Juana. In fact, there's only one unambiguously decent character in the whole film, the detective Johnny Farragut, played by Harry Dean Stanton. Sailor and Lula are both too immature to be good. The overabundance of villains is actually a problem, for *Wild at Heart* is simply too dark and too violent for many people to enjoy wholeheartedly.

As *Wild at Heart* unfolds, flashbacks take us further and further into the past, and at every level we find Marietta Fortune pulling the strings. In Lula's eyes, her mother is the Wicked Witch of the East in *The Wizard of Oz*. It was Marietta who paid Bob Ray Lemon to kill Sailor. She did it because she discovered that Sailor had been a driver for her sometime boyfriend and business associate Marcello Santos (J. E. Freeman). One night Sailor was waiting in Santos' car outside the Fortune house when it went up in flames. It turns out that at Marietta's bidding, Santos had doused her husband Clyde (Lula's father) with kerosene and struck a match. When Sailor got out of jail and ran off with Lula, Marietta put both Santos and her current boyfriend, detective Johnny Farragut, on their trail.

There was just one problem. Santos' condition for helping was to kill Johnny Farragut, whom he regards as a danger to his and Marietta's criminal dealings (probably drugs) with a Mr. Reindeer of New Orleans. Marietta says no but realizes that Santos might well do it anyway. But she doesn't warn Farragut because she can't bring herself to admit to him that she broke her promise not to call Santos.

It is classic narcissist behavior. Marietta's entire life is about projecting bland Southern gracious living clichés. She can't admit or take responsibility for her errors without compromising her carefully crafted image. The conflict between her fear for Johnny and her inability to admit error leads to a bizarre and hilarious psychotic episode where she in effect commits symbolic suicide, cutting her wrists and throat with lipstick (one of the tools of maintaining her image), then painting her face with it. At that point, she calls Johnny and tells him she has made a terrible mistake. But she refuses to tell him about it on the phone, telling him she will fly to New Orleans and tell him in person the next day. Of course this leaves Farragut in grave danger and probably cost him a night of sleep. Then she vomits in the toilet and begins laughing. The whole drama of death and resurrection has been a catharsis. How does Lynch come up with this stuff?

When Marietta and Johnny meet the next day for dinner, Marietta again refuses to confess and decides that she will just get Johnny out of harm's way by getting on the road that night. But when he returns to his hotel room, he is kidnapped then murdered by three horrifying thugs dispatched by Santos and Mr. Reindeer. At the end, though, Farragut only feels compassion for Marietta. It is genuinely tragic. He is a good man brought down because he was utterly blind to the depths of Marietta's deceitfulness and manipulation.

Marietta's reaction to Farragut's disappearance is classic. She refuses to call the police, because that would require admitting the true nature of the problem—and also, she probably has lots of unfinished business with the police. When she is given a note, obviously left by the kidnappers, that Johnny has "Gone fishing with a friend, and maybe buffalo hunting," she immediately interprets it in a face-saving way. He was not kidnapped because of her doing. He was a coward who fled because he was incapable of a serious relationship. When Santos shows up, it is pretty much obvious what has happened, so again to save face, she basically demands that Santos lie to her, which he gladly does. Marietta then cheerfully pivots to Santos, who will now be her partner in tracking down Sailor and Lula. It is a truly breathtaking portrait of how a malignant narcissist operates. She will pile up lies and corpses without end, as long as she maintains her positive image.

One villain like Marietta is really enough for a film, but in *Wild at Heart* there are two. Halfway through the film, Sailor and Lula bump into Willem Dafoe's Bobby Peru ("Just like the country") in Big Tuna, Texas. Peru has been dispatched by Santos and Reindeer to kill Sailor. Bobby Peru is one of the most viscerally repellent characters ever brought to the screen. That's a teaser, not a spoiler.

The mysterious Mr. Reindeer (played by W. Morgan Sheppard) is another fascinating study. He's a man entirely ruled by his appetites. When we first encounter him, he's wearing a tuxedo, sitting on a toilet, drinking tea, and watching a little striptease in his bathroom. He's just an expensively upholstered tube. He seems to live in a brothel, surrounded by attractive young women. The madame warns them sternly that they are there to show Mr. Reindeer a good time. "Do not bring misfortune upon yourselves." In another scene, he is flanked by two topless bimbos talking about a stolen comb. One of them holds a tray with a bottle of Pepto Bismol on it. In yet another scene, he is at a dinner party, surrounded by well-dressed whores, but he only has eyes for Grace Zabriske's Juana, a twisted, crippled grotesque (one of Johnny Farragut's killers).

Beginning with the title sequence—an extreme closeup of a match flaring up, followed by a vast, swirling vortex of flames, to the sumptuous opening strains of Richard Strauss' "Im Abendrot"—*Wild at Heart* is one of Lynch's most sensuously beautiful movies: a screen as wide as America filled with strikingly composed images filmed in a way that imbues seedy bars, cheap hotels, and bleak landscapes and cityscapes with a voluptuous shell pink, sunset, or neon luster.

Although I would have preferred more original music by Angelo Badalamenti, who composed the unforgettable score of *Twin Peaks*, Lynch's choices cannot be faulted, especially his selections from Strauss and Penderecki and Chris Isaak's haunting and iconic "Wicked Game" and "Blue Spanish Sky."

I have grown so fond of *Wild at Heart* that I am frequently surprised at the strong negative reactions of people to whom I have introduced it. I hope I can do a better job of preparing you. Because *Wild at Heart* does have its flaws.

For instance, Lynch loses a lot of people early on, in the scene with the Idiot Punk at the rock concert. The film veers into bizarre fantasy when Sailor stops the concert with a hand gesture, humiliates the punk, and then turns the speed metal band

Powermad into a backup group while he croons Elvis' "Love Me" to an audience of screaming, swooning females. Are we supposed to believe this is possible for a guy who just got out of jail and who, even if he did know the band, could not have rehearsed with them? People who routinely suspend disbelief in vampires and space travel throw up their hands in disgust. But you just have to be patient.

Beyond that, *Wild at Heart* is just a bit too weird on top. There are eccentrics, cripples, and freaks at every turn, and a lot of them have nothing to do with the plot.

Finally the film is really too violent and gross: sadistic murders, including a man lit on fire and two exploding heads, bloody gunshot wounds, a severed hand (you'll laugh in spite of yourself), two bloody car accidents, the rape of a 13-year-old-girl, an abortion, what basically amounts to the rape of the same woman at 20, while she is pregnant, during which she has an orgasm, etc.

There were three exploding heads in the first cut, but the murder of Johnny Farragut in the middle of the film was so gross that 80 people walked out of the first test screening—100 walked out of the second screening—so Lynch cut it. For the sake of the people around him, I hope David Lynch saves all of his darkness for the screen.

Viewers draw the line in different spots, but virtually everyone who watches this movie thinks "This is too much"—too much weirdness, too much violence, too much blood—well before the final frames. Lynch described *Wild at Heart* as "a picture about finding love in hell," but for most people there's too much hell there to be redeemed by love.

My answer, though, is that these are problems with our world, not with *Wild at Heart*. And because the movie dives so deep into darkness, the ending is all the more satisfying.

I have watched *Wild at Heart* more than 20 times, but in the last viewing before writing this, I realized that I had never before watched it without wincing—closing my eyes or looking away—in certain spots. So it took me decades to finally look at every frame of this, my favorite David Lynch film.

David Lynch has not made many films, and *Wild at Heart* falls somewhere in the middle of the pack. But *Blue Velvet* is certainly the paradigmatic "Lynchian" film: an innocent young man leaves the garden of childhood naïveté, encounters diabolical evil, finds his strength, and triumphs over it in the end—with all the bizarre touches we expect from Lynch.

In *Wild at Heart* the protagonists aren't that innocent, and there's a whole lot more diabolical evil to endure before the happy ending. The same moral order is there, but it is distant. The horror is far more prevalent and oppressive. But of all Lynch's other works, *Wild at Heart* is still the closest to the paradigm of Lynchian perfection, and that should count for something.

Does *Wild at Heart* have a political message—or at least a political lesson it can teach us? Yes, and it is a conservative one. First, it is a very bleak portrayal of the desire-dominated world created by liberal individualist snakeskin salesmen: a world swarming with criminals and freaks and awash in substance abuse, sexual libertinism, and obnoxious music. It is a veritable *Garden of Earthly Delights*.

We sympathize with Sailor and Lula, and we see that they have decent sentiments, but they were so poorly nurtured and educated that they might have been better off raised by wolves. Sailor didn't have parental guidance because both his parents died while he was a child of cigarette- or alcohol-related illness, and Lula was raised in the midst of a gang of criminals, one of whom raped her at the age of 13.

Furthermore, neither Sailor nor Lula is particularly good at reasoning, so their desires and their *thumos* keep getting them into trouble, and in the modern liberal democratic wasteland trouble abounds. Lynch clearly believes that there is a moral order to the world. Sailor and Lula are just too thick to know it by reason.

But the moral order can capture their imaginations, shape their sentiments, and set them off in the right direction in the guise of a narrative, namely *The Wizard of Oz*. In the wasteland, the only myths we have are movies. When the moral order clothes itself in myths, we have religion.

Yes, *Wild at Heart* is a religious film. Only magic can redeem these characters, and only Christian or post-Christian sentimentalists would want to. In truth, inadequacies of nature and nurture doom them, and their son, to just more of the same.

Yes, *Wild at Heart* is grotesque and obscene. But religious art has long employed the grotesque and obscene. Just look at Bosch.

Thus *Wild at Heart*'s ultimate message is: Liberalism is the road to hell, not paradise—and only a Good Witch can save us now.

Counter-Currents, February 2, 2019

ZOOTOPIA

Disney's *Zootopia* is cute, clever, and entertaining. But in terms of its message, it is pure evil. *The Angry Birds Movie* is plausibly interpreted as a pro-nationalist, anti-immigration, anti-Muslim allegory, whether that was the intended meaning or not. *Zootopia*, however, is clearly intended as pro-diversity, anti-nationalist propaganda. But worse than that, *Zootopia* is basically a syringe of mental vaccine against race realism, which will make white children who absorb its message less likely to observe and act upon racial differences. Thus it will make them more likely to fall victim someday to non-white predators. And parents are paying for the privilege of injecting this poison into the brains of their children. But then what else is new?

Zootopia is the story of Judy Hopps, a cute little bunny girl with wide blue eyes and a perky, can-do attitude who grows up on a carrot farm in the countryside and dreams of becoming a policewoman in the big city of Zootopia.

At the beginning of the movie, a voice-over explains that in the past, animals were ruled by their instincts. Predators ate prey, and prey feared predators. But, over time, they evolved beyond these instincts and created a society in which predator and prey live side-by-side in harmony, and everyone is free to be anything he or she wants. So cute little bunny girls from the country can even dream of being big-city cops.

Unfortunately, some animals aren't entirely thrilled by the progressive narrative. Of course they would never challenge it openly or righteously. Instead, they speak furtively and apologetically. Judy's parents, for instance, discourage her from her unrealistic dreams and fear for her safety in the big city. They even give her a canister of fox repellent, just in case, because foxes can't be trusted. It's in their biology, you see. And remember Gideon, the fox bully from Judy's childhood who talks like a white Southern hick? Judy takes the fox repellent, just to humor her parents.

Judy goes off to the city. Because of an affirmative action initiative, she gets in the police academy. As one might expect, the police department is full of large, strong, aggressive animals like water buffalo, rhinos, and tigers. So Judy will have to work really hard to pass the tests and fit in. But in Zootopia, biology is no barrier to realizing one's dreams. Think *G.I. Jane* with bunnies.

Unfortunately, however, there are deep-seated biological prejudices in the police department that lead the police chief to think that a five-pound bunny might not be able to arrest a panther or a musk ox. So, upon graduation, Judy the "token bunny" is assigned to write parking tickets.

Judy is disappointed, of course, because there are bigger crimes to solve. For instance, a number of predators have recently gone missing. But orders are orders, so she dedicates her perky, can-do attitude to writing parking tickets. Then she encounters Nick Wilde, a fox with an adorable little fox pup, who is being discriminated against by elephants who refuse him service at their ice cream parlor. Foxes, you see, have a reputation for being sly con artists, and the elephants are stereotyping him just like Judy's parents would. Judy uses her badge to intimidate the elephants into serving the fox. Serves them right, the bigots. But then she is outraged to discover that the fox is actually—true to stereotype—a con artist.

Now it is tempting to regard this discovery as a little red pill for the audience. But that would be a mistake, for as the movie progresses, we learn that the sly fox has a good heart. He's a *Mensch*. Yes, he is a bit of a scoundrel. But it turns out that his trickery and connections can be used for good ends as well. So he teams up with Judy and helps her solve the missing predators' case, and at the end of the movie, he becomes a police officer himself, while Judy becomes a bit of a foxy trickster. She even teams up with Mr. Big, the organized crime boss in Zootopia, who uses illegal methods to help Judy's investigation. And this delicious feast of Jewish moral ambiguity and subversion is rated G, because to turn a human being into a liberal, you have to get them young

And as for Gideon, the childhood bully fox, even Judy's parents like him. He's grown up to be an artisan pie baker. (I kid you not.) Gideon explains to Judy that his bad behavior in the past was due to psychological issues. Keep moving folks, nothing biological to see here.

This is the intellectual equivalent of a vaccination. A typical vaccine protects us from infection by a disease-causing microorganism by boosting our immune system against it. Our immunity is boosted by injecting a small amount of the dangerous microorganism itself, which has been diluted, killed, or otherwise denatured. In *Zootopia*, a small amount of truth, namely that certain predatory types might actually act according to their natures, is acknowledged. But then it is shown not to matter.

The truth about foxes is diluted by the NAXALT (not all X are like that) fallacy, which basically argues that since "Not all foxes are like that," due to the inevitable existence of outliers on bell curves, we have to act as if "*All* foxes are not like that," i.e., we are somehow morally obligated to treat every member of a group as an outlier, even though this is obviously untrue, because there are always more average specimens than unusual ones.

The same pattern is repeated on a larger scale in the search for the missing predators. It turns out that the predators have gone savage, reverting back to their predatory nature. Mayor Lionheart of Zootopia, who is a predator himself, has been covering up the outbreak of savagery to protect predators against stereotypes. After all, Zootopia is only 10% predator, 90% prey. We can't have the majority thinking that 10% of the population is criminally inclined, can we? Even if it might be true. Judy, however, suggests that maybe the cause is biological, that predators are reverting to their savage ways.

If this is true, then perhaps the solution is to quarantine or segregate predators, which is an end to Zootopia's idea that all different species can live in the same society peacefully. Indeed, the movie shows quite clearly that biological diversity makes it necessary to separate animals. For instance, Zootopia is divided into different habitat zones, from tropical rain-forest to Arctic tundra. Why? Because animals are biologically adapted for certain environments and cannot live comfortably in others. Zootopia is also segregated by size. It has a special neighborhood for small rodents, who obviously can't have elephants traipsing up and down their streets. Obviously, Zootopia is only workable because of a certain amount of segregation.

One of the most amusing scenes is when Judy is in a hurry and goes to the Department of Motor Vehicles to run a license plate. It turns out that the DMV is staffed entirely by sloths, who march to an entirely different drummer. I used to have the same sinking feeling when I would visit the Atlanta Post Office, which is staffed entirely by sloths as well. And what do the predators eat if not prey? Can lions and bears subsist on tofu? The natural conclusion is that there would be less petty frustration and bloody conflict if different kinds of animals lived in societies of their own. The only possible Zootopia is a world in which each species has a homeland of its own, rather than being all mixed together.

The separate habitats, the inter-species conflicts, the cover-up of minority crime, and Judy's suggestion that the cause of crime may be biological all seem like a massive red pill. But it turns out to be another vaccination. For the climax of the movie proves Judy to be wrong about the cause of crime and the mayor to be right to cover-up the crisis, in order to prevent people from drawing the same mistaken conclusion that Judy announces.

The punishment for Judy's candor is swift and righteous. She is denounced and shamed for transgressing the sacred dogmas of liberalism. Her fox friend, Nick, takes it personally and becomes sulky. The obvious truth that predators are biologically predisposed to prey on others is said to be tearing Zootopia apart. Judy feels terribly guilty.

Then we discover that the real cause of the predators going feral is a drug. It turns out that Assistant Mayor Bellweather, a sheep, has hatched a conspiracy to drug predators, making them turn feral, in order to create fear and division in Zootopia so she can rise to power on a prey-supremacist platform. Fortunately, the plot is uncovered, the criminals are arrested, and a cure is found for the poison. Lesson: if lions can't lie down with lambs, that's probably the lambs' fault.

Judy concludes that her reference to heredity, although superficially plausible, was ignorant, irresponsible, and small-minded. She concludes the movie with a speech about what she has learned. She thought that Zootopia was a perfect place where everyone gets along and you can be anything you want to be. But she learned that it is not perfect. There are problems. But they are not caused by biology, which society cannot change. Instead, they are caused by things like ignorance, fear, psychological issues, and simple mistakes—all of which can be fixed. So, in the end, we can all get along and be anything we want to be. But it just takes a little bit of effort. In real world political terms, this is a repudiation of utopian liberalism for PC social engineering.

The fact that different species evolved for different environments and have different, conflicting forms of life, is not an insuperable problem. It is just as superficial as different human languages and customs and religions. (And nobody fights about them, right?) Superficial diversity only gives rise to color and comedy. Deep down, we're all just the same, lion and lamb alike.

The real-world analogies are clear: Some racial groups may indeed have a genetic disposition to predatory behavior, whether it be brutish (like blacks) or sly (like Jews). It seems daring to acknowledge this, of course, but denial is becoming increasingly threadbare and alternative race realist explanations are becoming more widespread. So instead of outright denial, the Left is now taking a subtler approach. Race realism must be acknowledged, but in a diluted and denatured form, to vaccinate people against accepting the real thing.

Biology may be real, but we can safely ignore it because of NAXALT, emotional blackmail, moral shaming, the alleged social usefulness of some biological predispositions (Nick's sly foxiness), and plausible alternative explanations, like evil members of the majority using drugs to make some groups act like animals in order to seize power by dividing society (diversity good, division bad). Got it? Sure, it sounds dumb when stated so baldly, but this is a movie for children, and many grownup liberals actually hold exactly such childish beliefs.

Zootopia is genuinely witty and highly entertaining, but its message is far worse than the mindless, mechanical shitlib shilling that we have come to expect from Disney. It is a calculated attempt to inoculate specifically white children against race realism. Judy Hopps and her family are characterized as European Americans. The entire movie is calculated to appeal to whites, right down to the artisan pies. Which means that someone, somewhere at Disney is aware that white racial consciousness, fueled by awareness of human biodiversity, is on the rise. Thus they have created a movie to fight us. That's the bad news. The good news is: *They're afraid.*

Counter-Currents, June 16, 2016

INDEX

Numbers in bold refer to a whole chapter or section devoted to a particular topic.

2001: A Space Odyssey, 22, 76, 109
300 (film), 97, 190
'80s, **168–71**

A
abortion, 29, 203
Abrams, J. J., 133, 136, 147, 151–52, 155
Adam & Eve, 115
Addison, John, 102
Adele, 145
Affleck, Ben, 14, 16
Afghanistan, 78, 79, 184
Africa, 14, 17–19, 26, 81, 108, 153
Aghdashloo, Shohreh, 73–74, 121
AIDS, 33; see also HIV
Akira, 87
Alien, 1, 2, 87
Alien: Covenant, **1–3**
alienation, 174
Aliens, 1, 2
Allen, Barry, 96
Alt Right, 11
Amazons, 95, 96
Andress, Ursula, 103
androgyny, 170, 178
Angry Birds Movie, The, 206
anime, 117
Annis, Francesca, 47
anti-Semitism, 3, 4, 8, 20, 34–35, 114
anti-sex films, 29–30, **61–70**

Apollo Program, 149
Aquaman, 96
Arabia, 42
archeofuturism, 41
Arkham Asylum, 9, 176
Armenia & Armenians, **120–22**
Armenian Genocide, 120, 121
Arquette, Patricia, 31
Arrakis, 42–44, 46, 49–52, 66
Arrival, 22
artificial intelligence, 40
Aryan mind, hacking, 8, 111
athleticism, 175, 182
Atlanteans, 95, 96
Atlas Shrugged, 16
Atreides (noble house), **43–50**
Atreides, Duke Leto, 41, 55, 85
Atreides, Lady Jessica, 47, 50–52, 55–56
Atreides, Paul, 41–42, 45, 47, 54–55, 86
atrocities, 121, 138
Aurora, 115–16
Auschwitz, 8, 36, 130
Avasarala, UN Deputy Undersecretary Crisjen, 72–74
Avatar, 178

B
Babe franchise, 103
Babylon Five, 147
Badalamenti, Angelo, 202
Bale, Christian, 121
Ballard, J. G., 28

Bane, 103
Barbarella (film), 48, 178, 179
Barton Fink, **4–8**, 110, 112–13
Batman Begins, 193n2
Batman v Superman: Dawn of Justice, 11, **13–16**
Batman, compared to Nite Owl II, 182
Batman, compared to Superman, 13, 15–16; see also *Batman v Superman: Dawn of Justice*
Batman: The Dark Knight Returns, **9–12**, 13; see also *The Dark Knight Returns*
Battlestar Galactica, (2003–2009), 71
bell curves, 81, 208
Beery, Wallace, 5
Bene Gesserit, 40–42, 45–48, 52, 54, 59, 86
Bene Tleilax, 40, 42, 46
Bergman, Ingmar, 151
Berle, Milton, 102
Bernard, Viola W., 165
berserker, 197
Besson, Luc, 178
Beyond Thunderdome, 103
biotechnology, 90–91
Black Panther, **17–21**
Blackhawk Down, 3
blacks, 18–21, 26, 71, 81–83, 108, 134, 153, 161, 171, 175, 210; see also negroes
Blade Runner, 3, 22–24, 168
Blade Runner 2049, **22–24**
blank slate theory, 163, 166
Blofeld, Ernst Stavro, 145–46
"Blue Spanish Sky," 202
Blue Velvet, 39, 45, 168, 194, 204
Böcklin, Arnold, 2
Bollywood, 14, 74

Bond, Commander James, CMG, RNVR, 103, 145–46; see also James Bond franchise
Bond girls, 103, 145
Borg, 56, 147
Born Together—Reared Apart: The Landmark Minnesota Twin Study, 163
Booth, Frank, 199
Boseman, Chadwick, 18
Bosch, Hieronymus, 106, 205; see also *Garden of Earthly Delights*
Boyega, John, 153, 158–59
Bruckheimer, Jerry, 151
Bruegel, 106
Budapest, 1
Buddhism, 40, 119, 131
bug-chasing, 32
Burton, Amos, 72, 73
Buscemi, Steve, 112
Buttercup Dew, 1n1, 3
Byrne, Gabriel, 110

C
C-3PO, 118
Cage, Nicholas, 194
Caine, Michael, 27
Caladan (home of House Atreides), 41, 42, 43, 46
Calrissian, Lando, 142, 157
Cameron, James, 1
Camus, Albert, 125
Cannes Film Festival, 4, 196
Carradine, David, 85
Casino Royale (2006), 145
Cavil, Henry, 16
Chani, 51, 52, 55, 56
Chatham, Wes, 73–74
Chapterhouse Dune, 42
Chewbacca, 142, 152, 154

Index 215

Children of Men, **25–27**
Christ (Jesus), 16, 86, 140, 185–86, 191
Christian allegory, 16, 24n2
Christianity, 40, 138–39
Christie, Gwendolyn, 158
CIA, 19, 78
civil rights, 20, 82–83
Clarke, Emilia, 143
Clockwork Orange, A, 76
Coburn, James, 102
Coen Brothers, 4–8, 110–14, 178
Cohen, Leonard, 97
Cold War, 81, 180, 192
colonialism, 20, 139, 178–79
Comer, Anjanette, 99
Contact, 87
Corey, S. A., 71
Costello, Jef, 145n1
Counter-Currents, 117
Cox, Julie, 55, 56
Craig, Daniel, 145
Crash (Cronenberg film), **28–33**
Crichton, Michael, 88, 91
Crimebusters (masked vigilantes and superheroes), 181, 184; see also Minutemen; Watchmen
Cronenberg, David, 28–33
Crouching Tiger, Hidden Dragon, 46
Cuarón, Alphoso, 25–26
Cushing, Peter, 135
Cyborg (comic book character), 96

D

D'Annunzio, General Gabriele, Prince of Montenevoso, Duke of Gallese, OMS CMG MVM, 170
Dafoe, Willem, 168–70, 201
Dance of Reality, The, 85
Dalí, Salvador, 85, 106
Damon, Matt, 107, 108
Dark Knight Returns, The, 9, 12; see also *Batman: The Dark Knight Returns*
Dark Knight Rises, The, 135, 193n2
Dark Knight Trilogy, 193n2
Dark Knight, The, 175
David (android), 1–2
David Irving v Penguin Books and Deborah Lipstadt, 34–38
De Laurentiis, Dino, 39, 48, 53
De Vries, Piter, 48, 55, 85, 86
Dean, James, 31
Death Star, 133–36, 152, 156
Debussy, 2
Deep Space Nine, 147
DeHaan, Dane, 179
Del Toro, Benicio, 159
Delevingne, Cara, 179
Demiurge, 62, 65
Democratic Party, 20, 21
Denial, **34–38**
Denying the Holocaust, 34–35
Dern, Laura, 158, 194
determinism, genetic vs. environmental, 162–64, 167; see also heredity
DiCaprio, Leonardo, 179
Dionysus, 191
Dirty Dozen, The, 134
Disney, 20, 87, 93, 133, 136, 141–42, 144, 156, 160–61, 210–11
Dissident Right, 77
Diversity, 60, 72, 92, 108, 133, 148, 159, 178–79, 206–11

Do Androids Dream of Electric Sheep?, 24
Doctor Zhivago, 120
Dr. No (film), 103
Dr. Strangelove, 180
Driver, Adam, 138, 153, 158
DuBois, W. E. B., 20
Indivisible by Two: Lives of Extraordinary Twins, 163
Dune (fictional planet), see Arrakis
Dune (Alejandro Jodorowsky film), **85–87**
Dune (David Lynch film) **39–53,** 54–55, 58, 87
Dune Book, 87
Dune Messiah, 39, 43, 47, 54, 56–57
Dune & Children of Dune (Sci-Fi Channel mini-series), **54–58**
Dunkirk, **59–60**

E
Edwards, Gareth, 135, 136
egalitarianism, 12, 91, 108, 109, 163; 192–93
Ehrenreich, Alden, 141, 143
Eisenberg, Jesse, 14, 16
El Topo, 85
Elephant Man, The (film), 49, 194
Elgar, Sir Edward William, 1st Baronet, OM, GCVO, 58, 60
Eliot, T. S., 117
Empire Strikes Back, The, 93, 133, 137, 144, 151, 154, 156, 159, 168
England, 60
English Patient, The, 121
Eno, Brian, 55
"Entry of the Gods into Valhalla," 2

Entwined Lives: Twins and What They Tell Us About Human Behavior, 163
Enya, 58
Esther, Queen, 111
Eraserhead, **61–70**
Ereignis, 31
Ethiopia, 17
ethnonationalism, 18–19, 164; see also nationalism; White Nationalism
ethnostate, 18
eugenics, 40, 78, 90, 193
Evans, Chris, 179
Evans, Richard, 35
Exorcist, The, 168
Expanse, The, **71–74**

F
Farragut, Johnny, 200–202, 203
Farrakhan, Louis, 20
fascists, 71, 117, 180, 185, 193
fascism, pop, 193
Faulkner, William, 6
Fassbender, Michael, 1, 2
Faustianism, 89, 108, 116, 149–50
Faye, Guillaume, 41
feminism, 10, 17, 25, 35, 89, 103, 105, 133, 153
feudalism, 39–40
Fifth Element, The, 14, 168, 178
Filoni, Dave, 144
Finney, Albert, 110, 146
Firefly, 74
First World War, 120
Fishburne, Lawrence, 116
Fisher, Carrie, 137, 153, 158
Flash Gordon, 168, 179
Flash, The, 96
Ford, Harrison, 22–23, 143, 153–54

Fortune, Marietta, 194–95, 198, 199–201
Foss, Chris, 85, 87
Fountainhead, The, 16
Frankenstein, Dr. Victor, 2, 32
Frankenstein (creature), 10, 32
freedom, personal, 198
Freeman, J. E., 111
Fremen, 42, 44–45, 50–52, 55
French Connection, The, 168
Freud & Freudianism, 32, 70, 165–66
Freud, Anna, 165
Friedkin, William, 168, 170
Frontiersman (archetype), 88, 93, 107
Futurism, Italian, 59

G

G. I. Jane, 2, 200
Gadot, Gal, 15–16
Galland, Edward, 162–67
Garden of Earthly Delights, 204; see also Bosch, Hieronymus
Garfield, Andrew, 138
Garvey, Marcus, 20
Gattaca, 78, 80
genetic engineering, 40
Genetic Similarity Theory, 162–64
George, Terry, 120
Germans (Second World War era), 59–60
Giannini, Giancarlo, 56
Gibson, Mel, 103
Gibbons, Dave, 180
Giedi Prime (home of house Harkonnen), 43, 46, 48, 50, 52
Gielgud, Sir John, 98
Gifford, Barry, 195

Giger, H. R., 48, 49, 85, 87
Girl with the Dragon Tattoo, The, 154
Glass, **75–77**
Gleeson, Domhnall, 154, 158
globalization, 149–50
Gnosticism, 24n1, 61–69
Godzilla (2014), 135
Golden Path, 57
Goldsmith, Jerry, 2, 147
Goebbels, Dr. Paul Joseph, 114
Good Kill, **78–80**
Goode, Matthew, 192
Goodman, John, 6
Gordon, Commissioner James, 9–11
Gosling, Ryan, 23, 179
goy & goyim, 6, 7, 96, 111–12, 159
Grand Politics, 141
Gravity, 25

H

HAL-9000, 2
Halleck, Gurney, 45, 49, 56
Hamill, Mark, 154, 158
Hannibal (film), 2
Happy Feet franchise, 103
Harden, Marcia Gay, 111
Hardy, Tom, 103, 106, 145
Harkonnen (noble house), 43–44, 48–49, 51, 85
Harkonnen, Baron Vladimir, 44, 46, 48–49, 52, 55–56, 85, 87, 200
Hakonnen, Feyd, 48, 52, 56, 85
Harrelson, Woody, 143
Hawat, Thufir, 45, 51, 52, 55
Hawke, Ethan, 78–80
Hawking, Steven, 176
Hayasaka, Fumio, 123
hedonism, 29, 44, 198

Heidegger, Martin, 31
Herbert, Frank, 39–53, 54–60, 85–86
heredity, 163–66, 209; see also determinism, genetic vs. environmental,
Heretics of Dune, 42, 48
Hero (film), 46
Hidden Figures, **81–84**
Hinduism, 40, 61
Hitler, Adolf, 34, 59, 178, 186
Hitler's War, 38
HIV, 32; see also AIDS
History of Violence, A, 28
Holocaust denial, 34–35
Holy Mountain, The, 85, 86
honor, 45, 110, 118, 128, 131, 196
honor culture vs. guilt culture, 131
Hood, Gregory, 16
Howard, Bryce Dallas, 89, 92
Howard, James Newton, 176
Howard, Ron, 89
Hunter, Tab, 102
Hurt, William, 55

I

IQ, 81, 93, 96, 150, 161, 163
I, Claudius (TV series), 47
Identitarianism, 141
Idiot Punk, 198, 202
Importance of James Bond & Other Essays, The, 145n1
individualism, 9, 198, 204
"Im Abendrot," 202
Inquisition, 138
irony, 58, 155, 175
Irulan, Princess, 42, 52, 55, 56, 85
Irving, David, 34–38
Isaac, Oscar, 121, 158

Isaak, Chris, 202
Isherwood, Christopher, 98
Islam, 40, 42, 104, 169
Isle of the Dead, The, 2
Isolationism, Wakandan, 18–20
Israel, 12, 79

J

Jackson, Peter, 15
Jackson, Samuel L., 75, 172, 176–77
Jagger, Mick, 85
James, P. D., 25
James Bond franchise, 103, 145–46, see also Bond, James
Japan & the Japanese, 117, 123, 125, 131, 138–40
Jason Bourne franchise, 145
Jewish Board of Family and Children's Services, 165
Jewish culture, 155, 190
Jewish ethnic networking, 35
Jews, 7–8, 20, 36–37, 60, 101, 111–14, 122, 131, 161, 210
Jodorowsky, Alejandro, 48, 85–87
Jodorowsky, Brontis, 85, 87
Jodorowsky's Dune, **85–87**
Johnson, Greg, 12n1, 24n2, 28n1, 122n1, 149n1, 150n2
Joker, The, 9–11, 14, 175, 187
Jones, Felicity, 133–34
Jovovich, Mila, 179
Judeo-Bolshevism, 8
Jurassic Park, 88
Jurassic Park III, 88
Jurassic Park franchise, 92
Jurassic World, **88–91**
Jurassic World: Fallen Kingdom, **92–94**

Justice League, **95–97**

K
K-2SO, 135
Kali Yuga, 194–95
Keene Act, 182–83, 187–89, 192
Kennedy, John F., 181, 187
Keeslar, Matt, 56
Kek, 140
Kellman, David, 162–67
Kent, Clark, 14–15, 189
Kerkorian, Kirk, 122
Kier, Udo, 85
Killer Bob, 200
Killmonger, 18–19
Kingdom of Heaven, 3
Kirby, Jack, 17, 20
Koenig, Walter, 147
Komitas (Soghomon Soghomonian, ordained and commonly known as Fr. Komitas), 121
Kosmogona, 199
Koteas, Elias, 30
Kravitz, Zoë, 79–80
Krige, Alice, 56
Krishna, 191
Kurosawa, Akira, 123
Kurzel, Jed, 2
Kwisatz Haderach, 47–48, 50
Kynes, Dr. Liet, 50, 51, 55

L
Ladd, Diane, 194, 199
Last Man (Nietzschean), 76
Latin America, 183, 187
Lawrence of Arabia (film), 51
Lawrence, Jennifer, 115, 116
Lawrence, T. E., 42
Le Bon, Charlotte, 121
Lean, David, 120
Lear, Amanda, 85
Lecter, Hannibal, 2
Lee, Stan, 17–20
Left, the, & Leftists, 25, 60, 81, 108, 140, 149, 159, 161, 166, 168, 180, 187, 210
Leia, Princess, 137, 152, 153, 158, 160
Lenin, Vladimir, 193
Lerner, Michael, 5
Lesotho, 17
Liberace, 102
liberal democracy, 12, 20, 39–40, 76, 204
liberal humanism, 97, 189
liberalism, 21, 139, 148–50, 187, 205, 209, 210
Lin, Justin, 147
Lindelof, Damon, 1
Lipstadt, Deborah, 34–37
Lord of the Rings, 46
Los Angeles, 98, 169
Lost (TV show), 1
lost boys, 170
Lost Highway, 195
Lost World, The, 88
Louis Wise Adoption Agency, 162, 164–65
Lovecraft, H. P., 185
Loved One, The (film), **98–102**
Loved One, The (novel), 98, 99, 100
Lucas, George, 41, 49, 133–34, 136, 142, 144, 154–55, 161
Lucifer, 2
Luthor, Lex, 14–16, 96
Lynch, David, 39–53, 54–55, 61–70, 86, 111, 156, 194–203

M
"M," 146
MacDonald, Kevin, 20, 29n1
MacMillan, Kenneth, 44

MacNeice, Ian, 55
MacNeil, Peter, 31
Mad Max: Fury Road, **103–106**
magic, 41, 46, 54, 85, 86, 92, 96, 117, 133, 143, 153, 159, 176, 204–205
Magma (rock band), 85
Mahoney, John, 6
Malick, Terrence, 24
Man of Steel, 13, 16, 95
Man in the Planet, 62–69
Manhunter, 168
Mann, A. Wyatt, 17
Mann, Thomas, 5
Mansfield, Jane, 31
Mao, Jules-Pierre, 72, 73
Mao Zedong, 193
Martian, The, 3, **107–109**, 116
Marvel, 17, 20
Marxism, 5, 24, 25, 105, 183
Mary Sue character, 133–34, 160
masculinity, 145; see also paleomasculinity
Masterpiece Theatre, 120
Masters of the Universe, 87
materialism, 54, 68, 76
Maul, Darth, 143
Mayer, Louis B., 5
McDowell, Roddy, 102
McEvoy, 76
McGill, Everett, 51
Mendelsohn, Ben, 135
Mengele, Dr. Josef, 165
mentats, 40, 45–46, 48
Merchant-Ivory films, 121
messiah, 42, 52, 54, 86
Metabarons, The, 86
MGM Studios, 122
Miami Vice, 169
Middle East, 12, 42
Mifune, Toshiro, 123, 124

Miller, Frank, 9, 13, 190
Miller, George, 103
Miller's Crossing, **110–14**
Milton, John, 2
Minghella, Anthony, 121
Minutemen (masked vigilantes), 181, 185, 186; see also Crimebusters; Watchmen
miscegenation, 72, 143
Miyagawa, Kazuo, 123
Moebius, 85
Mohiam, Reverend Mother Gaius Helen, 41, 45, 47, 48, 50, 55, 56, 86
Moore, Alan, 180, 190
moral order, 69, 123, 194, 204; see also myths; religion, function of
Morgan, John, 22n1
Moriarty, P. H., 55, 56
Morley, Robert, 98
Morse, Robert, 98
Mrs. Doubtfire, 109
Muad'dib (Paul Atreides), 51, 52
Multiculturalism, 60, 148–50
Mutants (gang), 10
Mystery Man, 199
myths, 115, 146, 156, 191, 195, 204; see also religion, function of; moral order

N
NAACP, 20
Nance, Jack, 48, 61ff.
NASA, 81, 83, 107–108
National Public Radio, 28
National Socialism, 8, 140
nationalism, 60; see also ethnonationalism; White nationalism

Nature's Thumbprint: The New Genetics of Personality, 166
NAXALT fallacy, 207, 210
Nazis, 13, 34, 36, 81, 165, 186, 193
Neeson, Liam, 138
negroes, 82, 108; see also blacks; booty-twerking & mudiking, 82; Magical, 17
neomorphs, 2
Neubauer, Alexander, 166
Neubauer, Peter S., 165–66
New Frontiersman, The, 180, 185
Newman, Alec, 55, 56
Newman, Thomas, 145
nihilism, 25, 69, 105, 194–95
Nixon, Richard, 180–83
Nolan, Christopher, 16, 59–60, 95, 156
Numinous, The, 17, 141

O
O'Bannon, Dan, 85, 87
O'Connor, Flannery, 4–5, 98
O'Meara, James J., 168
O'Toole, Martin, 34
Oakland (Calif.), 17, 19
Odets, Clifford, 5
Oldman, Gary, 178
Operation Nemesis, 122
Original Sin, 198
Osiris, 191
Ottoman Empire, 42, 120
Owen, Clive, 26

P
paganism, European, 154
paleomorphs, 2
paleo-masculinity, 88, 116, 175; see also masculinity
Palmer, Leland, 200
particularism, 139

Passion of the Christ, The ,140
Pavich, Frank, 85, 87
Passengers, 22n1, **115–16**
Pearce, Guy, 1
Pearl Harbor, 11
Penderecki, Krzysztof, 199, 202
Penguin Books, 36, 37
Perot, Ross, 178
Petersen, William, 168–70
Phillips, Sian, 47
Pine, Chris, 148
Pink Floyd, 85
plenitude, principle of, 174
political correctness, 9, 16, 35, 71, 72, 92, 138, 140, 147, 171, 178, 210
potentiality, actualization of, 174–75
Portman, Natalie, 179
Portuguese, 138
Pratt, Chris, 88–89, 92, 115–16
prescience, 48, 50, 54, 57
Presley, Elvis, 203
Prince, 176
Princess Mononoke, **117–19**
pro-family films, 90, 92
pro-natalist films, 89, 109
Proust, Marcel, 86
Prometheus, 1–2, 87
Promise, The, **120–22**
purdah, 104, 105
Purim, 111

Q
Qi'ra, 143
Quantum of Solace, 145

R
R2-D2, 118, 151
race realism, 206, 210
racism, 83, 160, 193

Raiders of the Lost Ark, 87
Rand, Ayn, 109
Rashomon, **123–32**
rationality, 110
Ravel, Maurice, 123
Reagan, Ronald, 10–11, 168–69
Reagan, Tom, 110, 112
Realism vs. relativism; see *Rashomon*
Red China, 108
red pill, 207, 209
Regency, 109
Reindeer, Mr., 200–202
religion, function of, 195–96, 204; see also moral order; myths
Republic, The, (Plato), 196
Requiem for a Dream, 30
Rey, 151–53, 157, 159–61
Reynolds, Ryan, 179
Richards, Keith, 29
Richardson, Tony, 98, 99
Ridley, Daisey, 153
Right-wing views, 9–11, 25, 180–93, 204
Rise and Fall of the Third Reich, The, 35
Robinson Crusoe, 115
Rogue One: A Star Wars Story, 22n1, 115, 116, **133–37**, 142, 144, 156
Rommel, Gen. Johannes Erwin Eugen, 38
Roosevelt, Franklin D., 11–12
Rushton, J. Philippe, 164n1

S
Saddam Hussein, 42, 79
Sade, Marquis de, (Donatien-Alphonse-François, Comte de Sade), 28
Salter, Frank, 164n1

Sarandon, Susan, 57, 58
Sardaukar (terror troops), 43–44, 45, 46, 49, 51
Schwartz, The, 135, 155
Scorsese, Martin, 138, 140
Scott, Ridley, 1–3, 22, 107
Scott-Heron, Gil, 82
Segal, Nancy, 163
segregation, 82–83, 207–209
self-actualization, 153, 175
separated at birth policy, 163, 165–66
sex, 28–33, 61–69, 99, 100, 186, 196, 197
Seydoux, Léa, 145
Seydoux, Michel, 85
Shaddam IV, Emperor of the Known Universe, 42–43, 51, 52, 56, 85
Shafran, Robert, 16267
Shaloub, Tony, 6
Shelley, Percy Bysshe, 2
Sheppard, W. Morgan, 202
Shirer, William L., 35
Shore, Howard, 29
Shylock, 4, 110
Shyamalan, M. Night, 75–77, 172–77
Sicario, 22
Silence, **138–40**
Sin City, 26
Skyfall, 145, 146
"Skyfall," 146
Skywalker, Luke, 152, 154, 157, 160
slavery, 104, 160, 178
Sleeping Beauty (fairy tale), 115
Smith, Sam, 145
snake (symbol), 198
Snoke, Supreme Commander, 151, 157, 161
Snyder, Zack, 11, 13, 16, 95–97,

180–81, 190
Socrates, 196
Solo, Han, 141–43, 152–53, 156
Solo: A Star Wars Story, **141–44**
Son of Trevor Lynch's White Nationalist Guide to the Movies, 1n2, 23, 85, 168n2
Sons of Batman, 10–11
Sophia, 65–66
Southern, Terry, 98
Southerners, 195
space program (American), 81–82, 108
Spacing Guild, 40, 42, 45
Spader, James, 29
Spectre, **145–46**
Split, 76–77
Stalin, 83, 193
Stalker, 22
Stander, Lionel, 101
Stanton, Harry Dean, 200
Star Trek (1960s TV show), 23, 147, 149
Star Trek franchise, 147–50, 151
Star Trek II: The Wrath of Khan, 147
Star trek IV: The Voyage Home, 147
Star Trek V: The Final Frontier, 147
Star Trek: Beyond, **147–50**
Star Trek: Enterprise, 147
Star Trek: The Motion Picture, 147
Star Trek: The Next Generation, 147
Star Trek: The Undiscovered Country, 147
Star Wars (A New Hope), 23, 41, 133–34, 136–37, 144, 148, 154, 156, 178–79
Star Wars Cantina, 141, 148, 178–79
Star Wars Trilogy, 87
Star Wars: Attack of the Clones, 144, 156
Star Wars: Rebels, 143
Return of the Jedi, 144, 156
Revenge of the Sith, 136, 142, 144, 156
Star Wars: The Clone Wars, 143
Star Wars: The Force Awakens, 93, 142, **151–55**
Star Wars: The Last Jedi, 93, 142, **156–61**
Star Wars: The Phantom Menace, 154, 156
Star Wars Universe, 93, 133–37, 141–44, 151, 154–55, 156, 158, 159, 161, 176
steampunk aesthetic, 49, 106
Steiger, Rod, 100
Steppenwolf (comic book character), 95, 96
stereotypes & stereotyping, 207–208
Stewart, Patrick, 45, 56
Stilgar, 51, 55, 56
Stockwell, Dean, 45, 168
Storm Troopers, 142
Stranger, The, 125
Straight Story, The, 51
Strauss, Richard, 202
subjectivity vs. objectivity; see *Rashomon*
Sucker Punch, 16, 94
Superman, compared to Batman, 13
Superman, Nietzschean, 12, 13, 76
Swanson, Gloria, 85
Swaziland, 17
Switzerland, 20
Sydow, Max von, 50, 151

T
Tarkin, Grand Moff, 135–37, 154
Taoism, 40
Terminator, The, 87
terrorism, 25, 26, 78–79, 135, 169, 176
Thalberg, Irving, 6
Thelma and Louise, 2
Theron, Charlize, 103
Thor, 17
Three Identical Strangers, **162–67**
thumos, 196–98, 199, 204
Titanic, RMS, 99, 115
Todd, Jason, 9, 11
To Live & Die in L.A., **168–71**
Tootsie, 109
Traditionalism, 97
Trevor Lynch's White Nationalist Guide to the Movies, 28n1, 190n1, 193n2
Trevorrow, Colin, 92–93
Triumph of the Will, 154
Trump, Donald, & Trumpism, 18, 140
Tudyk, Alan, 135
Turkish internet trolls, 122
Turner, Tina, 103
Turturro, John, 4, 8, 110, 112–13, 168–69
Twilight, 15
Twilight of the Cockroaches, 117
Twin Peaks, 45, 51, 194, 202
twin studies, 163
Tyldum, Morten, 115
Tyler, Brian, 58

U
Unbreakable, 76–77, **172–77**
Unger, Deborah Kara, 29
USSR (Soviet Union), 10, 81, 184, 185

V
Vader, Darth, 135–37, 151–53, 157
Valerian & the City of a Thousand Planets, **178–79**
Vangelis, 24
velociraptors, 88–89, 93
Venice Film Festival, 123
Victorians, 49, 109
Viet Nam, 181
Viet Nam War, 187
Villeneuve, Denis, 22–24, 46, 51–53
virtue-signaling, 83
Vishnu, 191
von Stuck, Franz, 62

W
Wagner, Richard, 2, 3
Wakanda, 17–21
Wallfisch, Benjamin, 24
Waltz, Christoph, 145
Wang Chung, 168
Wardle, Tim, 162–67
Warner Bros, 94
warrior ethos, 44, 86, 154
Watchmen, 181–83; see also Crimebusters; Minutemen
Watchmen (film), **180–93**; anti-feminism, 191; characters: Captain Metropolis (Nelson Gardner), 181, 182, 186; Chess, Roy, 184; Comedian, The (Eddie Blake), 181–83, 186, 187, 188–92; Dollar Bill, 181; Dr. Manhattan (Jon Osterman), 182–85, 188–89, 190–91, 193; Glass, Dr. Milton, 190; Grice, Gerald, 188; Hooded

Justice, 181, 196; Knot-Tops, 183, 186, 189; Moloch (supervillain), 183–84, 187; Nite Owl I (Hollis Mason), 181–82, 185–86; Nite Owl II (Dan Driberg), 183–84, 186–88, 189–90; Ozymandias (Adrian Veidt), 182, 187–88, 192–93; Rorschach (Walter Kovacs), 182–85, 187–88, 189–90, 192, 193; Roche, Blair, 188; Silhouette, 181; Silk Spectre I (Sally Jupiter), 181–82, 186, 191; Silk Spectre II (Laurie Jupiter), 184, 186, 191–92; Slater, Janey, 183–84; Weaver, Wally, 184, 190; far-Right politics of, 180, 186, 189, 193; plot: 183–85; climax and denouement, 185–86; redemptive role of love in, 191–92

Watchmen (graphic novel), 180–81, 184–85, 189–90, 192

Waugh, Evelyn, 98–99

Wayne, Bruce, 9–11, 14, 96, 189

weirding way, 40, 46, 54

Weisz, Rachel, 34, 36

welfare statism, 18, 19, 21

Welles, Orson, 85

Whedon, Joss, 94

Whitaker, Forest, 133, 135

White nationalism, 21, 26, 113, 122, 150; see also nationalism; ethnonationalism

White Nationalist Manifesto, The, 25

White supremacy, 83

"Wicked Game," 202

Wicked Witch of the East, 200

Wild at Heart (film), 111, **194–205**

Wild at Heart (novel), 195

Wilde, Oscar, 34–37

Williams, John, 88, 136, 154, 158

Willis, Bruce, 75, 76, 172, 178

Winters, Jonathan, 99, 101

Wise Blood, 98

Wizard of Oz, The, 194, 195–96, 199, 200, 204

Wolper, Bartholomew, 10–11

Woman in the Radiator, 65–68

women, 3, 25, 50, 81, 83, 89, 90, 103–108, 116, 120, 127–28, 153, 162, 167, 173, 181, 191, 202

Wonder Woman, 15–16, 96–97

Wright, Lawrence, 165

"Writing's on the Wall," 145

wuxia, 46

X

X, Malcolm, 20

xenomorphs, 1–3

Y

Y Tu Mamá También, 25

Yaitanes, Greg, 56–58

Yared, Gabriel, 121

Yemen, 79, 184

Yindel, Ellen, 10–12

yoga, 40, 54

Young Turks, 120

Z

Zimmer, Hans, 13, 24, 59–60

Zootopia, **206–11**

About the Author

Trevor Lynch is a pen name of Greg Johnson, Ph.D., Editor-in-Chief of Counter-Currents Publishing Ltd. and Editor of *North American New Right*, its webzine (http://www.counter-currents.com/) and occasional print journal.

He is the author of *Confessions of a Reluctant Hater* (San Francisco: Counter-Currents, 2010; second, expanded ed., 2016); *New Right vs. Old Right* (Counter-Currents, 2013); *Son of Trevor Lynch's White Nationalist Guide to the Movies* (Counter-Currents, 2015); *Truth, Justice, & a Nice White Country* (Counter-Currents, 2015); *In Defense of Prejudice* (Counter-Currents, 2017); *You Asked for It: Selected Interviews*, vol. 1 (Counter-Currents, 2017); *The White Nationalist Manifesto* (Counter-Currents, 2018); and *Toward a New Nationalism* (Counter-Currents, 2019).

He has also edited many books, including *North American New Right*, vol. 1 (Counter-Currents, 2012); *North American New Right*, vol. 2 (Counter-Currents, 2018); *Dark Right: Batman Viewed from the Right* (with Gregory Hood) (Counter-Currents, 2018); and *The Alternative Right* (Counter-Currents, 2018).

His writings have been translated into Czech, Danish, Dutch, Estonian, French, German, Greek, Hungarian, Norwegian, Polish, Portuguese, Russian, Slovak, Spanish, Swedish, and Ukrainian.

www.ingramcontent.com/pod-product-compliance
Lightning Source LLC
Chambersburg PA
CBHW031141160426
43193CB00008B/211